Welcome

Even though, supposedly, the worst of the credit crunch is long gone, many of us are still facing unprecedented demands on our finances. Bigger heating bills, pay freezes, more VAT: we seem to be earning less, yet paying more. Rarely has the need to earn a few extra pounds been so prevalent.

That's where eBay comes in. With over £1,000 per second changing hands on eBay across the world, it's become a favoured shopping destination of many. For buyers, it's a chance to snap up some great deals, and save valuable pounds on items against the high-street price. Furthermore, it's a treasure trove of items you simply wouldn't be able to get anywhere else.

For sellers? Where else would you be able to offer your wares to over 230 million people through just one website? Not for nothing have many people gone on to base successful businesses around the eBay service.

And yet it's not quite as simple as it seems. Is that bargain as good as it looks? Are you about to get scammed? How do you make your auctions more appealing to buyers? And what are the pitfalls that you need to avoid?

That's where we come in. Across the jam-packed pages of this guide, we're going to look at the secrets of being a successful buyer and seller on eBay. There's no lashing of gloss paint here; we're going to look as much at the cons as the pros. However, with some common sense, the advice we've got to offer and perhaps even the assistance of one of the many eBay aids reviewed in this book, you can get the deals you've been hoping for. What's more, you might just be able to do your bank balance a bit of good too.

Happy bidding!

Simon Brew

Contents

Chapter 1
Why Use eBay?

If you're brand new to eBay, then start right here, as we look at just what it can do for you, and how things have changed…

Chapter 2
What You Need To Get Started

So you're ready to take the plunge? Here's what you need to get up and running on eBay

Chapter 3
Introductory Selling

It's not tricky to get an item on eBay, but making a successful sale is another matter. Luckily, we've got lots of help right here

Chapter 4
Advanced Selling

If you're looking to do more than just sell a few items through eBay, then there's added help at hand, and a few tips and tricks worth knowing…

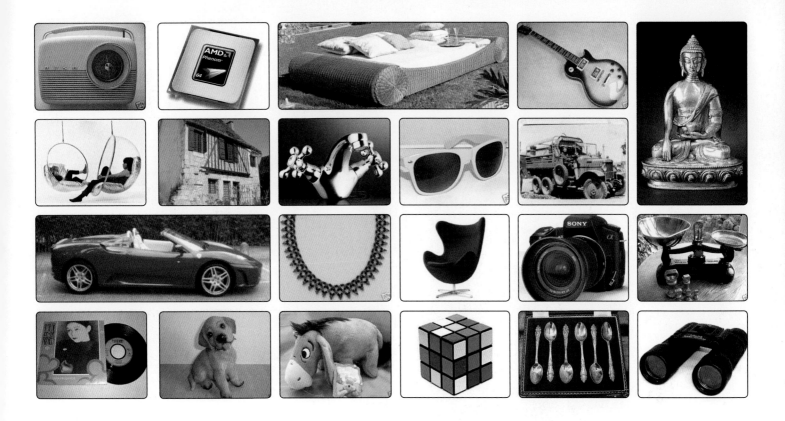

Chapter 5
Buying Through eBay

It's easy to pay over the odds on eBay, but armed with our advice there are great deals to be had

Chapter 6
PayPal

What is PayPal and how much is it going to cost you to use?

Chapter 7
eBay Alternatives

eBay doesn't have the monopoly on buying and selling. Here are some other places for your to promote your wares…

Chapter 8
Reviews

Lots of eBay services, programs, websites and more put to the test!

Case Studies

Chapter 1
Why Use eBay?

Why Use eBay?

It's the world's most successful auction website by far. So what makes it so special and how does it differ from its competitors?

When it comes to buying and selling online, there's really only one name that springs to mind: eBay. Like Google, eBay has managed to make a nonsense word familiar simply by being the best at what it does. It's a name that's always in the news for one reason or another - perhaps because of someone's astounding success story, or thanks to something weird, wonderful or controversial turning up for sale. But what is it about this online auction site that draws so many people in?

WORLDWIDE CAR-BOOT SALE

The early popularity of eBay brought about possibly the most socially significant change to the way people buy and sell things since credit cards were invented. Sure, in the past people might have gone to jumble sales and picked up a few second-hand bargains, but even the biggest car-boot sale pales into insignificance when compared with eBay. Imagine having access to everything that anyone in the world might want to sell, whenever you want, from the comfort of your computer.

When you log into the site, you might not have any idea what you want to buy, or you might have something specific in mind. Either way, you're likely to be able to find something to bid on, or buy outright. It's worth bearing in mind, however, that the sale of certain items is prohibited, and eBay removes contentious sales pretty quickly. The current list of prohibited items includes material deemed offensive in some way, illegal or sexual services, and the likes of lotteries and prize draws (you can find the full list at **pages.ebay.co.uk/help/sell/policies. html#prohibit**) For most of us, though, all of that is no great loss. And for pretty much anything else, eBay's still your best bet, warts and all.

ONLINE DEPARTMENT STORE

Not everything on sold on eBay is second-hand, and in recent years, that's been the dramatic change on the service. Retailers increasingly have an eBay arm to their business (and the increasing number of high-street stores on eBay has been a source of complaint in recent times), or will pass excess stock on to traders to sell on eBay, so the products won't have been used, or even taken out of their boxes. A PowerSeller logo beside an eBay trader's name indicates that this is someone who takes eBay seriously, sometimes running their entire business through the site.

eBay is also great fun just to browse around. Half the fun of shopping is browsing, and eBay has enough on offer to fill hours and hours of your life. It's all too easy to get drawn into a never-ending cycle of finding something you like, clicking through to the seller's shop to see what else they've got, then browsing through categories. Because any search is likely to bring up a variety of different options, it's easy to get carried away, looking at things that you never knew you wanted, and perhaps even buying a few.

◄ All kinds of things you didn't know you wanted are for sale

12 cornflake crispies

Item condition:	**New**
Time left:	18d 20h (11 Aug, 2010 15:43:05 BST)
Quantity:	1 2 available
Price:	**£4.00** Buy It Now
	Watch this item
Postage:	£3.00 Royal Mail 1st Class Standard See disco See all details Estimated delivery within 2-3 business days.
Payments:	*PayPal*, Postal order or Banker's draft, Credi See details
Returns:	Returns accepted	Read details

Zoom unavailable   🔍 Enlarge

eBay Buyer Protection

OPOSSUM TAXIDERMY ARM GAG GIFT WEIRD

Item condition:	--
Ended:	May 14, 2010 19:32:25 PDT
Bid history:	3 bids
Winning bid:	**US $11.50**
Shipping:	**FREE shipping** US Postal Service Parcel Post | See all details
	Estimated delivery within 3-10 business days.
Returns:	7 day money back, buyer pays return shipping | Read details

eBay Buyer Protection
eBay will cover your purchase price plus original shipping.
Learn more

GET RICH QUICK

Of course, the biggest attraction for many people is the promise of a quick and easy way to make money. Something about eBay appeals to the same part of our brains as TV programmes like *Bargain Hunt* and *Cash In The Attic*; the idea that we might be sitting on a fortune is irresistible to most of us. Whereas once upon a time, people just held on to their valuables in order to pass them down to their children, nowadays we just have to know: is it worth much? And if it is, who might want to buy it?

In the past, some truly bizarre and often worthless items have been sold for enormous amounts of money on eBay, which can only be encouraging to would-be salespeople (it seems to happen less often now, sadly). One of the biggest items ever sold was a dismantled US Navy fighter jet, which sold for around $1 million on the US site. But that seems downright conventional when you consider that some people have managed to flog empty jars containing 'ghosts' (or even their own souls) on eBay. It's hard to argue with that kind of creativity.

It's much more enterprising, in any case, than those who've sold toenail clippings, a place at the birth of their child, or even their virginity. All of these are testament to the possibilities of eBay. Many of these items, of course, contravene eBay's terms and conditions, but that doesn't mean they still don't manage to turn up from time to time.

SOCIAL NETWORKING

As social networks go, eBay is never going to match up to the likes of Facebook and Twitter, but there is, nevertheless, a social side to the auction website. Buying something from an online store is usually a pretty impersonal experience; on eBay, you'll find yourself not only bidding against other people - and some auctions can get pretty frenzied - but you're also buying from a real person. The seller's screen

▲ eBay's social side has even led to marriage

name and feedback ratings are right there in front of you (in some detail), and new eBay users might find monitoring their feedback becomes an obsession.

And the social aspect goes beyond trading messages with fellow eBayers. Some people have even met their future spouses on the site. One man, who was bidding on an ornamental eagle, ended up meeting the seller and falling in love with her. Another couple who met on the auction site actually ended up getting married at eBay's Annual User Conference in New Orleans a few years' back. So while a relationship might be the last thing you're looking for on eBay, stories like this prove it's not beyond the realms of possibility.

DON'T BE SCARED!

As overwhelming as eBay might seem at first glance, it's easy to get around once you know how. That said, it's far from a perfect beast, and it pays to have advice and help in your corner. With that in mind, coming up, you'll find comprehensive advice from some of the UK's eBay experts, and plenty of case studies to show you how it should (and shouldn't) be done.

MEMORABLE EBAY AUCTIONS

KATIE MELUA'S MOVEMENTS

A printout of Katie Melua's work diary was found backstage at the Guilfest 2004 festival, and sold on eBay. It caused great concern to her management, as it offered the star's travel and accommodation details for the following few months. As one of her staff said to a national newspaper, "These sensitive documents will cause her a lot of trouble if they get into the wrong hands."

What Can It Do For You?

Whether you're just doing a spot of shopping or looking to set up your own business, eBay has something for everyone

eBay can be used for a variety of different purposes, and not everyone uses it in exactly the same way. You may never use all of eBay's features and functions, or you might use one now, and a different one later. Chances are, though, there's at least one way that eBay can be useful to you.

The three most obvious reasons for signing up to the site, and their relative advantages compared with the alternatives, are examined here.

CLEARING OUT THE GARAGE

Most people have a sizeable amount of 'stuff' that just sits in their house, taking up space. Over the years, unwanted gifts, impulse buys, and gadgets of all kinds fail to find their place in your life, and end up finding their place in the back of a cupboard, or in the attic or garage. You could round it all up and take it to a local charity shop, but some of it might be valuable, and wouldn't it be nice to make some money from it?

eBay obviously isn't the only solution, but it's easier than placing an ad in the paper or going to a car-boot sale. Instead of having to drive to a field at 6am on a weekend morning, you just log into a website, sit back, and wait for people to buy your items. There's also less haggling, and more structure; you're less likely to get ripped off using eBay because of the various procedures put in place. eBay's rules make sure both buyers and sellers know where they stand legally right off the bat.

The other advantage is that you'll be reaching a much wider audience. Even if you're only willing to pay the postage on sending items out to bidders located in the UK, you'll be able to offer your items to people across the country, not just those who read your paper or attend your markets. That means you're more likely to find someone who's interested and, perhaps even more importantly, someone who's willing to pay you a price you're happy with.

MOVING YOUR BUSINESS ONLINE

Almost all businesses now have websites; the Internet is an important, if not a necessary, part of most business strategies. However, getting started can be quite daunting; websites can be expensive, difficult and time-consuming to set up, and if you want to be able to sell your products through your website, that adds an extra dimension of difficulty. It's easier, not to mention cheaper and quicker, to set up an eBay shop instead. Yes, you'll have to pay a fee to eBay in order to trade in this way, but it's likely to be a much smaller sum than you would otherwise spend on web development and maintenance.

There's also the fact that eBay has a built-in audience. People will already be logging into the site to shop, and might choose to look there before they'd look at individual websites. For existing customers, or people who have already heard of your business, you can link

▶ eBay provides a way for sellers to keep overheads low, so even low-cost items can be profitably sold

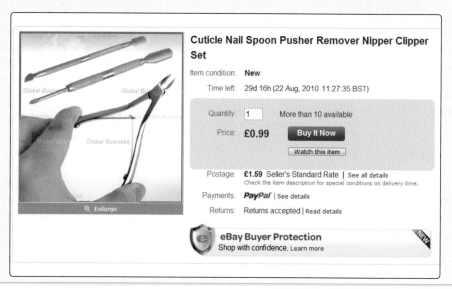

Cuticle Nail Spoon Pusher Remover Nipper Clipper Set

Item condition:	**New**
Time left:	29d 16h (22 Aug, 2010 11:27:35 BST)
Quantity:	1 More than 10 available
Price:	**£0.99** Buy It Now
	Watch this item
Postage:	**£1.59** Seller's Standard Rate	See all details
	Check the item description for special conditions on delivery time.
Payments:	**PayPal**	See details
Returns:	Returns accepted	Read details

eBay Buyer Protection
Shop with confidence. Learn more

UK Coca Cola Cherry Coke 150ml 'picnic' can 1998, empty

Item condition: **New**

Quantity:	1 4 available
Price:	**£4.00** Buy It Now
	Watch this item

Postage: £1.25 Royal Mail 2nd Class Standard | See all details
Estimated delivery within 4-6 business days.

Payments: **PayPal**, Postal Order or Banker's Draft, Personal cheque, Credit card | See details

Returns: Returns accepted | Read details

eBay Buyer Protection
Shop with confidence. Learn more

▲ Even things normally reserved for the dustbin can end up on eBay

longer want (although the service is used more and more by big name business now), much of it will be a lot cheaper than you'd expect to pay if you found the item in a shop. Similarly, sellers who run most of their business through eBay will have lower overheads than traders who work from shops, so again the price you pay will probably be lower. And if not many other bidders are interested in the item you want, you could nab some real bargains.

There are any number of tricks and tips that can help you find the best deals, some of which will be covered later in this book. There's also a huge amount of satisfaction to be found in winning an auction and carrying off your prize, especially if it's something that's no longer on general sale, or something you've wanted for a long time and have never been able to find.

The fact that you can search auctions based all over the country - or even the world - widens your net and increases your chances of bagging a bargain. You can set your highest bid level at a price you're willing to pay, which means you can ensure you don't spend more than you're comfortable with, and you'll soon learn that even if you lose one auction, another one will be along shortly.

from a main site to your eBay auctions (and vice versa), so they won't have to look very far to find what they're after either.

The most difficult part of moving a business online is probably finding a way to handle payments. With eBay, that's already taken care of: eBay's associated payment system, PayPal, is easy to use, reliable, and trusted by most web users. It's often more secure than other payment methods, with a much smaller margin for error.

FINDING A BARGAIN

As previously discussed, eBay is a prime location for finding pretty much anything, from antiques to records, from books to imaginary friends. It's a marketplace on an almost unimaginable scale. Because a lot of eBay sales come from individuals selling things they no

GETTING STARTED

By now, you should have some idea why people love eBay so much (and you may be drawing up plans of your own to buy and sell). The rest of this book, then, will explain exactly how to use the site, and warn you of any pitfalls you might encounter on your travels.

The Pros & Cons Of eBay

There are a number of advantages and disadvantages to using eBay. Here, we take a look at what they are

It's difficult to imagine the Internet without eBay now. For many people, it's a tool without which they couldn't run a business; for others, it's a last chance to find a must-have item not available on the high street (usually at a premium price). Many users will evangelise for hours on end about how brilliant it is, even those left cold by some of the increasing number of changes to the service over the past few years. But eBay isn't without its flaws. As with any service or marketplace, you'll need to keep your wits about you.

COMMUNITY SPIRIT

There are five 'fundamental values' that underpinned eBay, which used to be published on the site, although they've been removed in recent times. However, the guiding philosophy always used to be:

- We believe people are basically good.
- We believe everyone has something to contribute.
- We believe that an honest, open environment can bring out the best in people.
- We recognise and respect everyone as a unique individual.
- We encourage you to treat others the way you want to be treated.

The removal of these values from the site doesn't necessary mean that eBay no longer works to them, it's just it seems shyer about telling you so. That said, while it was never the case that eBay's founders didn't mean what they said, not everyone is always well-intentioned, and not everyone is trustworthy. Even if you assume that eBay employees adhere to these principles, that doesn't mean every single person doing business on the site will.

For every story about someone finding a treasure on eBay, there's a counter-story where someone got caught out by a hoax. Both are, of course, as rare as each other. A once common hoax is for sellers to pretend to sell some new and expensive consumer electronic item, but in fact only be offering the box; the photograph may well depict the real equipment, but somewhere buried in the listings will be a mention that only the box is up for auction. Fake Apple iPhones were listed on eBay before the real thing was available in the shops, and though these types of auctions are usually removed posthaste, you can't rely on eBay to catch all the fakes immediately.

In the summer of 2009, meanwhile, English 20 pence coins were attracting opportunists en masse. A small batch of said coins were minted without the date, and some eBay sellers grabbed the headlines when they tried to charge up to £5,000 - with free postage! - for collectors looking to pick up such a rarity.

More recently, there are cases of people paying by PayPal, then instantly coming around to collect goods in person. Once they've got them, they claimed to PayPal that their account had been hacked, and thus the payment was cancelled. Thus, the seller has been left with no item, and no money.

▲ Sometimes you can get more than you bargained for

▲ Bob Geldof wasn't happy when Live 8 tickets appeared on eBay

BAD EGGS

Those were extraordinary cases; a more common eBay issue is a seller who just doesn't produce the promised item, or sends something in worse condition than they'd originally said. There are measures that can be taken against these people, but it's discouraging nonetheless. And, of course, it works both ways: sometimes, people bid on items but never pay for them, forcing the seller to relist the item and start all over again.

Some eBay sales might not seem illegal, but still fall foul of the rules and regulations. Tickets for the inauguration of President Obama in 2008, for instance, were blocked by eBay. Furthermore, tickets for Michael Jackson's memorial concert were to be found on eBay at one point. Tickets for other concerts or events are listed for sale on eBay all the time (aside from football tickets, which eBay prohibits), and though these are perfectly fair game and have often been put on sale by genuine fans who can't attend the event for one reason or another, sometimes they're scalped or counterfeit tickets. It's important to think about what you're buying when you use eBay.

RINGING THE CHANGES

Another problem with eBay is that the rules can change at any time. For example, one of its policy changes meant that UK listings didn't automatically show up in searches performed on the US site. American customers could still browse UK listings, but they'd have to click through to the advanced search functions.

Obviously, this had a massive effect on UK traders who regularly sold to Stateside customers, and although eBay publicly apologised, it didn't change the policy back. According to eBay, this system made the listings more relevant to customers, and it was happy with its decision. After all, UK customers hadn't been prevented from using the US site; they'd just have to pay an additional listing fee to make sure that US bidders saw their items. This isn't a reason not to use eBay, but it might be a reason to avoid depending on it too heavily.

A year or two back, eBay introduced a policy that meant UK sellers weren't allowed to charge postage and packaging for DVDs. For those already on tight margins, not being able to charge postage was a controversial move, which was popular with buyers, but led to some sellers moving away from eBay altogether, no longer able to compete with the big-name sellers. Fortunately, said policy has since been reversed, although limits are still in place.

Not all policy changes are so controversial. For example, a policy change to the jewellery section of the site meant that sellers could only describe their wares as diamonds if they met certain criteria - in other

▲ For all its advantages, it pays to exercise caution on eBay

words, if they really were diamonds. Other look-alike gems, such as cubic zirconia, had to be clearly labelled; if the word 'diamond' was used in the listing, 'imitation' or 'simulated' had to precede it. Undoubtedly, this change would have upset some sellers, but it's clearly for the good of the customer.

More recently, eBay has altered its policy on the way it calculates final fees. The service used to offer tiered final fees to private individuals, but in a claimed effort to simplify things, it's now charging a flat 10% on all Buy It Now auctions. This, inevitably, meant that many prices actually went up, causing many to amplify complaints that eBay was more interested in business customers than private sellers. That's not the case, but eBay did itself few favours with its new flat rate policy, and it's left many despondent with the service.

BUSINESS SENSE

It's important to take into account the fact that eBay is, ultimately, a business, and it's a hugely successful one at that (in spite of the growing criticisms that it's faced in recent times).

People often talk about eBay as if it's a purely altruistic organisation, but it's not. Yes, it's an exciting service with potentially a lot to offer, but before you do anything else, you should make sure you've read the terms and conditions. eBay does offer protection against fraud, and will help out in most disputes, but clearly it's better to avoid getting into them in the first place. Prevention really is better than cure.

MEMORABLE EBAY AUCTIONS

VAMPIRE KILLING KIT

Ridiculously superstitious horror fans had the chance to bag a Vampire Killing Kit. It contained a crossbow with four silver-tipped arrows, an ebony wooden stake, a large bottle of holy water, various surgical instruments and more, all in a solid mahogany box. It sold for $4,550.

eBay By The Numbers

Not all eBay auctions are successful. More than half end without a single bid. What are people after? We check out the top searches

It's been a tough couple of years for eBay, financially. It, along with many businesses, suffered as part of the credit crunch, and it's also lost business as a result of criticisms aimed at it. However, it's still in rude health. Revenue for 2010 was over $9bn, although its PayPal business is accounting for more and more of that. Even so, it's still, clearly, a massive place to do business.

By mid-2009, eBay was reporting 233 million members, with around half that number in the US (which is one of 37 markets in which eBay has a presence). In the UK there are 14 million active users, 40.62% of whom visit eBay.co.uk at least once a month. Recent figures estimate that 178,000 users in the UK use eBay to run a business or as their primary or secondary source of income, posting items in 13,000 categories (there are 50,000 categories worldwide). Across the world more than $60 billion worth of merchandise is traded and $1,900 (approx £1,155) is spent via eBay every second.

WHAT WORKS?

So what kind of items are most popular, and what are buyers looking for? The largest stores tend to sell DVDs, Blu-rays, phones and books, but a glance at eBay's 'Pulse' data (which you can find at **pulse.ebay. co.uk**) reveals that it's technology that's still being actively hunted down; mobiles phones, games consoles, iPads, and iPods continually dominate the top ten, with only furniture and clothes regularly making in-roads in the chart. The 'Collectables' category still remains popular, though, where Hornby items, Pokemon, postcards, flags, medals, Betty Boop, enamel signs and Guinness figure highly. It's not the most lucrative, however. For that, you need to look at motor vehicles. Then again, they do cost more to actually buy on the whole!

The total number of 'collectable' items actually increases when you take into account other categories being used to advertise them. In the 'Cars, Motorcycles & Vehicles' category, for example, classic cars are the third most popular search term. Not for nothing is one of the key terms most used when listing products on eBay the word 'vintage'.

Given eBay's past reputation as a place to get items stupidly cheap, these statistics aren't surprising, but the situation is very different now that the world has latched on. Whereas it used to be possible to sneak in at the last second and put in a winning bid, or find an auction that nobody else had stumbled on, it's getting increasingly hard to find genuine bargains on the most popular and top-selling products. Also, most sales tend to be Buy It Now only, sadly, which has taken some of the fun away too.

What eBay's popularity boom has done, however, is make far more items available than ever before. Not only are there a lot more auctions based in a lot more places, the range of items has widened as people realise that there's a market for just about anything. Some of the stranger auctions (and eBay.co.uk has broken the barrier for having had ten million items available at any one time) include a heart-shaped potato (which, incredibly, sold for $1!), a method for communicating with ghosts, squirrel underpants, a time-travelling egg, and a log shaped like the Mercedes Benz insignia. You can be certain that in the ten years of eBay.co.uk and more in the US, there have been some strange old auctions.

If all this sounds like the whole set-up is somewhat strange, then that would be an understandable conclusion to reach, but it's one of the reasons why eBay is one of the best places for selling anything from anywhere. Whatever's in the loft, or whatever someone has a desire to put in the loft, it's almost guaranteed to be on eBay. Sometimes, the more obscure the better.

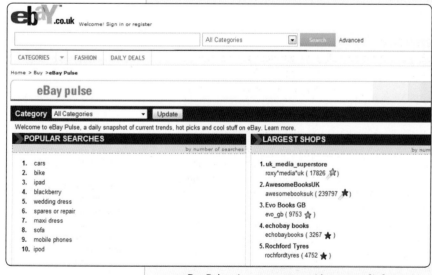

▲ **eBay Pulse gives access to a wide source of information**

Categories

Most popular eBay categories by revenue:

eBay Motors	$16.5 billion
Consumer Electronics	$4.9 billion
Clothing & Accessories	$4.5 billion
Computers	$4 billion
Books/Movies/Music	$3.1 billion
Home & Garden	$3.6 billion
Sports	$2.6 billion
Collectibles	$2.7 billion
Business & Industrial	$2.2 billion
Toys	$2.1 billion
Jewellery & Watches	$2 billion
Cameras & Photo	$1.5 billion
Antiques & Art	$1.4 billion
Coins & Stamps	$1.3 billion

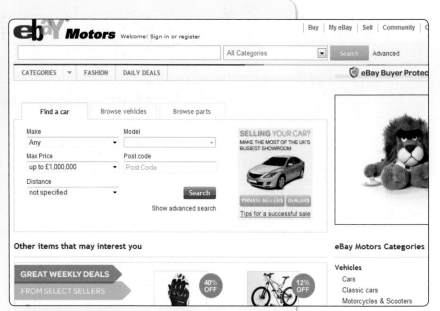

▲ eBay Motors has grown year on year

In that sense, it's not hard to see why so many people choose eBay over other auction sites such as CQOut (**www.cqout.com**). Although there was initially some competition when the idea of Internet auctions appeared (names such as QXL, Yahoo! Auctions and Amazon Auctions have all fallen by the wayside), it was eBay that out-muscled every other name. This was pretty surprising in the case of Yahoo! Auctions, which was a free service and has now closed completely in the UK. The sheer scale of eBay, which makes other sites look positively minuscule in comparison, means that using those other sites is a bit like going to a small-town local market with a handful of stalls, rather than a county-advertised car-boot sale that fills an entire field.

SUCCESS OR FAILURE

This, of course, isn't without its problems. Over half of all listings on eBay end without getting a single bid. Putting an item up for sale doesn't necessarily mean that the ideal buyer is going to find it within the allotted time, or pay the price demanded, or that they haven't found an alternative lot in better condition or closer to where they live. In car-boot terms, it's like being stuck on a wallpapering table in the furthest corner from the entrance, half-an-hour from the burger van and in a large puddle. Fortunately, you don't have to pay the listing feeds of old if your item doesn't sell.

Still, some eBay users prefer Amazon when it comes to selling books, CDs and DVDs. Amazon user James said, "The great thing about Amazon is that you get far longer to sell the item, and if you don't manage to find a buyer, you haven't lost anything. You can pay quite a lot of money to eBay for a relatively

unsuccessful ten-day listing, whereas on Amazon you get 60 days for free. Although Amazon does take a hefty fee on completion of a sale, you tend to make it back on the postage. Sometimes you can sell a book for a penny and still get more for it overall than you would have done on eBay - had you sold it at all."

However, with Amazon, you are generally - although not always - at the mercy of which products it already currently sells. "Amazon is no good for more obscure things, and sometimes I haven't been able to list modern titles with ISBN codes. That's frustrating for both the seller and any potential buyers, especially if it's something you could get from Waterstone's or HMV. Amazon is fantastic if you're dealing with specific and reasonably easily available items, but eBay wins when it comes to rare or just downright odd."

BIG MONEY

eBay Motors is arguably the greatest success story from the site as a whole. It has 12 million monthly unique visitors and, once the site had established a level of trust, sales rose from $1.5bn (£760m) in 2002 to $18bn (approx. £10bn) in 2008. A staggering 34% of all online automotive minutes are spent on eBay Motors, making eBay the top online automotive site based on the percentage of minutes users are surfing auto listings. eBay used to have an attached feeling of paying your money and taking your chances, but little by little it became the weapon of choice for those having no luck in the classified ads. Ironically, eBay now does classifieds of its own, as well as auctions, and, given the weight of traffic flowing, it seems a more attractive prospect than the local paper (or even some of the bigger ones, such as Loot).

DID YOU KNOW?

A Shropshire businessman who had been burgled spotted some of his possessions on eBay. As a result, police raided three addresses in Shrewsbury, recovering goods worth up to £7,500.

▶ AuctionSniper: another of the many sniping tools available to download from the web

This counts even more so if the item that contains a motor isn't necessarily a car. If you ever fancy buying an aeroplane, there's no shortage here. Helicopters, fighter jets and even a Russian space shuttle have appeared over the years, along with the necessary consumables, simulators and ejector seats. The most expensive item ever sold was a private business jet for $4.9 million. Is eBay unique? Certainly.

EASY TO USE?

But just how easy is it to use? Is buying really that simple? If someone's only got a few items to sell, is it worth them even signing up? What if they have a whole shop full of stuff and would like an Internet-based outlet as well?

Signing up is easy enough. You provide a username and password, exactly like registering with any other site, and then some personal details. The one 'detail' you might balk at providing is a credit or debit card, but this is a standard procedure, which has been in place for years to help combat fraud and misuse of the service. Verify your account by checking your e-mail for the automated message, and the process is complete and you can start bidding. It's that fast.

Bidding is equally easy, which has been the downfall of some addicted users. You read the item description, put the maximum amount you're willing to pay into the box and confirm your bid. You don't even have to worry about going back and bidding again, as the proxy system means that eBay will do it for you.

"I was long attracted by eBay, and one day decided to take the plunge," said Bill Dove, who lives near Falmouth, Cornwall. "I began selling some of my old board games that I had stored in my loft and cupboards for years. That was in 2000. I had a large

collection and really needed to downsize to create more space, and the extra income proved very useful. But I remember buying as well and having to wait at the computer while an auction was ending, eager not to miss out."

'Sniper' software will ensure that you aren't outbid at the last second, and there are various auction management programs and websites that will help to keep track of multiple auctions (you'll find a round-up of some of your options at the back of this book). eBay's own interface is detailed enough to keep any user up to date with all their activity, and you can even have warnings sent to your mobile phone if you're in danger of losing an item.

Paying for things is a lot easier than it used to be. Years ago, when you won an auction, you usually had to pay by cash or postal order, which was not good if you were buying from the States. International money orders are expensive, so if there was something you really wanted from over the pond, you'd hide some cash in a letter or padded envelope.

▲ The Bidnapper sniping tool

Thankfully, the days of putting bank notes in the post and hoping the mail sorters were honest are over. eBay introduced the PayPal system as a means of payment, and then liked it so much it bought it. Completing a transaction is now as straightforward as pressing 'Pay Now', entering the relevant amount and hitting 'Send'. If the seller's on the ball, it's possible to get the item as early as the next day. And it's not just auctions; hundreds of thousands of eBay Shops are online, allowing you to purchase directly as from any other Internet store, and often delivering much quicker.

SELLING WORK

Selling is a different matter, of course, and requires some work. You'll have to choose a category, write up a description, include a photograph (which increases your chances of success), decide starting prices and which payment methods you'll accept. eBay seller James said that this has got easier: "You can put in your item title now and eBay will try to identify a category that's relevant. If it can't, and to be honest it often doesn't, you just choose from a list and then some subcategories. It can take a while to put a page together, but sometimes the simplest ones are the best anyway. People hate having to wade through loads of unnecessary detail when all they really want is a photograph and a price."

It's then a case of sitting back and watching the bids roll in - or not, if the number of unsold auctions is anything to go by. Common advice states that waiting for an appropriate time to list an item can really help, as does Jenny's experience from when

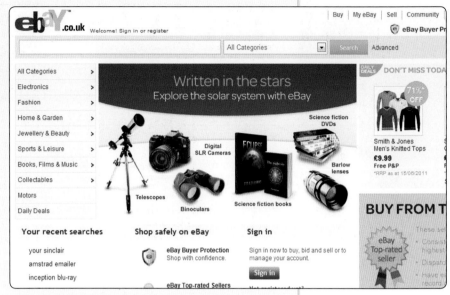

▲ eBay just about remains the number one way for people to get rid of their old belongings

she sold a copy of a Derren Brown book for three figures. "I saw some copies a while back and knew that they were already quite rare, so I bought one with the intention of reading it and then reselling it when his new series started. I did exactly that and sold it for more than twice what I paid for it. Looking at prices now, I got in at exactly the right time. He went off the TV and nobody has sold one for that amount since."

James agrees: "Sporting goods can be a real balancing act. Do you just sell them, or wait for the team or player to start doing well? What if they get injured? What if you miss that window of opportunity? Selling things can be very difficult if you don't know all the ins and outs. That's fine if you want to attempt getting rid of some junk or you don't care about getting the maximum possible amount for your items, but tough if you're dealing with Collectables - which, of course, is what eBay's all about."

If you want to give eBay a try, you have nothing to lose; just stay sensible and alert and follow some simple rules. If you're buying, know what you want, and know how much you're willing to spend. If you're selling, do a bit of research, and have some idea of what you can realistically expect. Factor in the amount in fees that eBay will slice off too, so you know how much will end up in your pocket.

If you manage to keep your head, then you're far likely to be successful using eBay than someone who gets caught up in the moment, and puts common sense aside. And consequently, you're also far more likely to pick a bargain, or make a few welcome extra pounds on the side.

Facts & Figures

1995: The year eBay was founded in the US

233 million: The number of registered users worldwide

49%: The amount of revenue eBay pulls in from America alone

$1,839: The sum, per second, eBay users worldwide trade on the site

6.4 million: The number of new listings added each day

39%: The amount of goods now sold at a fixed price

632,000: The number of worldwide stores

Five billion: The number of feedback comments left

MEMORABLE EBAY AUCTIONS

TREASURE TROVE

The British Museum is keen to point out that treasure hunters who find valuables such as gold and silver coins or Roman jewellery and sell them on eBay are breaking the law. Items found in this way should be reported to the authorities as treasure trove, and the Museum has set up the Portable Antiquities Scheme (PAS) to police eBay for such items.

The Evolution Of eBay

How did a computer programmer's home page grow into the world's biggest online auction site, and arguably the dot-com boom's greatest success story? Let's take a look...

Like many web users in the mid-90s, Baltimore-based Franco-Iranian computer programmer Pierre Omidyar had a home page. And like many home pages, it was pretty trivial. It even included a tongue-in-cheek 'tribute' section dedicated to the Ebola virus. But it was soon to grow into something massive. The 28-year-old coder became interested in the technical issues involved in setting up an online auction site, where sellers and buyers could interact independently of the facilitator. He added a test-of-concept feature, which he called AuctionWeb, to his website and went live with it on America's Labor Day weekend in 1995.

The very first item sold on AuctionWeb was a broken laser pointer, listed for sale by Omidyar himself. His expectations for the auction were low, believing it would only make a few cents, if it sold at all. This first, trivial listing was intended to test how his new subsite performed with a live auction rather than to sell the product. But to his astonishment, it went for $14.83. "You do realise it's broken?" Omidyar e-mailed to the winning bidder. "I'm a collector of broken laser pointers," he replied.

Omidyar had never intended AuctionWeb to take off to any great degree. He was more interested in the

▲ eBay Motors was launched in 1999

technical side of things than running it as a business. Yet as the laser pointer auction proved, he was onto something big. Sellers began listing all manner of items on AuctionWeb, which soon took over his entire domain. When it became too big even for this, he moved the site to a new, more expensive business domain. He tried to register www.echobay.com, after his consultancy firm, Echo Bay Technologies, but the URL was already taken, so he chose a shortened version; ebay.com was born!

According to eBay, "from day one, Omidyar built eBay around what remain the company's core values" that people are basically good, that everyone has something to contribute and an open environment brings out the best in people. According to the website, "The success of eBay underscores the truth of these values, and is at the heart of eBay's continuing success."

EARLY GROWTH

The budding auction site grew and grew. In early 1996, Omidyar started charging a fee based on the final sale price. He wasn't sure whether the users would accept this, but the money soon came rolling in. Monthly profits reached $10,000 by June, having doubled for four consecutive months. It was time to quit his day job and devote his full-time attentions to eBay, which took on its first employee around now, a

▲ eBay's head office in San Jose, California

part-timer called Chris Agarpao. He was soon joined by the company's first president, Canadian-born businessman Jeff Skoll. By the end of the year, eBay boasted 41,000 registered users, and a Gross Merchandise Volume (the total value of all goods sold on the site) of $7.2 million. eBay soon entered its first third-party licensing deal, licensing its SmartMarket Technology to a company called Electronic Travel Auction, which sold plane tickets and other such travel products.

By 1997, aided by an investment of $5,000,000 from a venture capital firm, the company had grown to 41 employees. It's said that in the early days they sat on folding chairs, and used self-assembly desks they had to screw together themselves. Unlike other hungry dot-com start-ups, Omidyar was keeping costs as low as possible, even though business was growing at a phenomenal rate. eBay was hosting over 200,000 auctions a month, compared to 250,000 auctions for the whole of 1996. Collectors found the site especially useful, with the market for Beanie Babies alone surpassing $500,000 a year. Registered users crossed the 341,000 mark, and gross sales exceeded $95 million. Feedback stars made an appearance too, joining the feedback forum introduced the previous year. In September, the

AuctionWeb name was dropped and the entire site branded under the name 'eBay'.

In March 1998, Harvard Business School graduate Margaret Whitman joined eBay as CEO to further develop and expand the business, which she went on to do with a series of shrewdly planned buyouts. The personalisation tool, My eBay, was launched to make it easier for both buyers and sellers to manage their accounts, and the eBay Foundation was set up as a charitable institution. In September, just three years after selling that broken laser pointer on his home page, eBay went public. Omidyar and Skoll became instant billionaires. By now the company boasted 138 employees, 2.1 million registered users and had a Gross Merchandise Volume of $740 million.

INTERNATIONAL REACH

1999 saw some major changes to the online auction site. First of all, it went international, with local versions of eBay launching in several countries. Germany was first, with www.ebay.de launching in June. The UK and Australia got their own eBay sites in October. The march towards world domination had begun. eBay Motors was also launched that year. This specialist site, found at www.motors.ebay.com, offers an online marketplace for cars, vans, motorcycles, boats, collectables and other vehicles, as well as parts and accessories. The 'Buy It Now' option was introduced, enabling sellers to sell at a fixed price instead of going through the auction process, and a partnership with AOL was launched. eBay paid $75 million to become AOL's official auction site for four years, giving it prominent placement on several sites owned by the ISP, including AOL.com, Compuserve, instant messaging service ICQ and the newly acquired Netcenter Web portal of Netscape Communications Corporation. By now the auction site, which was still only four years old, had 640 employees and ten million registered users.

eBay started the year 2000 as the net's number one e-commerce site, a position it cemented with a series of new international launches. In April, the auction site opened a Canadian branch, with France following in October and Austria in December. eBay Taiwan

▲ PayPal introduced Buyer Protection in 2003

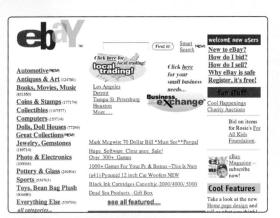

▲ eBay's front page in April 2000

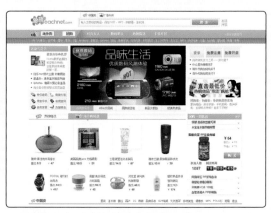

▲ eBay China is now found at www.eachnet.com

▲ By 2006, the categories list began to show the range and diversity we know today

▲ eBay UK, as it is today. Easily navigable, with lots of categories to choose from

launched this year too. But one wing of the company which wasn't doing so well was Billpoint. An online payment system bought by eBay in May 1999, Billpoint was intended to take some of the risk out of paying for goods won on eBay. By February 2000, it was processing 4,000 payments a day, but start-up company PayPal was getting through 200,000 daily transactions. Ironically, most of these were generated by eBay sales. Yet this was a minor glitch in an otherwise unqualified success story. By the end of the year, the auction site had around 1,900 employees, which was triple its 1999 workforce, and 22 million registered users.

In another charitable move, eBay launched Auction for America on 17th September 2001, to raise money for the victims of the terrorist attacks on the Pentagon and the World Trade Center six days earlier. eBay Stores was also launched that year, as were new international marketplaces in Ireland, Italy, Korea, New Zealand, Singapore and Switzerland. eBay was going from strength to strength. In the past year, its registered users had almost doubled to 42 million, and its employees swelled to 2,500.

The phishing scam that hit the site in 2001 was much less welcome. A spam e-mail claiming to be from eBay encouraged users to follow a link and enter their registration details into what was a fake version of eBay's home page. eBay issued a warning.

PAYPAL

By the summer of 2002, eBay had already acquired and swallowed up eight companies, mostly rival online auction sites. But its most significant acquisition came in October of that year. PayPal, by now a near monopoly in the independent online payments market, was bought by eBay for $1.5 billion. By the time of the buyout, PayPal was already the payment system of choice for around 50% of eBay users and, under the eBay umbrella, it continued to grow. Competing services such as Citibank's c2it and Yahoo!'s PayDirect soon closed as PayPal became as dominant in the online payments market as eBay was in online auctions. In 2008 it processed transactions of $60 billion in total, an increase of 27% over the previous year. Naturally, PayPal's position as the de rigueur payment method for eBay made life easier for eBayers. Sellers could get away with offering only one payment type without risking their auction prices, and buyers knew their PayPal accounts were valid anywhere on eBay.

eBay Facts & Figures

Here are some things you may not know about eBay:

- A women's dress is sold every 18 seconds, a mobile phone every six seconds and a major appliance every minute.
- eBay currently enjoys approximately 84 million active users worldwide.
- More than $1,900-worth of goods are traded on the site every second.
- eBay UK currently has over 15 million users, with over 70 million items listed at any one time.
- 45% of active UK Internet users visit eBay.co.uk at least once a month.
- eBay has localised websites in 30 countries.
- Since 2005, there have been over 1.5 million

charity auctions on eBay, raising more than £18.3 million.
- In 2008, the last year for which we have complete figures, the company had a turnover of $8.46 billion and a net income of $348 million.
- You can buy just about anything on eBay, which today has over 13,000 product categories, but a few items are prohibited. These include live animals, bootleg or pirated movies and music,

By 2003, eBay had topped 5,700 employees, up from 4,000 the previous year. There were around 95 million registered users, and 40 million people with PayPal accounts. And still the company continued to grow, opening a Hong Kong site in December. PayPal introduced Buyer Protection in this year. Now, if you bought an item on eBay and it didn't arrive or was significantly different to how it was described in the auction, you could appeal to PayPal and possibly get your money back (including the postage), subject to adjudication by PayPal. The maximum amount covered was boosted to $1,000 the following year. eBay UK reached a major milestone in 2003 too. Come December, it crossed the 100 million listings barrier.

2004 was another year of expansion and acquisitions, as eBay opened local sites in Malaysia and the Philippines and bought out the Bazee marketplace in India, and Rent.com closer to home. eBay also opened its China Development Center in Shanghai to accelerate technology innovation. By now it employed 8,100 staff worldwide, and enjoyed 135 million registered users.

The following year, eBay made its biggest purchase to date, paying $2.6 billion in cash and stock for Internet telephony leader Skype. Other acquisitions included Verisign Merchant Gateway and Shopping.com, and there were launches in Poland and Sweden. eBay was growing at such an incredible rate that in 2006, the company boasted 222 million users and 13,200 employees. The following year, the UK site reached another milestone, crossing the one billion listings mark. Also in 2006, eBay made available some of its programming interfaces, allowing third-party developers to build applications that work with eBay.

CHANGES

Two changes made in 2008 got a mixed reception from eBay users. At the beginning of the year, the feedback system was changed so sellers could no longer give negative feedback on buyers. The move was made due to complaints from buyers that they couldn't leave deservedly negative feedback without risking a retaliatory strike, but sellers complained they now had no recourse against a miscreant buyer. In December, the site abandoned its live auctions, which had been run in association with an auction house and allowed eBay users to bid through eBay, just as they would if they were at the venue. According to Jim Ambach, vice president of Seller Experience, live auctions were no longer part of eBay's immediate focus and were therefore retired.

While users might gripe and groan about changes in the rules and alleged lack of support when there's a problem, almost everyone agrees the site has grown in user-friendliness over the years. As Pennsylvanian eBayer Colleen Allison put it, "I've sold more on eBay in the last four months than I did in the previous three years combined, and it has definitely become more user-friendly."

And the site is growing in popularity on this side of the pond too. eBay UK, which celebrated its tenth anniversary in the autumn of 2009, today offers more than 17 million live listings at any one time. 45% of active UK Internet users visit eBay.co.uk at least once a month, and it's been estimated that 178,000 users run a business as a primary or secondary source of income. And with 13,000 categories to choose from, there's an excellent chance you'll find what you're looking for.

It seems eBay has come on a long way since it sold that broken laser pointer over a decade ago...

Chapter 2
What You Need To Get Started

Your eBay Toolkit

You've decided to give eBay a try, but don't know where to begin.
In this chapter, we show you what you need to get started

Given that eBay's an online service, the place to start with your toolkit is a computer with Internet access. Although there are now apps for mobile phones and tablets that enable you to access eBay while on the move, for best results a computer and a broadband connection can't be beaten. Dial-up is a possibility but doesn't come recommended.

You'll also need a web browser like Microsoft Internet Explorer or Mozilla Firefox so you can access eBay and the wider web. It's also advisable to have some kind of anti-virus protection and firewall installed on your computer. eBay ensures that all your personal details are encrypted using secure communication software, but it's always a good idea to protect your interests at your end.

BRING AND BUY

In addition to a computer to sit behind, a potential eBay buyer also needs a roof over their head, or at least a front door with a number or name on it. A postal address is required to receive the items you buy. To purchase said items, you'll also need a

suitable form of payment, which is not as blindingly obvious as it may sound, because it depends entirely on the seller's preferences. Some sellers will happily accept traditional forms of payment such as cash (how quaint!), postal orders and cheques. However, the vast majority of sellers prefer to receive online payments, because they're processed much more quickly and securely. Some sellers will only accept online payments using services like PayPal or Nochex.

What does this mean? Well, eBay policy now states that all sellers must offer PayPal as a payment method, so you can easily pay for any item online, although you will need a credit card or bank account to facilitate the payment. If you don't already have a PayPal account, one will be created for you. All you need to do is specify whether you want to draw the funds from a credit card or debit account. It's simple, and because the transaction is completed immediately, you can be sure that your items are winging their way towards you much more quickly.

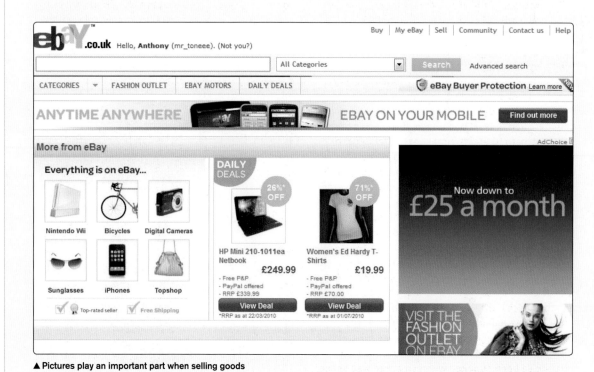

▲ Pictures play an important part when selling goods

▲ A computer is obviously one of the key requirements for any potential eBay user

THE HARD SELL

If you intend to sell items on eBay, then you also need a PayPal (or similar) account. Again, you'll need to link your online account to a credit card or bank account. As a seller, it's recommended that you verify your account. There's more information on PayPal at the end of this chapter.

An essential piece of equipment for every seller is a digital camera, as it enables you to take photographs of your items and use them to illustrate your listings. After all, people like to see exactly what they're buying. When eBay was in its infancy and digital cameras were still very much a luxury item, very few sellers uploaded images, but these days you'd be committing commercial suicide if you didn't provide at least one image. If you don't have a digital camera, then it's almost essential to get or borrow one. You'll also need some means of transferring the photos from your camera to your computer - check your camera's documentation for further details.

eBay charges you for uploading multiple pictures (only one photo per listing is free), so if you'd like to display more than one picture it's a good idea to acquire some personal web space and host the images yourself. If you're planning to sell regularly, then this will work out cheaper than having to continually pay eBay's image fees (and you won't be limited to the default 400 x 300 dimensions that eBay rather stingily resizes your images to). Check with your Internet service provider; you may find that you've been supplied with some free web space,

which will be useful for image-hosting purposes. We'll be coming back to images in more detail later in this book.

CHECK IT OUT

You should now have everything you need to start wheeling and dealing on eBay. An Internet-enabled computer? Check. A postal address? Check. A bank account and/or credit card? Check. A digital camera? Check. There's just one thing missing: an eBay account. Registering for an account is free and easy. Just follow our step-by-step guide and you'll become a member of the world's largest marketplace in a matter of minutes.

What's In A Name?

When you register with eBay, you must enter a User ID. This is your unique username that's displayed (rather than your real name) when you buy and sell on eBay. If you use eBay casually, your choice of User ID isn't overly important. It just needs to be something that a) you're not going to forget, and b) doesn't put people off. However, if you're planning on specialising in a particular area and bulk selling a certain type of product, you should choose a User ID that reflects your business. If you're not happy with your chosen ID, eBay lets you change it at any time (but not more than once a month).

How To... Set Up Your eBay Account

Whatever your reason for going to eBay, you'll need to get registered and set up your account. Here's how:

1 There are two types of eBay account: private and business. This guide covers the registration process for a private account. If the volume of items you sell increases, you can switch to a business account later. First, go to eBay directly or via a search engine.

2 The eBay home page bombards you with links and featured items. You can ignore all of this for now. Look at the top-left corner of the page and you'll see the welcome line, which reads, 'Welcome! Sign in or register.' You can browse eBay without becoming a member, but to buy and sell you must sign up to the site, so click 'Register'.

3 If it says 'Hello' followed by a username, then someone else uses eBay on the same computer, and they've asked for eBay to remember their login details for them. You must never use someone else's membership, so click the 'Sign Out' option to exit their account. You can now click the 'Register' option.

4 You're prompted to enter your details, but before you begin filling in the boxes, click on the 'Privacy Policy' link. As you'll shortly be submitting personal information, including bank account details, you should be aware of how eBay stores and uses this.

5 Don't get too hung up on the details; it's all pretty standard. Scroll down and click the 'eBay User Agreement' link when you seen it. This page displays eBay's terms and conditions, which all users have to

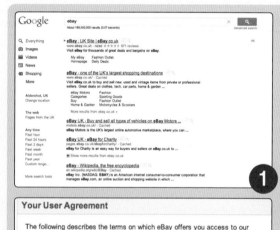

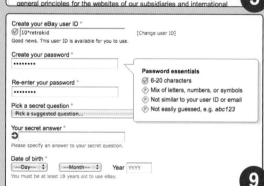

accept. Read through the details so you know where you stand as a user.

6 Okay, now you've got your head around all the legal stuff, you can return to the registration page and enter your details. The form should be familiar, as it's very similar to other online forms that you've no doubt completed in the past. All fields marked with an asterisk need to be completed.

7 Next, enter your name, address and telephone details. You must enter your primary phone number. There's no need to worry about receiving unsolicited calls, because eBay will only contact you by telephone in the event of there being a problem with your account. Similarly, you're also required to enter a working e-mail address.

8 The next step is to enter your User ID (see the previous information about suitable usernames). Enter your User ID and wait while the site checks it. If

the username you've opted for has already been taken by another user, the site will suggest several alternatives that you can choose from instead.

9 Once your User ID has been accepted, you then have to create a password to go with it. To ensure your chosen password is secure, a number of rules are imposed: it must be at least six characters in length; include a mixture of numbers, letters and symbols; not be similar to your username or e-mail address; and not easily guessable.

10 When you enter a password, eBay will instantly assess it and let you know if it satisfies all of the rules. If any red flags appear, you must tweak your password until four green flags are displayed. When eBay is happy with your password, you must re-enter it in the box below for verification purposes.

11 In case you forget your password later, you must enter the answer to one of the secret questions. If

you then request for your password to be sent to you, eBay will ask you your chosen secret question and will only supply the password if the correct answer is given.

12 Next, enter your date of birth using the day and month drop-down menus, then tap the year into the final box. This step checks that you're 18 or over. If you're under 18, then you're not legally allowed to buy and sell on eBay. Sorry, kids!

13 To ensure you're a real flesh-and-blood person and not an evil account-registering robot, you must enter the numeric verification code in the box. If you're struggling to decipher the jumble of numbers, click the 'Refresh this image' link until a clear code appears.

14 Tick the box at the bottom to confirm you've read the User Agreement and the Privacy Policy, and understood the terms of use, then click the 'Register' button at the bottom of the page. eBay will then send a confirmation e-mail to your chosen e-mail address.

15 Open your e-mail application and wait for the message to land in your inbox (it may take a short while to arrive, so don't worry if it doesn't appear immediately). When it does, click on the 'Confirm Now' button on the e-mail to confirm that your e-mail address is correct.

16 If for some reason nothing happens when you click on the link, you'll notice that a Confirmation Code is also included in the e-mail. Copy this code and then click the link displayed below. You'll be taken to a screen where you can paste the code and confirm your e-mail address. Click 'Register' when done.

17 Once your e-mail address has been confirmed, you will be automatically signed in under your User ID. You can now begin to browse, bid for and buy items. However, if you wish to sell items on eBay you must follow some additional steps, in order to create a seller's account.

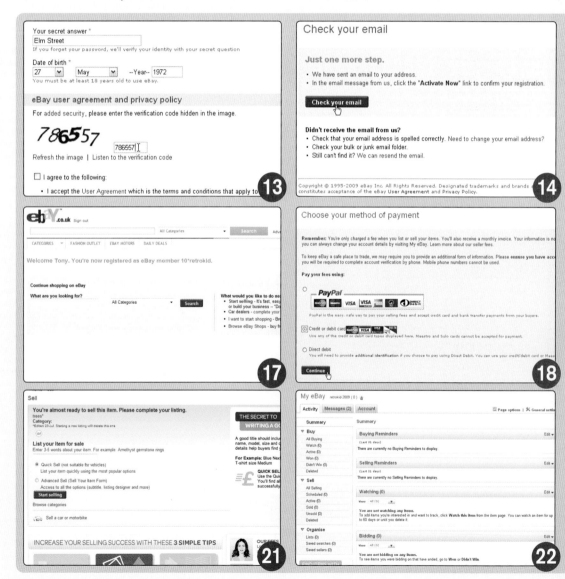

18 As a new eBay user, before you can list your first item, you'll be prompted to register as a seller. You will incur fees every time you sell an item, so you have to select a method of payment from the three available options: PayPal, credit/debit card, or direct debit.

19 If you choose to put your debit or credit card on record, carefully enter the card details, making sure all the fields are filled in. The billing address for the card must match the address you registered with. If you need to amend the address, click the 'Change' link.

20 As an extra security measure, eBay will confirm your landline telephone number with an automated call in which you're given a confirmation code. Click the 'Call Me' button, then answer the call and jot down the four-digit code. Enter the code on screen to continue.

21 Once you've chosen how you wish to pay for your eBay selling fees, you will become a registered seller and be returned to the selling screen. All fees you now incur will be paid automatically on a monthly basis.

22 It's important you keep your personal details up to date. If you need to make a change, click the 'My eBay' option found at the top of every eBay page. Here you can monitor items you're watching or selling, view messages, change preferences and update your details.

23 Open the 'Account' tab at the top of the page and click the 'Personal Information' link. You'll see all the information you entered when you registered. To make a change, click the 'Edit' link to the right of the detail you wish to amend. You will be prompted to re-enter your password for each change.

24 If you should forget either your User ID or password, go to the Register screen and you'll see links that you can use to request a reminder. For your password, you'll need to answer your secret question and enter various personal details.

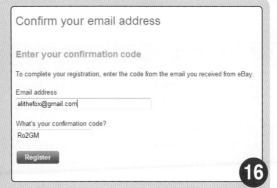

Get To Grips With PayPal

If you're going to be a good eBayer, it's worth getting yourself an account with its most popular payment system

PayPal is eBay's own online payment system that enables you to send and receive funds via the Internet. Essentially, it acts as a monetary middleman between the buyer and the seller, ensuring that the transaction is both speedy and secure (neither party has access to the other's personal banking details). It should come as no surprise, then, that it has become phenomenally popular as a payment method on eBay, with reports suggesting that more than 90% of all

eBay purchases are handled through the service that PayPal offers.

No longer must buyers post off cheques or postal orders and then be forced to wait for the funds to clear at the other end before receiving the item. No longer must sellers trudge into town to cash these bothersome bits of paper at their local bank. Instead, the funds are transferred between parties in less time than it takes to simply click a mouse button.

How To... Set Up A PayPal Account

As well as being a convenient way to pay for goods on eBay, PayPal is also used by many other sites to transfer money. And if you want to be an eBay Seller, it's compulsory to offer it to your buyers. To set up an account, just follow these six simple steps, and you'll be ready before you know it.

1 To begin, simply go to **www.paypal.co.uk** and click the orange 'Sign Up' button on the left of the page. Choose your country from the drop-down menu and select the type of account you wish to open; this example shows you how to open a Personal account, which is ideal for buying and selling online.

2 Begin by entering your e-mail address. In PayPal, your e-mail address is the equivalent of your eBay User ID. Whenever you sign into the

site, you will have to enter your e-mail address and password, and during all transactions your e-mail address is displayed. Your password must be at least eight characters long.

3 Fill in the rest of the form (all fields are mandatory). Your address must match the billing address of the debit or credit card you plan to link your PayPal account to. A telephone number is required so that PayPal can contact you quickly should a problem arise with your account.

4 Carefully enter the details of your credit or debit card. The CSC is the identification number usually found on the back of your card. Browse the PayPal Service Description, User Agreement and Privacy Policy pages, and when you're happy, click 'Agree and Create Account'.

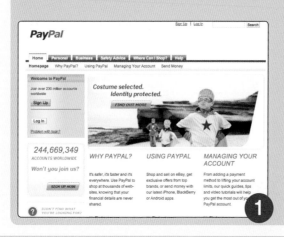

COUNTING THE COST

For the buyer, PayPal is a completely free service. It costs nothing to open an account and nothing to send money to other users. You simply link your PayPal account to your bank account or debit/credit card and PayPal will automatically withdraw and transfer funds when you wish to make a payment.

The seller, however, must pay a fee each time they receive a credit or debit card funded payment. This fee is typically around 3% of the total amount. Some users begrudge paying these charges, particularly as PayPal is owned by eBay, and eBay already charges sellers a listing and final percentage fee. The way they see it, they're getting hit in the pocket twice. However, the majority of people don't mind paying a bit extra, as PayPal really does take the hassle out of receiving payments, and the service's added security is also a valuable asset.

HELD TO ACCOUNT

PayPal offers three different types of account: Personal, Premier and Business. Business is self-explanatory, but what's the difference between Personal and Premier? In short, a Personal account is ideal for those who'll be shopping more than selling. You can accept payments from other users, but there's a monthly volume limit. A Premier account is essentially the same, but there's no limit, so if you plan to sell regularly on eBay, a Premier account is recommended. If you're not sure, begin by opening a Personal account, and you can upgrade to either a Premier or Business account later.

It should be pointed out that while PayPal is preferred by most eBay users, alternative online payment systems such as WorldPay and Nochex are available. The alternatives are covered elsewhere in this guide.

5 PayPal will validate your credit or debit card details and, provided everything is okay, you will see this success screen. Your PayPal account is now active and you can use it to pay for items online and send money to other PayPal users. The final step is to get your account verified.

6 By verifying your account you will lift the spending limits imposed on unverified accounts. It's easy to do and basically involves adding a bank account and supplying additional business information. To do this, sign into your account and click the 'Get Verified' link, then follow the steps.

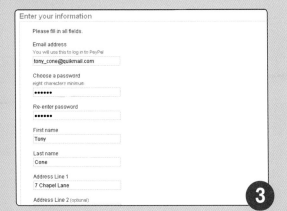

Case Study: **Luzern Solutions**

eBay can be a great way for businesses to expand, as this electronics company explains...

Not every business starts off on eBay. Some are already established and then use the auction site as a way of opening up a fresh frontier. It's what Irish company Luzern Solutions (**stores.ebay.co.uk/ LuzernTech**) did and, with around 87,000 feedbacks to its name, it's doing pretty well.

Luzern offers a range of electronic goods whether they be televisions or computers, as well as a range of consumer items. The company was once particularly strong when it came to selling refurbished products and it used to specialise in PDAs and smartphones but it has since expanded.

That said, selling refurbished products is an idea worth exploring. Doing so takes advantage of the problems companies face when people return items to a shop. Often the returned item has been removed from its original packaging, so the shop cannot then resell the product as new. The shop will return the goods to the manufacturer, which then has to work out what to do with them.

That's where a refurbished seller steps in. It snaps up the opened goods, refurbishes them, ensures they're in great shape and then ships them out to lucky eBay punters. Nowadays, however, Luzern partners with leading brands and retailers including Acer, Creative, Palm, Philips, LG and Sony.

Luzern sells a lot of stock through eBay, although it also has a stand-alone website. Although it has a range of Buy It Now offers, it typically starts its auctions at the low possible price of 99p and it does not include a reserve. This means buyers have complete influence over the resulting price and there are substantial savings to be made.

Operations director Shane Manton said, "We believe Luzern has many advantages over high-street electrical stores. In the high street, you pay what the retailer demands, but through eBay we offer open auctions where you can get a real bargain and that encourages people to buy.

"And I would also say that feedback is vitally important. It says everything about your service. We take it very seriously."

LuzernTech's strength also lies in making its presence known. It has regular auctions each day, never ending before noon or after 11.30pm. Its research shows that ending auctions outside of those times tends to lower the final price the item fetches.

The large number of goods for sale each day also means buyers have a higher chance of clicking on one of its offerings. Even if the buyer does not decide to bid on that particular item, he or she may be tempted to click on the link that takes you to the Luzern eBay shop. And then the buyer is presented with a huge range of goods from which to chose.

Mr Manton said, "Auctions allow you gain reasonable volume of customers and, of course, auctions are a true reflection of the open market worth of a product. The internet allows you the potential to get to the maximum audience. The web is so vast it's often difficult to ensure they find you, yet eBay makes it easier."

The eBay shop runs alongside Luzern's own website, which offers items at fixed prices in both pound sterling and euros. But Mr Manton says eBay is an important part of the business.

The eBay shop is well branded and easy to navigate. It clearly states what Luzern is and does and it has a list of all the items up for auction. The site also includes the all-important 'About Me' icon, a quick click on that shows the extent of the company's operation.

We Ship to Mainland UK & Ireland Only
Monday to Thursday 8.30am to 5pm
Friday 8.30am to 4pm

Customer Services
+44 (0) 203 3185 987
+353 (1) 811 9080

customer.care@luzernsolutions.com

Luzern

Enter keywords here... **Search**

Accessories Bluetooth-Headsets Buy It Now Camcorders/Cameras GPS Home Cinema Systems Laptop Bags LCD TV's Lighting Mobile Phones

HIS AND HERS
TOMMY HILFIGER
WATCHES

Categories

Accessories

Audio - HiFi

Philips 40" LCD TV 40PFL5605H Full HD Pixel Plus HD USB

▲ Luzern sells a wide range of good via its eBay store

As well as company information, the site aims to give buyers even greater confidence in making a purchase from the shop. There's a bunch of links that explain the warranty, terms of sale and shipping costs. There's also a 'Frequently Asked Questions' section.

Luzern only accepts eBay payments via PayPal. It does not accept cash or cheques and says this makes payment more accountable and prevents the hassle of bounced or forged cheques or having to wait for cheque clearance.

Luzern is a PowerSeller and, as such, is regarded as a pillar of the eBay community. The powers-that-be at eBay say PowerSellers are exemplary members with 98% positive feedback and an excellent sales performance record.

Mr Manton advises looking for outside help in expanding your online venture. In 2003, Luzern secured investment from Enterprise Ireland, an Irish government-supported enterprise agency. Similar

▶ Shane Manton, Luzern's operation director

enterprise schemes operate across the UK and Ireland, although there are fewer today.

So what are the secrets of Luzern's success? Mr Manton said, "Our main selling points are great prices, quality of product and service. You can't go wrong with those three."

▲ Luzern's eBay Shop supports its stand-alone business

▲ eBay gives Luzern's customers the chance to bag a bargain

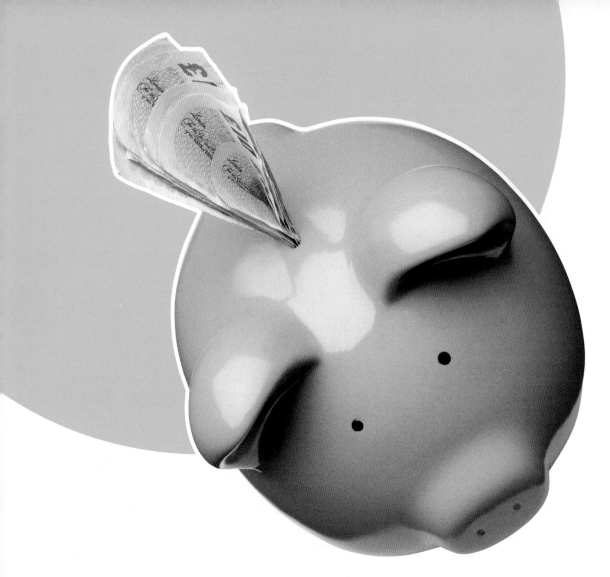

Chapter 3
Introductory Selling

Let's Start Selling

Your listing is your virtual shop window, so if you want to draw in the punters, it pays to spend some time making it look good

It's easy to start selling on eBay: just click 'Sell' in the menu bar (the menu bar appears in the top-right corner of almost every page, so you'll seldom have trouble finding it). There's no messing about; you're whisked immediately into the listing wizard. Jump right in, using the steps below to guide you through the various options and stages. You don't need to be signed into your account in order to begin a listing, but sooner or later in the process it'll become essential, so you might as well log in before you start.

CHOOSE A CATEGORY

First, you need to choose the category in which your item will appear. There are more than 30 main categories and several thousand subcategories, so it's essential to take your time and choose carefully. If you list your item in anything but the most appropriate category, untold numbers of potential bidders might never find it.

Pinpointing the right category for your item can be achieved in one of two ways. One method is to type some keywords into the text box. Maybe you've been clearing out your cupboards and you've unearthed a still unopened model kit. Your keywords in that case might be 'knight rider model car' (unless it's a Lancaster bomber, of course). When you're done, click 'Start selling'. You're now taken to a 'hit list' of likely categories. Tick the box beside the one you think fits the bill (very often this isn't the one at the top). Once you're happy with your choice, click 'Continue'.

The second method of choosing a category is to browse for it manually. To do that, click 'Browse categories' (available on both the initial selling page and the 'hit list' page). Now you can explore every single main category and every single subcategory. Drill down through the lists until you reach what seems most appropriate. Click 'Continue' when you're done.

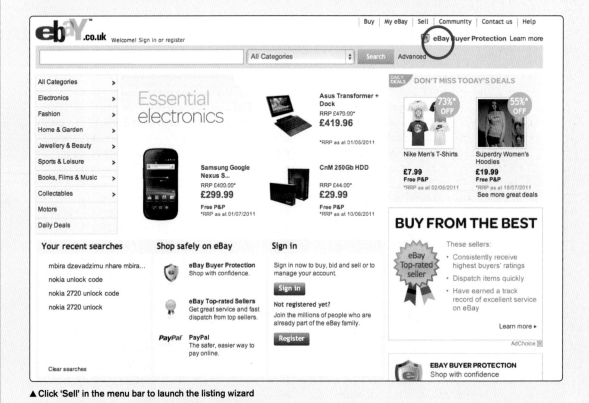

▲ Click 'Sell' in the menu bar to launch the listing wizard

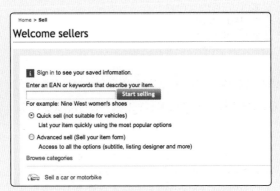

▲ One way to select a category is to enter some keywords

▲ Tick the most appropriate category

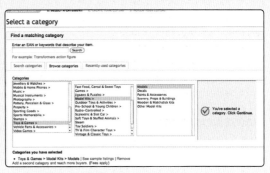

▲ You can list your item in two categories

It's a good idea to satisfy yourself that you've chosen your category wisely. To do that, click 'See sample listings', a link that appears near the bottom of the page once you've made your selection. A list of recently completed auctions then pops into view. Does your item sit well with what else is on offer? Are other people with listings in Toys & Games > Model Kits > Models selling vehicles from 1980s TV shows? If not, a rethink is probably in order.

Tip: When starting a listing, you'll probably notice there are two approaches: Quick Sell and Advanced Sell. Advanced Sell, the default, is the traditional approach, and the one shown throughout this guide. Quick Sell is a relatively new approach, where the listing process is semi-automated and you're offered only a limited set of options and upgrades. It's best used only for very simple listings.

ADD A SECOND CATEGORY

Sometimes the item you're selling might be appropriate for two different categories. When that happens, you can list it in both. Take the Knight Rider model, for instance. Examples of this item can regularly be found not only in Toys & Games > Model Kits > Models but also in Toys & Games > Diecast & Vehicles > Other Diecast & Vehicles. That might seem a pretty poor choice, but who cares? If this is where people are looking for such things, it's as valid a category as any.

If you use the keyword method to select a category, adding a second one is as simple as putting ticks in two different boxes. If you use the browsing method, you need to click 'Add a second category and reach more buyers', a link near the bottom of the page. You can then drill down through the categories and subcategories again.

The snag with listing in two categories - and it's a big one - is that most of your listing fees get doubled (but not your selling fees). Usually, you pay the same as you would for listing two separate

items. The only fee that remains single-rated is the one charged for scheduling (an option covered later in the chapter).

COMPOSE YOUR TITLE

Now it's time to look at one of the most important aspects of selling on eBay: the task of building up your actual listing. The first job is to compose a title. This is the heading that buyers will see when they're looking through lists of items.

Imagine a shopper called Mr Browser. He wants to buy a music CD. He walks into a record shop, wanders up and down the aisles, flicks through the racks, and sooner or later finds the title he's looking for. It's as good a method as any, and Mr Browser uses just the same technique when shopping on eBay. He picks a category that looks appropriate, roots through the subcategories, peruses the pages of auction headings, and eventually finds an example of the item he wants to bid on. Mr Browser is why listing your item in the right category is critical.

Then there's Mrs Specific. When she wants a music CD, she walks into a record shop, heads immediately for the counter, asks the assistant for the location of the desired title, and plucks it straight off the shelf. On eBay, Mrs Specific doesn't bother with categories. Instead, she enters some keywords into the search box. The only auctions

Help buyers find your item with a great title Add or remove options | G

★ **Title** ⓘ

Knight rider model car

Subtitle (£0.35) ⓘ

Collectors item

Condition ⓘ

Used

EAN

4263345 330027

4263345330027

▲ For the title and subtitle, you get just 55 characters apiece

Item specifics ⓘ

Add more information to help buyers find your item in search results. Buyers can popular item specifics to refine their search and locate your item faster.

Type Remove

Cars

Model Remove

Subtype Remove

Brand Remove

Aoshima

▲ Item specifics can help your item appear in more searches

she's then given to look through are those with titles that contain her keywords (and such auctions might be spread across a dozen different categories). Mrs Specific is why your auction title needs to be just right.

You've only got 55 characters to play with, so think carefully about what you write. The art of creating a solid title is covered in 'What Makes A Good eBay Listing?' elsewhere in this book.

ADD A SUBTITLE

Adding a subtitle is optional. It costs £0.35. You get a further 55 characters, but bear in mind that they're only scanned in searches if a buyer elects to search both titles and descriptions (one of many optional search criteria). Most buyers don't bother. Don't worry too much about keywords, then; be free and loose. As with your title, the art of a good subtitle is covered elsewhere in this eBay guide.

SELECT ITEM SPECIFICS

Next you need to complete the item specifics. These are presented in the form of drop-down menus, the headings for which depend on the category in which you're listing your item. For Toys & Games > Model Kits > Models, the headings are Type, Subtype, Model, Scale, Brand, and Condition. The Condition menu, which offers choices of New and Used, is common to all categories (even Antiques, oddly enough).

Often the choices in a menu aren't suitable. For example, in the Brand menu for Toys & Games >

Model Kits > Models, there's no Aoshima. That's bad luck if you're listing a plastic K.I.T.T. from one of Japan's top model makers! When this happens, though, you can select 'Other'. This opens up a free-form text box in which you can enter anything you like. Alternatively, you can opt to specify nothing; just leave the menu on '-'.

Tip: Many sellers don't bother with item specifics, preferring instead to leave them all blank. However, when buyers perform searches, they can opt to only see results that fulfil certain criteria. One of those criteria is whether or not an item is new or not. If yours is, then be sure to say so under the Condition heading. Do that at the very least, because if you don't, your item could easily be missed unwittingly by thousands of potential buyers.

UPLOAD A PICTURE

They say a picture is worth a thousand words. Nowhere is that more true than in the world of eBay. An item illustrated with at least one good image will receive hugely more interest - and perhaps higher bids - than an otherwise identical item described by words alone.

Your first picture is free. To get started, click 'Add pictures'. This opens a new window, and you're presented with two tabs: Standard and Basic. You can also get a third tab by selecting the self hosting box under 'Add or remove options'. The Standard tab is your best bet (and the one used in this guide). The Basic tab is similar but it lacks the handy editing tools that allow you to alter a picture's size, rotation, contrast, and brightness.

In the new window, click 'Browse'. This will bring up a dialogue box that enables you to leaf through the folders on your hard drive and other storage devices. Once you've located your chosen picture, double-click the filename or highlight it and click 'Open'. You can add up to a further 11 pictures (under '2', '3', '4', and so on), though each one after the first carries a price of £0.12. When you've added all you want, click 'Upload'.

GIZZMOHEAVEN UK SELLER	8GB SANDISK SD SDHC MEMORY CARD FOR CASIO NIKON CANON BRAND NEW	FREE DELIVERY	UK SELLER	CLASS 4	Top-rated seller	Buy It Now	£7.75 Free
All in 1	ALL IN ONE MEMORY CARD READER MINI SD MMC M2 XD CF		1 Bid	£3.49 Free
GIZZMOHEAVEN UK SELLER	2GB SANDISK SD MEMORY CARD FOR CASIO CANON IXUS KODAK	Top-rated seller	Buy It Now	£3.68 Free

▲ Examples of listings with and without subtitles

Bring your item to life with pictures   Add or remove options | Get help

You can add another picture for free. ⓘ

(Add pictures)   Remove all pictures   Your pictures: 1 | 11 more d

1

« » 🗑

ⓘ 1 out of 1 images are not optimal.

ⓘ Good news. Gallery picture is free. Add a picture and we'll show your item to buyers in se
results. ⓘ

▲ To add an image, click 'Add pictures'

If you prefer, your free picture can be one that's hosted on the web. This is useful if your Internet account comes with free web space or if you're signed up with a photo-sharing site such as Photobucket (**photobucket.com**) or Flickr (**www. flickr.com**). To use this service, click 'Add pictures' and then use the Self Hosting tab. In the text box, enter the full URL (web address) of where your picture is located. To finish, click 'Insert Picture'.

Sadly, the Self Hosting option is a mere shadow of what it once was. Until recently, you could add up to six pictures, but now you can only add one (the free one). Don't go thinking you can add one picture via Self Hosting and then several others by uploading them from your hard drive; it's either one method or the other. It's a great shame. The mind boggles at why eBay has crippled what used to be such a valuable service.

Tip: The maximum picture size is 4MB if you use the Basic tab and 8MB if you use the Enhanced tab (there's no limit if you use Self Hosting). To help them load quickly in bidders' browsers, pictures are automatically compressed when they appear in your actual listing (though this doesn't apply to Self Hosting, so be careful). You can use any of the following formats: JPG, BMP, GIF (both static and animated), TIF/TIFF, PCX, and PNG.

DECIDE ON PICTURE UPGRADES

As standard, your first picture appears in small form at the top of your listing and in larger form near the bottom. Additional pictures appear near

Standard | Copy web files | Self hosting | Basic

Self hosting   For better results, we recommend you copy the web files to eBay.

Your first self-hosted picture has been copied to the eBay server and will display on your item page. If we can't copy it, we display the original.
Enter the URL (web address) of picture to link to on a web server
http://

Select optional picture upgrades

ⓘ Good news. Gallery picture is free. Add a picture and we'll show your item to buyers in search results. ⓘ

Gallery Plus (£0.95)
☐ Display a large picture in search results — capture special details or different views for buyers.

(Insert picture) Cancel

▲ If you prefer, you can host your free picture on the web

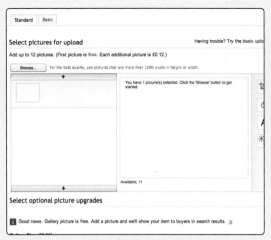

Standard | Basic

Select pictures for upload   Having trouble? Try the basic uplo

Add up to 12 pictures. (First picture is free. Each additional picture is £0.12.)

(Browse...)   For the best quality, use pictures that are more than 1000 pixels in height or width.

You have 1 picture(s) selected. Click the 'Browse' button to get started.

Available: 11

Select optional picture upgrades

ⓘ Good news. Gallery picture is free. Add a picture and we'll show your item to buyers in search results. ⓘ

▲ If your image is on your hard drive, use the Standard tab and click 'Browse'

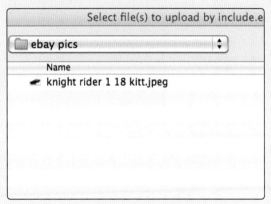

Select file(s) to upload by include.e

📁 ebay pics   ▲▼

Name

🖼 knight rider 1 18 kitt.jpeg

▲ Leaf through your folders to find the right image

the bottom in a cluster of clickable thumbnails. If you'd like more control and sophistication, you need to use one or more of eBay's picture upgrades. These are described below.

FREE **Gallery:** With the Gallery upgrade, a thumbnail of your item gets shown beside your title on search results pages. Buyers can then see what you're selling without actually having to open up the full listing. Until last year, Gallery used to cost £0.15, but now - hallelujah! - it's free. Previously, without it, all that appeared against your title was a camera icon (so long as your listing actually contained a picture at all).

£0.95 **Gallery Plus:** Gallery Plus is essentially the Gallery option gone large. As with Gallery, a thumbnail image of your item gets shown beside your listing's title on search results pages, but there's a big difference -quite literally. If an interested eBay user hovers over the Enlarge link, the image pops up in its own box,

▲ Multiple images are shown below your main image as an interactive slideshow

▲ You can choose to enlarge the image to take a closer look as well

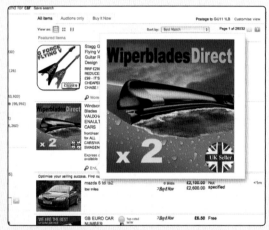

▲ Go large with Gallery Plus

greatly magnified - up to 400 x 400 pixels. Additional pictures in the listing are shown in the box as thumbnails, and the buyer can also magnify those as well.

£0.60 Supersize: If you want any potential bidders to see your item in greater detail, you can pay for the Supersize upgrade. When they click on a picture (perhaps a thumbnail in the cluster at the bottom of your listing page), it will then display at up to 800 x 800 pixels (assuming your pictures are at least that size

to begin with). The standard size is only up to 400 x 400, so the result it truly impressive. Be aware, however, that Supersize isn't available if you're also using the Self Hosting option.

FREE Picture Show: As with Gallery, the Picture Show upgrade used to cost £0.15, but now you get it automatically for free if you're including at least two pictures. It replaces the item image at the top of your listing with an interactive slideshow. This cycles through your images one by one, and buyers can stop it, start it, move forward, and move back. If you also buy the Supersize upgrade, buyers can view the slideshow in a separate window, where the images are displayed at up to 800 x 800 pixels. Note that Picture Show isn't available if you're using the Self Hosting option.

£0.90 Picture Pack: Normally, if you bought five extra pictures and the Supersize option, you'd pay £1.20. With the Picture Pack upgrade, you pay just £0.90. With eleven extra pictures and Supersize, Picture Pack costs £1.35, whereas buying the upgrades separately would set you back £1.92. If you really believe your listing can't survive without every picture upgrade going, Picture Pack can save you a fair few pennies. Note that Picture Pack isn't available if you're using the Self Hosting option.

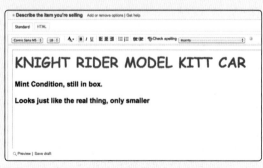

▲ The Standard window provides basic formatting tools

▲ Use HTML to truly customise your listing

▲ £0.07 buys you a theme

▲ Themes can really help spruce up a listing...

▲ ...but be sure to choose one that's appropriate!

COMPOSE YOUR DESCRIPTION

Next up is the main attraction: your item description. A poor description can mean low bids and even no sale. A fabulous description can send the bidding through the roof. The lowdown on putting together something perfect is covered in greater detail towards the end of this chapter.

You can enter your description using either the Standard window or the HTML window (click the tabs to switch between the two). Private sellers usually use the Standard window. To help bolster and brighten your text, there's a toolbar giving you basic word-processing functions - font, size, colour, bold, centre, and so on. You can also insert bullet points and give your spelling the once over.

The HTML window allows you to build up your description like a web page. This is the approach often taken by business sellers; it requires some effort and a little bit of skill, but the results tend to be more professional. You don't get any editing facilities, however, so your best bet is to use a separate website designer and then copy and paste your HTML from there. A simple but workable solution (and it's free!) is the Composer applet built into the Mozilla SeaMonkey suite (**www. seamonkey-project.org**).

Tip: With some simple HTML, you can adorn your description with as many (web-hosted) pictures as you care to include - any size, any position, and all for free. Why not run a Google search and track down an introductory HTML tutorial?

ENHANCE YOUR LAYOUT

Does your listing look drab or boring? If you think so, you can apply a theme. This gets you a fancy border, a background and some clipart. You can also specify where your pictures go - top, bottom, left, or right. The price is £0.07. It's an upgrade that works best on a Standard description, but you can also use it if you've gone down the HTML route.

There are dozens and dozens of themes to choose from. If you're selling a kettle, for example, you could use In The Home-Kitchen. For a model of

Michael Knight's K.I.T.T., it might be fun to go for Entertainment-Fun and Games. There's a preview link, so you can see what your choices look like in the flesh. Have a play!

PICK A VISITOR COUNTER

A visitor counter - otherwise known as a hit counter - indicates how many buyers have checked your listing out. Only unique visits are recorded; if the same buyer visits multiple times, you get just the one hit. The counter, if you choose one, appears at the bottom of your description.

There are three types to choose from: Basic Style, Retro-computer Style, and Hidden. The Hidden counter is visible only to you; buyers never see it. Sometimes an auction with a lot of hits (several hundred) can pull in the bids, because buyers get the impression your item is something

---

Visitor counter ⓘ
Basic Style ▾ `01234`

Visitor counter ⓘ
Retro-computer Style ▾ `01234`

Visitor counter ⓘ
Hidden ▾ Thanks for looking!

▲ Examples of the three hit counters: Basic Style, Retro-computer Style, and Hidden

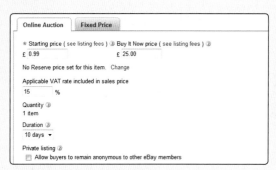

▲ Fill in your auction's starting price...

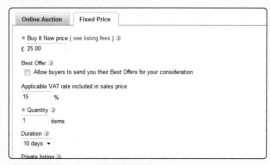

▲ ...or choose to sell at a fixed price

▲ A standard auction in action (with the Buy It Now option)

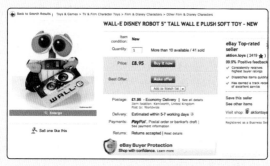

▲ A fixed-price 'auction' in action (with the Best Offer option)

special. Conversely, an auction with scarcely a handful of hits (half a dozen) can put buyers off (perhaps your item has something wrong with it?). If in doubt, choose Hidden.

Always have a counter of some sort; it's good to know what interest your auction's attracting. Indeed, a counter is such a useful feature it's a miracle eBay doesn't charge for it!

THE STANDARD AUCTION

There are two sorts of listing: auction and fixed-price. Select the one you want by simply clicking on the appropriate tab. This section deals with auction listings.

An auction is exactly what you'd expect: people bid against each other over a set period of time and the person who bids the highest in that time wins the item. First, then, you need to enter your item's starting price. The figure you enter here can determine the 'insertion fee' eBay will take for hosting your auction. This fee is also dependent on what you're selling.

For mobile phones with contracts, the insertion fee is a flat £7.95, regardless of your starting price. It's a similar story for property; the flat fee there is £35. For media items (books, magazines, CDs, DVDs, videogames, and the like), there's no insertion fee at all if your starting price is £0.99 or lower (except if you're a business seller, where it's £0.05). For media items starting at £1 or higher, the fee is £0.10. For every other type of item (including mobile phones without contracts), the

insertion fee rises with the starting price, as listed in the scale below:

- £0.01-£0.99 = Free (or £0.10 if you're a business seller)
- £1-£4.99 = £0.15
- £5-£14.99 = £0.25
- £15-£29.99 = £0.50
- £30-£99.99 = £1
- £100+ = £1.30

If you're worried your item might sell for below its worth, you can specify a reserve price. To do that, click the 'Change' link, which opens a separate window that allows you to enter the desired amount (£50 is the minimum). If the bids on your item fail to reach this figure, the item remains unsold. Of course, there's a fee for this upgrade (in addition to the insertion fee). For property, it's a flat £2. For everything else, it depends on the reserve's size:

- £50-£4,999.99 = 2% of reserve
- £5,000+ = £100

If you want, you can also specify a Buy It Now price (though to do so you need a verified PayPal account and a feedback rating of ten or higher). This enables a buyer to cut out the bidding process altogether and click a button to purchase your item immediately (thus ending the auction). As soon as someone makes an opening bid, however, the Buy It Now button disappears; your listing continues as

DID YOU KNOW?

Approximately 15% of eBay deals are cross-border transactions, with the seller in one country and the buyer in another.

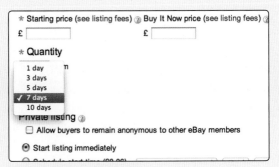

▲ Choose your auction's duration

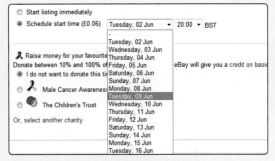

▲ Specify when you'd like your auction to begin

a standard auction. If you've set a reserve, the Buy It Now button will remain in place until the reserve's been met. There's a fee for all this, naturally, and the amount you'll pay depends on your Buy It Now price (which must be at least £0.99). The rates are listed below:

- £0.99-£4.99 = £0.05
- £5-£14.99 = £0.10
- £15-£29.99 = £0.15
- £30+ = £0.25

Tip: If your item is a road vehicle, caravan, boat, or aircraft, it falls under the umbrella of eBay Motors (this applies equally to fixed-price listings, covered next). The fee structure in that case is somewhat different to that outlined above. For more detail, see **pages.ebay.co.uk/help/sell/motorfees.html**.

THE FIXED-PRICE 'AUCTION'
A fixed-price auction, also known as a Buy It Now (or BIN) auction, really isn't an auction at all. You see, there's no bidding. None at all. It works similarly to the Buy It Now option in a standard auction (and, like there, you need a verified PayPal account and a feedback rating of ten or higher). Basically, you set your price (£0.99 is the minimum) and then a buyer, if he or she likes what's on offer, simply clicks a button to 'win' your item. The insertion fee is always a flat amount, regardless of your selling price, but, as shown below, there are different figures for different types of item:

- Mobile phones with contracts = £7.95
- Property = £35
- Media = £0.20
- Everything else = £0.40

With a fixed-price auction, there's also the option to adorn your listing with a Best Offer mark. With this, if a buyer likes your item but doesn't want to pay the full price, he or she can click 'Make Offer' and submit a suggested figure. It's a bargaining tool. eBay forwards you an e-mail with the offer

and you have 48 hours to accept or decline (unless the auction finishes sooner). The best thing about this upgrade is that there's no fee!

Tip: You should only alter the VAT rate from the default if you're a VAT-registered business selling an item at net price (this applies equally to standard-auction listings). Private sellers sometimes erroneously alter the rate to 0%, believing VAT isn't relevant. Don't make this mistake; potential buyers might get confused and think VAT will be slapped on to the final price!

THE LONG AND THE SHORT OF IT
Your listing can run for three days, five days, seven days, or ten days. For standard auctions (but not fixed-price ones), a one-day option is also available (so long as you've got a feedback rating of five or higher). For fixed-price auctions (but not standard ones), there's a 30-day option too. The snag with that, though, is that it trebles every listing fee except the insertion fee. The default length is seven days, but if you'd like to change that, simply make your choice from the Duration drop-down box.

Ordinarily, your auction begins immediately after you submit your listing. That means it'll finish at the same time of day it begins and one, three, five, seven, ten, or 30 days later (depending on what duration you've chosen). If you prefer, you can set up a schedule. For £0.06 (and as long as you have a credit or debit card linked to your account for billing purposes), you can have your auction start at any time you choose and on any day up to three weeks into the future. Simple use the relevant drop-down boxes to do so.

KEEPING THINGS PRIVATE
At this stage, there's an option to make matters private. Ordinarily, the User IDs of all bidders and

> Private listing ⓘ
> ☑ Allow buyers to remain anonymous to other eBay members
> ○ Start listing immediately
> ● Schedule start time (£0.06)   Tuesday, 02 Jun ▾   20:00 ▾ BST

▲ If necessary, you can hide bidders' identities

▲ Charity begins at eBay

▲ Decide how your item will be delivered

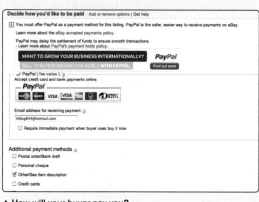

▲ Do you want to ship abroad?

buyers are available for everyone to see. If you tick the appropriate box, however, only you, as the auction's 'owner', will be able to see these IDs. Be aware, though, that doing this can attract suspicion, because people might wonder what you're hiding. Use this option only if you've got a genuine reason to keep your bidders' and buyers' identities a secret.

WANT TO GIVE GENEROUSLY?

If you're feeling particularly generous, you have the option of giving a portion of your sale's proceeds to charity. You can either choose one of the charities featured by eBay or, alternatively, you can click the link to choose your own. Doing the latter opens up a new window, from where you can select from over 3,500 institutions. The percentage you decide to give can be between 10% and 100% (in 5% increments), but the minimum amount is £1. By default, all donations are collected via the same payment method used to collect your eBay fees (in practice, PayPal or a debit or credit card), but you have the option to change this from within your account settings.

As an incentive, eBay reduces your insertion fee and final value fee by the same percentage as you donate. For example, if you donate 10% and your

insertion fee and final value fee total £1, you'll only be charged £0.90. Bonus!

MONEY, MONEY, MONEY

Next, you need to decide how the winner of your item will pay. This is a simple section to complete; you just tick the relevant boxes. PayPal used to be optional but, with the exception of listings for property, services, and eBay Motors, it's now compulsory. Be sure to enter the correct e-mail address here; you wouldn't be the first to discover payment has been made to someone else's account!

If you're running a listing with a Buy It Now price (either a fixed-price listing or a standard auction),

▲ How will your buyer pay you?

▲ What's your returns policy?

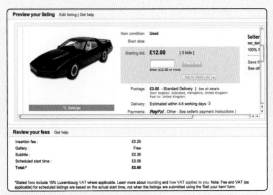

▲ Preview your listing and make final edits before putting it up

▲ Time to groan: see how much it's all going to cost

you can choose to display a message informing buyers that you require immediate payment (via PayPal). Tick the relevant box to enable this feature. If you do, when a buyer 'buys' your item, it'll remain unsold and available to everyone else until that buyer makes payment.

SHIPPING AND STUFF

Next come the shipping options. You need to decide what delivery service you're going to use, how much you'll charge your buyer for it, whether or not you're going to offer insurance, when you'll dispatch, and what countries or territories you're prepared to ship to. This section is another point-and-shoot affair. Simply tick the boxes, select from the menus, and enter your figures. If you're willing to dispatch your item within one business day of the sale and use an overnight delivery service, you can also choose to have a Get It Fast logo appended to your listing.

Rounding off this part of the process are a couple of free-form text boxes in which you can give potential buyers information not covered elsewhere. Declare your returns policy (will you accept unwanted items back for a full refund?) and maybe state the time-frame in which you expect to be paid after your item's sold.

LAST-CHANCE EXTRAS

Your listing is now nearly complete! Once you've filled in all the blanks detailed in the sections above, click 'Continue'. You're then given one last chance to take up some of the upgrades you've already been offered (eBay really, really wants you to take them!).

This is also the point when eBay sellers used to be offered a batch of new upgrades, such as Bold, Highlight and Featured Plus. However, these are no longer offered, and all that remains is Featured First, which is only available if you've been an eBay seller for some time and are able to meet certain criteria in terms of sales and feedback.

£44.95 **Featured First:** With this, your item really can move up the pecking order. When a buyer makes a search, Featured First auctions within the relevant category are randomly selected to appear on page one (in the Featured Items section), regardless of how long they've got left to run. In some categories, Featured First auctions are so few and far between that yours could be virtually guaranteed a page-one position for its entire duration. For your money, you get Gallery Plus thrown in, too.

Unfortunately, this powerful upgrade is only available to Top-rated Sellers. These are sellers that have opted into the PowerSeller program, and who meet a number of requirements laid down by eBay. These include at least 100 transactions and £2,000 in sales in the last 12 months and a positive feedback score of at least 98%.

As well as access to the Featured First option, Top-rated sellers receive the following privileges and benefits:

- Priority customer service
- Up to a 30% discount on final value fees
- Unpaid item protection
- Expanded seller protection from PayPal
- A badge on listing pages
- Increased visibility in Best Match search results

PREVIEW AND GO!

That's it. You're all done! You're now given the opportunity to preview your listing - to see exactly how it'll look to potential buyers - and also the chance to make any last-minute edits. Crucially, you're also shown the total amount of your hard-earned cash eBay will take in listing fees. If you've chosen a fixed-price listing, you're also shown how much you'll be charged as a selling fee (if your item sells). When you're happy, click 'List your item'!

What Makes A Good eBay Listing?

Getting your listing right is essential, so what can you do to make yours stand out from the crowd?

If eBay gave statistics of those items that sell well, they'd show that the impression presented by the listing is crucial in making sales and in attracting bids. Creating listings that give your items the very best chance is a vital skill that any successful seller needs to master. The listing performs a number of crucial functions, including:

- Giving clear and concise information about what's being offered
- Outlining under what conditions sale is offered
- Providing confidence that the seller is a good eBayer
- Giving buyers an opportunity to ask questions
- Initiating the mechanism to buy or bid

If your listing succeeds in this respect, then the chance of your item selling for what you want, or more, is dramatically increased.

MIXING A PERFECT EBAY CAKE
For a successful listing to meet all the requirements of the checklist above, it's worth comparing it to making a cake: if you leave out even a single important ingredient, then the flavour of the cake is impaired. With that in mind, before you start to create and edit a listing on eBay, it's worth collecting together all the information you need to sell your

item, putting most of it in a document, which you can easily cut and paste from in order to save time. You'll need to have handy:

- The title of your item
- The category it falls into (maybe more than one)
- The condition of the item - new or used
- A full description, telling the prospective buyer what they'll get for their money
- A listing template
- A picture, showing the item
- A starting price
- Planned duration of the sale
- Shipping cost details
- Accepted payment types
- Returns policy

You need to consider each of these things before listing an item, as they can all have an impact on how much money you get and the number of people that are likely to be interested. It may look an exhausting list, but it's actually quite straightforward, and much of it revolves around simple common sense. Let's go through it in a bit more detail.

TITLE
This is the single most important decision you need to make about any listing, as the title is the reason most

▲ The title is a valuable means to hook a customer. Which of these two listings is trying to give the most information?

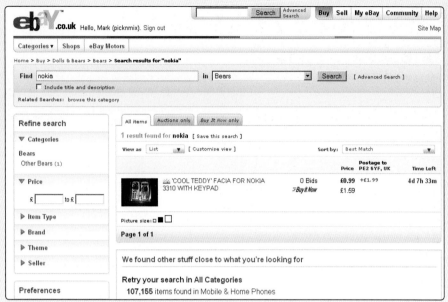

◀ This listing is for Nokia phone products. Not that many people will find it, because, for whatever reason, it's listed under the category of 'Bears'

potential customers will take a closer look at your item. A vague, incorrectly spelled or confusing title can easily get overlooked.

If other people are selling the same item, see what they're doing and follow the lead. You have 55 characters to play with in your title, so make the most of them.

For example, let's say the item is a golf club. In the title you need to get across the brand, model, style and condition, if you can fit that in. It's now common to use upper case, as it makes the title stand out more (although some potential buyers may equate this to shouting, and thus give your listing a miss). eBay also allows for a subtitle, but relatively few people use this feature, relying instead on the full description to provide any secondary information.

CATEGORY

As we've discussed, buyers that actively search eBay do it in two distinct ways. Some know exactly what they're looking for, and search for that item specifically (for instance, a 30GB Apple iPod).

Others know they want a type of item, but are unsure what brand/make they'd like (so they might, perhaps, search for an MP3 player instead of specifically requesting an iPod).

The second type of search is often category-based, and attracting those people requires that you put your listing in the right category for your item. If you're unsure, then try searching yourself, and see where similar items to the one you're looking to list have been placed.

eBay allows you to place the listing against multiple categories, at an extra cost, with an increased viewing count likely if you choose to do so. For most people,

though, just getting the category right is enough to attract interest.

There is a peculiar reverse logic that can also apply here. For whatever reason, items that appear in the wrong category can also get more attention. This is a risky strategy, as your item might be ignored, and you might seem an inept seller, but it can work. As a rule, research the correct category and use that one.

CONDITION

New is good, and used is less so. However, don't be tempted to suggest that an item is new when it isn't. You'll rightly upset the buyer who might be tempted to ask for a refund or to complain. Unless an item is new, never mark it as such. What you can do to help promote a used item is to mention in the title or description a few more details; for example, 'as new' or 'perfect condition'.

Unless it's an item where the age is actually a selling point, most people want new or at least new-looking purchases.

DESCRIPTION

If the item that you're selling is one that eBay recognises (such as a DVD or CD), then a short description of it will automatically appear at the top of the listing. However, this information on its own is rarely enough to answer all of a buyer's questions.

Getting all the relevant information in this section will help the potential bidder decide if they want your item, so it's worth taking the time to make it clear exactly what you're selling. In general, the more information you provide, the better the listing will be, but keep it relevant to the customer. They might not want to know that you've ended a relationship using

MEMORABLE EBAY AUCTIONS

A GERMAN BABY
A Bavarian couple put their baby son on eBay as 'a joke'. The authorities didn't see the funny side, and took the seven-month-old into care while they investigated the incident. eBay, of course, deleted the auction.

that phone, or that you're selling an item to pay a parking fine. A good source of information to use in this section can be found on the brand or manufacturer's website, if one exists. A bit of rapid highlighting, copying and pasting could save you plenty of typing. And unless you've got the wrong product, the details should be totally correct.

Please take note: eBay holds you responsible for making sure the information is accurate. Therefore, it's of real importance to get the description right and to not mislead people, otherwise there could be recriminations further down the line.

LISTING TEMPLATE

Built into eBay are a range of HTML listing template formats, which fall under the banner of the 'Listing Designer'. Although you're charged a small amount extra for choosing one of these templates, the overall impact it will have on your listing can be very positive, and thus worthwhile.

Templates give the layout of the listing more structure, colour, and the impression you've put more effort into presenting your product. The only problem with the eBay templates is that frequent users will have seen them all, and recognise them as such. But even then, it's hard to argue that they do any harm.

Third-party templates are an alternative, and they're available from a wide range of online locations. One of the biggest free suppliers is **www. auctioninsights.com**, where you'll find a free template creation tool. There are plenty of companies offering such templates, and other popular options are **www. auctionsupplies.com/templates**, **www. foamtemplates.com**, and **www.auctiva.com**.

Alternatively, a large number of software tools are available that allow you to create a listing away from

eBay, and then post it to the site in a single operation. These all have their own template designs from which you can choose. Some of these, such as The Seller Sourcebook (**www.sellersourcebook.com**), are online tools for which a subscription is payable for use.

Others, like eBaitor (**www.ebaitor.com**), Auction Ad Designer Pro (**www.freeauctionhelp.com**) and Auction Lizard (**www.auction-lizard.com**) provide a separate installable Windows application that creates the listing offline. The beauty of these tools is that you can work on a listing to the point where you're entirely happy with it before committing to upload it and make it live on the eBay site. It also allows you to reload old listings and tweak them for repeat use, which can save lots of time.

If you intend to build a business through eBay, or you plan on selling in significant quantities, then investing in a listings design tool might be a worthwhile exercise.

THE PICTURE

This one feature can be a real sale maker or breaker. A good picture can say a thousand words, and convince a buyer that it's exactly what they want to bid on. Conversely, a poor image can confuse matters and persuade people not to bid or buy. It's why we touch on images so much in this book, and we'll be going into pictures in a lot more detail shortly.

Included in the basic cost of an eBay listing is one picture, and you can add more for, of course, a fee. Extra pictures can enable your listing to show specific details of your item, and can be a necessity when selling something like a car or antique.

For low-cost items, using multiple pictures probably isn't particularly worthwhile, but for high-value items they can be invaluable in interesting your customers. A cheap way to get extra pictures and higher-resolution images into your listing is, as we've seen, to place them on a picture-hosting service and to provide a link in your description, so bidders can access those images.

Two sites that specialise in providing this service are AuctionPix (**www.auctionpix.co.uk**) and Vendio (**www.vendio.com**), but you can also use the general photography-hosting sites such as those run by Google, Yahoo! and Flickr.

If your sale item is new and unused, the best pictures can usually be sourced from online shops or the manufacturer's website, but if those aren't available you can take your own using any serviceable digital camera.

The maximum picture size that eBay will allow you to post is 800 x 800 pixels, so uploading anything bigger than that is pointless and time consuming. Ideally, take the images into a photo-editing application (such as Adobe Photoshop Elements or

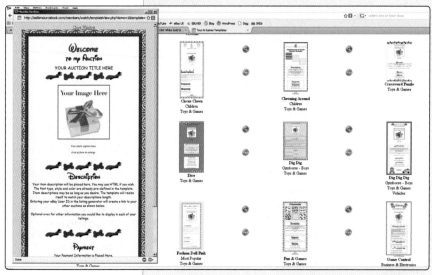

▲ A template can give your listing a more professional touch

▲ Given the choice between these two watches, regardless of price, which one would you be more interested in?

Corel Paint Shop Pro) and first crop out the superfluous parts of the image, and then scale the end product to get as close as possible to eBay's maximum size, without damaging the quality of your picture. After you've done this, save the image (usually in JPEG format) for uploading.

Adding a decent picture is one of the skills that many eBayers lack, and putting a good one on your listing could make a major difference. Try to follow these pointers:

- If you take the picture yourself, think about how it will look at a very small size alongside your item's title in a listings search.
- Close-up shots can easily be out of focus if your camera doesn't have a 'macro' feature, or you don't use it properly.
- Try finding a simple location to shoot, where the background won't distract the viewer. A blank wall or hardwood floor is ideal.
- If the item is small, like a coin, then put some other well-known object or a ruler in the shot so that the bidder can get an idea of scale.
- eBay has image-adjustment tools for picture brightness and contrast, but it's better to get these things right in a photo-editing application before uploading the picture.
- Camera flash can make some items difficult to see correctly. The best pictures are taken outside in natural light where possible.
- If it's important that the item you're selling is functional, you should show it working properly in a picture.
- Defects like scratches and marks can be shown in a photo to explain how minor or not they are.
- Never post a tiny or blurry picture. It only makes people suspicious.

These are merely a few simple pointers regarding how to use images in your eBay listings. We'll go into this topic of pictures in greater detail elsewhere in this book.

OTHER LISTING HINTS

If there's one single message for anyone creating a listing, it's simply this: don't put barriers between the item and the potential customer. It only takes one reason for them to click away to something else, so try not to give it to them.

The most common problem with any given listing is not providing sufficient information, leading the eBayer to assume it's either not the item they want or something they need. For example, if you offer Collection Only as a postage option, it's a good idea to explain why. Maybe the item is just too heavy or large to practically ship, but don't assume the potential bidder knows this; say it.

The other sticking point is with any limitations that you've set. These could be countries that you'll post to, payment types you'll accept, or a dozen other things. The more flexible you are in terms of these factors, the larger your potential audience will be. So only apply these restrictions if you must - if you don't feel comfortable with cheques, for example.

SUMMARY

Simple, common-sense rules apply. Present your sale item in the best possible light without exaggerating. Give as much information as possible and even encourage people to ask questions. Place the item in the correct category and be flexible about postage, international mailing and types of payments that you'll accept.

In short, give your items the best possible chance to sell, at the best price you can get.

Which Extras Are Worth Paying For?

eBay provides several optional add-ons to improve your listing, but which ones are you likely to need?

As a business, eBay needs to make a profit and will always look for ways to do so. One way it does it is to provide sellers with a range of optional extras for their listings.

The number of extras available was cut quite dramatically as of 30th September 2009. Previously, sellers could add effects like bold text and highlighting to their listings for a small fee. There was also an extra called Featured Plus, which has also been discontinued under these changes.

According to eBay itself, its reasons for doing so are as follows: "eBay buyers want an improved and consistent shopping experience that delivers a quick and satisfying result. These changes will eliminate buyer confusion and cut unnecessary costs for you." As odd as that sounds for a profit making company, it certainly makes for a more streamlined experience for both sellers and buyers.

In spite of this scaled back approach, there are still a number of extras and upgrades on offer, and they can dramatically expand the possibility of getting a sale or the amount you ultimately receive for an item. However, some of them are likely to be more suitable for you than others, so which ones should you choose and which ones you should leave alone?

THE STANDARD EXTRAS

£0.35 **Subtitle:** The subtitle provides key selling points about your item (benefits, accessories, etc.). You get 55 characters for anything that won't fit in the Title section.

The Pros: According to eBay, listings with a subtitle typically sell for 20% more, which would suggest, statistically, that if your product is worth more than a few pounds, it's a worthwhile exercise.

The Cons: Subtitles are not included in the results when somebody does a basic search. The only time subtitles will show up is when a bidder does a search by title and description. Also, it's not cheap for high-volume sellers.

Bottom Line: If the subtitle were referenced in a basic search, then using it would make more sense, but because it isn't, the subtitle probably isn't worth it for simple or low-cost items. Obviously, if you didn't fill the title line up, then adding a subtitle is a complete waste of time and money.

COST VARIES **Listing In Two Categories Or More:** Beware! This is an exceptionally dangerous feature, which eBay encourages sellers to use without them fully understanding the consequences. The problem with multiple categories is that each additional one multiplies the total cost for the listing. Two categories will double it, and three will treble it. That's not only the listing fee, but any extras you decide to take into the bargain.

Let's say your fees are £5. Selecting another category increases that to £10. With increases like that, your fees can rapidly spiral out of control.

The Pros: More people will see the item, which should drive up the number of bidders.

The Cons: The cost of the listing fee can negate what you make when you sell.

Bottom Line: A person listing a single low-to-medium-cost item should never use this feature. It's far better to list an item in one carefully chosen category and spend a little on extras than double or more the total fee. The only situation where it has any value is when you're listing multiples of the same items, with ten or more of them to sell. Then it might be worth placing it in more than one category, but only if you're supremely confident that it will help you sell more.

£44.95 **Featured First:** With a cost of £44.95 per item this isn't a feature for the faint-hearted or low-cost items. However, it's only available to Top-rated Sellers - an accolade that takes quite some time and effort to earn.

▲ With the Supersize picture feature, buyers can get a better look at your item without entering your listing

▲ The Highlight option which, along with Bold, was discontinued by eBay in favour of a simpler approach

The Pros: Puts you product above the rest, occasionally. Includes Gallery Plus!

The Cons: This isn't a guarantee of being 'first'. What it actually offers is the chance that it will appear on the first page in the featured items. It will be randomly cycled with other items listed with this feature. Also, it's only relevant when users sort by Best Match, so it's a clearly limited extra. As part of eBay's new Top-rated Seller scheme, it's an extra that you're unlikely to be using unless you're truly serious about selling through eBay.

Bottom Line: How useful this option is depends entirely on how many items a typical search for your item returns. The question you need to ask yourself is whether cutting the cost of your item by £44.95 will have a bigger impact on your profit than taking a chance on this.

Note: Items listed in the 'media' section can have this option for just £11.95.

GRAPHICS: PICTURES ON YOUR LISTING

A picture is, indeed, worth a thousand words, and takes much less time for an eBay customer to absorb. You get a single picture for free, which you should always take advantage of. But beyond that, what are the options?

£0.12 **Pictures:** In addition to the free picture eBay gives you as standard, you can add a further 11, each costing you another £0.12. These pictures will be presented as 'Standard' with a maximum resolution of 400 pixels along the longest edge.

FREE **Gallery Picture:** Shows a small preview of the first picture loaded in the search listing. Size is 64 x 64 pixels, from whatever size it originally was. This

option originally cost extra money, but it's now a standard eBay feature.

£0.95 **Gallery Plus:** This option displays a larger picture (standard resolution) in search results when a buyer's mouse hovers over the hyperlinked word 'Enlarge' under the gallery picture.

FROM £0.90 **Picture Pack:** (£0.90 for six pictures or £1.35 for seven to 12 pictures) This is a slightly confusing option, and the extra amount isn't just for the volume of pictures added. What it gives you is six or 12 pictures, plus Gallery and Supersize on those pictures you've uploaded.

For six pictures, that means you get Gallery listing and Supersize functionality for just £0.30. Inherently this then includes Picture Show for viewing all the item pictures at the top of your item page.

£0.60 **Supersize Pictures:** This will display the uploaded pictures to a maximum resolution of 800 x 800, which is more than twice the size of the standard resolution for £0.60.

EXTRA ENHANCEMENTS

£0.07 **Listing Designer:** A range of themed templates, providing layouts and graphics that enhance your listing. Simply select the one you like and preview its impact on your listing.

The Pros: Makes your listing more interesting.

The Cons: The eBay templates are well known, so things looking better may not fool anyone.

Bottom Line: Free templates are available elsewhere, so use them instead and save the money. They're not suitable for eBay businesses, where you need to create a unique identity and not use an off-the-shelf one.

£0.06 **Schedule Start Time:** Starting your auction the moment you finish the listing can often be a bad plan. For a little extra you can delay the start, which will correspondingly delay the finish. The best time for an auction to end is Sunday, while people are using the Internet at home. The worst days are Friday and Saturday. However, a bidding war isn't likely to break out if your item ends at 3am in the morning. The best time is between 9pm and 11pm in the evening. If you can't arrange for the item to be posted to fit with that time-scale, then spending a small amount of money to delay the start is almost certainly worth it.

Also, if you're selling something on the US eBay site, or which would be of interest to people in a specific country, think about the time differences that apply.

This isn't an advantage that helps a specific type of seller; everyone should be conscious of their timing, and schedule the best point to end an auction when they can. It could possibly be argued that this isn't relevant to those running Buy It Now listings, but many people do Ending Soon searches, so it can play a part even there.

The Pros: Allows your listing to start and end at the best times. It's a cheap option.

The Cons: You could save this small amount by being more organised.

Bottom Line: This is one extra you that should always use, unless you always post your auctions at the perfect time. As you can now save your listings before releasing them, this isn't the issue it once

▲ Featured First is a particularly expensive extra, so think carefully before you opt for it

was. If you have lots of items, the 6p this costs might eventually be significant, though.

PLAYING THE PERCENTAGES
If the advantages presented by eBay were guaranteed, using every extra would be a no-brainer. Alas, these numbers are only averages, and extras are most often used for selling high-value items, which can distort their benefits.

For someone starting out on eBay, it's a good plan to use extras sparingly, and only when you think they'll deliver a real benefit. Those running a business can experiment to find their true worth by selling the same things with and without the help of an extra. They'll be able to better judge if using them is a cost-effective investment, or merely filling eBay's pockets.

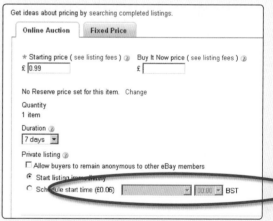

▲ For very little cost, you can choose when to start your auction. In most cases, this is worth paying for

▲ Setting up the options for a picture on eBay

Standard Picture Sizes On eBay

Picture Types	Resolution	File Size
List View	64 x 64 pixels	1-3KB
Thumbnail	92 x 76 pixels	2-5KB
Preview	200 x 150 pixels	10-20KB
Standard	400 x 300 pixels	30-40KB
Supersize	Up to 800 x 800 pixels	>50KB

Getting The Right Picture

A good picture can be an invaluable asset for an eBay listing. It could be the difference between a passing interest and a sale

The quality of your eBay listing and how you handle enquiries and fulfill orders builds confidence among your buyers - confidence in you. The photos that accompany your listings build up buyers' confidence in the item you're hoping to sell.

Great images can come out of inexpensive cameras. As long as you stick to a few rules, time spent on photos will pay off in increased sales. People may be put off by wordy or scant descriptions. If you're not the eBay poet you'd like to be, let your pictures speak for you.

BUYER FOCUS

Always have the buyers in mind as you snap your shots. Be sure they're properly lit from all sides so no area is obscured, and avoid harsh shadows on or around the item. Flash photography rarely improves shots, and glare can be a problem on reflective surfaces, so use ambient light when possible. It may be tricky in areas where it rains a lot, so plan photo shoots for sunnier days. Shoot outdoors if possible or indoors with lamps.

If the scale of an item is hard to judge, it's a good idea to put a recognisable object next to it. Coins are often used beside small items, and rulers and yardsticks can be placed with large items. Text descriptions of size are hard to visualise, and international buyers may not want to do conversions. Even if you think it spoils your photos, these types of visual aids are always appreciated.

IMAGE BASICS

Buyers want to identify merchandise at a glance. Remember, it takes them far less time to click away

from your page than to stop and find their glasses, so make your images stand out. Arrange and focus each shot so the item fills the available space, or crop it later, leaving a border of roughly 10% around the item.

Use the macro setting, if your camera has one, for very small items or close-ups of details in larger pieces, but be sure to use it properly. Choose high-contrast, solid, seamless, clutter-free backgrounds. Use light-coloured backgrounds for dark items, and darker shades for light items.

Include as much detail in each photo as possible, especially if there's a problem. Buyers need to know if an item is cracked, stained, torn or chipped. Sellers who post a zoomed image of a small flaw often get feedback comments of 'better than expected', when the item with its petite imperfection arrives. Those who try to hide or disguise damage in photos risk receiving negative feedback from buyers, which will reduce confidence from future potential buyers.

Be considerate of buyers' time and bandwidth. If your photos are slow to load, they'll move on. File sizes should be the smallest achievable without sacrificing quality. Keep in mind there are people who still have computer display desktop settings of 800 x 600 pixels, which is why eBay recommends dimensions of 400 pixels along the longest edge of your image.

Be aware, if you host your images outside of eBay's services, you'll be given an option to 'standardise your images' when you set up your page, meaning eBay will rescale each image to its recommended size. This can have disastrous effects on pictures you've worked hard

◄ A matchbox reveals this item's size instantly

◄ This seller brands their tattoo equipment photos with their name

◀ Near identical images from two completely different sellers

on. Resized images may contain unattractive moire patterns (wavy lines). Always preview your images at reduced dimensions before you approve any resizing.

REAL SELLERS' PICTURES

While you're learning to improve your photos, don't be tempted to copy images from other sellers. Not only will buyers notice, but you could lose your eBay account and face legal action.

To protect your own pictures from being used by other sellers you can add a watermark. eBay's image uploading includes the option of superimposing your User ID or a camera icon over your images.

Alternatively, you can use separate imaging editing software to customise your watermark. If you do opt for this method, try to place your mark where it's either impossible or too much trouble to remove, being sure not to obscure an important feature of your item. If it's stolen and altered, it'll be obvious which is the original and which was tampered with.

For example, the two rubber ducks above are from different sellers, yet the images are identical. However, the one on the right didn't bother to copy the entire shadow. If you're reselling new goods, manufacturers and wholesalers often have professional, free product shots available through their sites or on request.

USEFUL LESSONS

The best lessons are learned from other people's mistakes and successes. The examples on the following pages of eBay seller images demonstrate more right and wrong ways to photograph your wares.

Additional Tips

Take additional, high-resolution images of your items, even if you won't be posting them. They can be supplied to interested buyers on request to clinch sales, or kept as insurance and proof if the quality or condition of an item is challenged after the sale.

Be aware that newer web browsers and available add-ons and extensions make it possible for buyers to enlarge not only the text in web pages, but images as well. That enables sellers to post smaller pictures, and viewers can choose to enlarge them when they need to. This works to everyone's advantage, as long as the image quality is high enough. Test your images by resizing in a zoom-enabled Internet browser (such as Firefox or Opera) before uploading or linking them to your pages (you can simply drag and drop JPEGs onto an open browser window).

Don't become an urban legend! Be sure you're not capturing your own image in any reflective surfaces of your items or in the room. Photos have been forwarded through e-mails and put on sites over the years featuring alleged auction site sellers in the nude, caught in glass-doored china cabinets and gleaming steel kettles. Whether legitimate, intentional, accidental, or faked, they're a great reminder to scrutinise your pictures carefully before posting in public places.

In spite of the prior paragraph, remember that your photos always reflect on you. If you post haphazard, sloppy shots, buyers will assume you treat customers in the same way. Lazy photography can be just as damaging as negative feedback.

◀ This picture exposes more than any buyer needs to know

Picture Rights And Wrongs

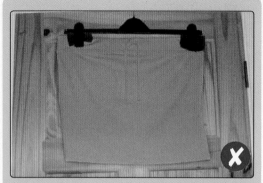

▲ This ladies' top, clamped and stretched across a hanger, and shot on the back of a door, doesn't look very attractive, or instil confidence that its buyer has any chance of looking attractive in it.

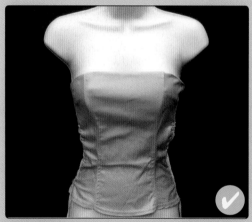

▲ Compare the first pink top to this seller's photo. This person has invested in a mannequin and shot against a high-contrast background, revealing the potential of the garment when worn.

If you don't sell enough to justify the expense of a mannequin or dress form, ask a same-sized friend to model the clothes. You don't have to include more than the torso, so your model can remain anonymous.

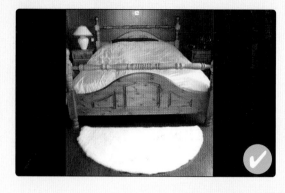

▲ Some items warrant breaking the rules. While most should be shot against plain backgrounds free from clutter or distracting elements, other items are more impressive in a setting, like this rug. It's a 'lifestyle' shot that demonstrates how it looks when used.

On its own, it would look like a non-descript semi-circular smudge of white. Here, it's accentuated against the dark wood and complements a tidy, attractive bedroom, so a buyer can picture it in their own home.

▲ Some items are more of a challenge to show at their best, like this 'original and trendy' cork picture frame. When there's little to work with, don't fail to adequately depict what is there. Nowhere in the description are dimensions mentioned or what hardware is included to stand or hang this 'envy of all your friends' frame.

◀ Part of eBay's advice is to photograph items 'at an angle'. That doesn't mean 'don't bother rotating images'. No one appreciates risking neck pain to view merchandise. This snap of a gargoyle ornament suffers from being on its side, and the damage is doubled by a muddled background. The cloth colour is too similar to the item colour, especially in shadowed areas. Buyers will struggle to tell where the ornament ends and the background begins. Its description includes 'sits on edge of shelf'. That's exactly where the photo should be shot.

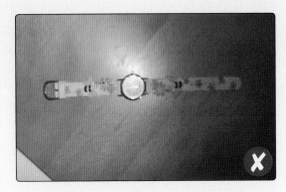

▲ This photo of a child's watch has multiple problems working against it. The glare from the camera's flash wipes out any detail on the glass face and strap design. It's impossible to tell the size or condition of the watch, and there's far too much space around the item, with distracting corners left in. It should be shot on a non-reflective surface like cloth, in natural light, without a flash and cropped much more tightly. Including a ruler in the shot would indicate length at a glance.

▲ This low-resolution rectangle of dingy brown is actually a 'caramel cream' shaggy chenille bathroom rug. It's been heavily compressed and pixelated, and smeared around the edges. It looks more like a coarse fabric doormat designed to strip mud off boots than the soft, luxurious surface a buyer would want to step on with bare wet feet. This picture would benefit from a 'lifestyle' setting like the rug opposite, with a high-resolution close-up of the velvety tufted pile as an inset.

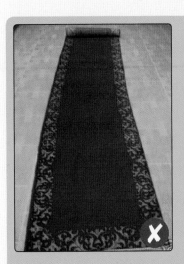

Extruded image (simulated)

Inset image

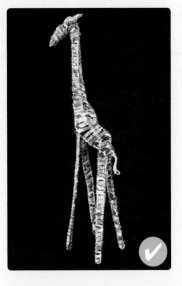

▲ The appeal and value of many items, like 'semi-antique' Persian rugs, are determined by original workmanship and present condition. This long, blurry shot doesn't show any detail whatsoever, only a vague indication of colour and pattern. Buyers need to know the exact condition of this item. They expect wear and tear on older, used items and, with certain things, this is even preferable to 'like new' condition.

▲ This seller wisely includes additional close-up shots of the pattern, weave, and worn areas, giving the buyer plenty to examine to make an informed purchase. If you're limited to displaying a single shot, by space or budget, you can include inset or 'extruded' images (zoomed or more detailed parts pulled from the main image) of a portion or section of a large item, like this revised image made from two of the seller's additional shots.

▲ This giraffe made from a soft-drink can is an ideal image for display. The high-contrast background and high resolution are perfect. It can be enlarged in a browser to full-screen dimensions without losing detail, is expertly lit, properly cropped with sharp focus, and shot at an interesting angle. As unique as the item is, the flawless photographic treatment makes it even more attractive.

Why Ratings And Feedback Matter

The rating system built into the eBay service is an important barometer of how trustworthy a trader is. Here's why

Quick reality check: when you use eBay you're trading with a complete stranger. Whether selling or buying, it's absolutely essential to get some measure of how reliable the other eBay member is. In short, will the goods/money arrive? This is why trading history is part of your eBay profile; it's used to determine whether or not to do business with you.

This might be something of a catch-22 situation if everyone required their buyer or seller to be experienced before trading, since it would not be possible to accumulate a rating without first having a good trading history. However, in practice, sellers of items under £100 are likely to accept business from almost anyone, allowing rookie users to build up their score. It's probably a good idea to start out buying smaller things on eBay to get the hang of it before taking the plunge and going for more expensive items.

As of mid-2008 an eBay member's reliability is scored only on the basis of buyer's feedback; you do not get ratings points for any purchases you make. However, you can read a member's feedback comments to get a measure of how good they are as a buyer.

HOW IT WORKS
Generally speaking, feedback - and thus, a rating - is given when a transaction is complete, the money has

been cleared, the goods are delivered and both sides are happy. If the buyer is paying through PayPal, the seller might give them their feedback straight away, since there's very little else required of the buyer, and receiving a thank you comment can encourage the buyer to reply in kind.

If something goes wrong with the transaction, then the feedback system is one way of informing other eBay users about the reality of dealing with this particular user. It should be pointed out that leaving negative feedback is not the first course of action to take if there's a problem. It's best for everyone to resolve matters with a positive attitude, rather than by resorting to 'revenge feedback'. Recent changes to the feedback system also include a three-day delay before you can give non-positive feedback, which can be time enough to cool off and maybe talk it over some more.

Feedback is an important part of the pseudo-gaming aspect of eBay. It's no coincidence that eBay describes a successful purchase as a 'winning bid', and awards a score to its members. Winning auctions and good feedback ratings are an important part of the eBay experience; it keeps people using the system and also provides a threat against misusing the service.

RATINGS
A feedback rating is composed of a choice of 'positive', 'negative' or 'neutral', along with a comment on the transaction. Generally speaking, a transaction should end with a positive result. Only very poorly managed transactions should be classed as neutral, and only in cases where there has been a complete failure, coupled with some sort of material loss on one side or another, should the transaction be rated as negative. Negative basically describes the other party as totally impossible to work with.

The comment in the feedback usually falls into one of two categories. It is either a stock 'thank you', which many people adorn with their own brand of hyperbole, or it's a description of what went wrong or, indeed, right with the transaction.

It is important, on the rare occasions where you need to deliver negative feedback, to make it

▲ Feedback profiles are central to the workings of eBay

absolutely clear why you're doing it. For example, you might write 'The seller sent me three poor excuses and then stopped replying to e-mails', which would clearly explain why no other person should deal with them. Conversely, writing 'This guy is a moron and needs help!', while it may be cathartic, is missing the point somewhat.

Some people seem to use the opportunity of giving feedback to wax lyrical about how much they enjoy using eBay. With some sellers, this can almost be an incentive to buy further items, just to see what they will write next.

THE RATING NUMBER

The ratings are compiled into a single 'score'. For every positive rating you get, your score is increased by one. For every negative rating, the score is reduced by one. Neutral, predictably, has no effect. However, an extra detail is that your score cannot be affected by more than a total of one by any individual eBay user in a given week. So, if you sold one hundred items to the same user and received all positive feedback, your feedback rating will still be one. Conversely, if you sold one item per week for a year to the same person and received positive feedback, you would score 52. To make things more complex, if the same user, in the same week, gives a variety of positive and negative ratings to the same seller, the overall positive or negative effect on that seller's feedback score will be determined by the balance of different ratings - a bit like the 'swing-ometer' showing how election results affect the political parties.

When reading a user's rating, do not just rely on the points total; there's also a description of the overall total percentage of positive feedback. A new feature of eBay is also the DSR (Detailed Seller Rating), which shows a star-based scoring system in terms of item description, communication, delivery time and how reasonable the postage charges were.

eBay sellers who trade in high volume and continue to receive a high percentage of positive feedback are designated as PowerSellers. This is a hard rating to achieve, but the confidence a buyer can feel with a PowerSeller is often reflected in increased sales. In addition, once you're a PowerSeller, it's harder for a buyer to leave you negative feedback.

IDEAL FEEDBACK RATINGS FOR BUYERS

As a buyer, if you have a choice of seller, you should prefer one with a long trading history and a large number and high percentage of positive feedback ratings. Ideally, you should find no negative feedback for your seller. If there has been negative feedback, it would be best if that transaction happened a while ago (you can see a breakdown of ratings received in the last one, six and 12 months).

Feedback Icons

You will notice an icon next to an eBay User ID. This icon represents how good that user's trading history has been. This table shows what they all mean.

Number of points	Icon
10 - 49	Yellow star
50 - 99	Blue star
100 - 499	Turquoise star
500 - 999	Purple star
1,000 - 4,999	Red star
5,000 - 9,999	Green star
10,000 - 24,999	Yellow shooting star
25,000 - 49,999	Turquoise shooting star
50,000 - 99,999	Purple shooting star
100,000 - 499,000	Red shooting star
500,000 - 999,999	Green shooting star
Over 1,000,000	Silver shooting star

You should also read the last few feedback descriptions, as they appear on the ticker on the profile page, to see what else buyers have to say about dealing with the seller. The Detailed Seller Ratings should be an honest appraisal of the seller, because they're left anonymously.

Look for comments and DSRs that describe items arriving rapidly and in excellent condition. If there has been any negative feedback, it might be worth trying to find out exactly what happened. It's possible that the cause of the negative rating was a particularly unreasonable buyer, and the seller's reply to the feedback, explaining their side of things, may give you a more balanced view of what happened and also how that seller treats their buyers.

Overall, though, it's in the interest of a seller to make sure that they get a satisfactory rating of their conduct on eBay. Feedback ratings are the primary way that a prospective trading partner gets to decide whether you look reliable, so every negative rating counts heavily.

RECEIVING NEGATIVE FEEDBACK

Having described the importance of a clean record on eBay, it's still almost inevitable that a transaction will go wrong, especially if you're dealing with countless members of the general public, not all of whom know how to use eBay properly. Should you receive negative feedback, there are two possible things you can do to deal with it.

MEMORABLE EBAY AUCTIONS

SNOW

Colorado resident Mary Walker opened an eBay auction for the snow she'd cleared off her drive. Bidding started at $0.99. "I figured eBay has ghosts and all sorts of weird stuff, so why not snow?" she said.

Leave Feedback

Your Feedback counts – share your trading experience with the eBay Community. Other members learn from your overall ratings, and buyers can leave specific Feedback about the item description, the seller's communication, and postage. Learn more

⊘ Sellers can no longer leave negative or neutral Feedback for buyers.
Buyers should leave honest Feedback without the fear of receiving negative or neutral ratings. Read more

Show Items: All | Bought | Sold   Find a transaction [Enter a User ID or item #] [Search]

Leave Feedback for 1 (viewing 1-1)

Pair of GUITAR STRAP BUTTONS END PINS PEGS spares parts - [View item summary]
Seller ▓▓▓▓▓ (14448 ☆) ★ Power Seller ⊞   Item # 120273259940
Ended: 20-Jun-08 12:37:32 BST

Rate this transaction. This Feedback helps other buyers and sellers. ⊘
⊙ Positive ○ Neutral ○ Negative ○ I will leave Feedback later

Please explain [Item arrived as described, in perfect condition and on time.]   20 characters left

Click on the stars to rate more details of the transaction. These ratings will not be seen by the seller. ⊘

How accurate was the item description?   ★ ★ ★ ★ ★
How satisfied were you with the seller's communication?   ★ ★ ★ ★ ★   ⓘ Remember – these Detailed Seller Ratings are
How quickly did the seller dispatch the item?   ★ ★ ★ ★ ★   anonymous, so please feel free to leave honest
How reasonable were the P&P charges?   ★ ★ ★ ★   ratings about your buying experience

◀ In the majority of cases, you'll be leaving positive feedback. Only in the worst possible scenario would you consider leaving negative feedback

First and foremost, you should respond. Your response will be listed alongside the complaint and allows you to give a more balanced view of what happened. It's not necessary to give your opinion of the other person involved. You need to portray yourself as a reasonable person to trade with.

If necessary, you may be able to appeal to eBay to have the feedback removed. It has very strict rules governing the removal of feedback and will only do so if there's a breach of those rules. See **pages.ebay. co.uk/help/policies/feedback-abuse-withdrawal. html** for the exact terms of feedback removal. In a nutshell, it will remove abusive or libelous feedback, along with feedback resulting from clearly malicious behaviour - like winning an auction purely for the chance to give negative feedback, rather than to buy the item.

AVOIDING NEGATIVE FEEDBACK
Prevention is the best cure. Even with the best will in the world, things can go wrong during the course of completing a transaction. If you keep the other party informed every step of the way, they're less likely to consider your service to be poor. This is not a recommendation to spam them with hourly updates (once every two hours is more than enough). However, if there are going to be delays, it's a good idea to keep the other person informed as you work through the problem.

Generally speaking, people are quite reasonable and respond well to being kept informed, even if it's bad news you're delivering. When you've completed your side of the transaction, contact the other person to make sure that they're happy and to offer assistance if they require it.

Leaving negative feedback is really a last resort for dealing with problems. If you're proactive, friendly and helpful throughout your dealings with other eBay users, the chances are that they'll give you a positive feedback rating, even if there were problems.

TIT FOR TAT
Amid some controversy, eBay changed its feedback system in 2008. Originally, the idea of allowing people to give mutual feedback made eBay seem like a self-policing community. However, the ability for a seller to reward a disgruntled customer with negative feedback, alongside the facility to mutually withdraw feedback, had resulted in a couple of phenomena. Firstly, there was a tit-for-tat effect when a buyer gave a negative rating and the seller immediately responded in kind. This discouraged some buyers from being honest, lest they get smeared in the process.

Secondly, the fact that a rating could be withdrawn had the possible effect of encouraging some people to bully their reviewer into agreeing to withdraw the feedback. One aspect of dealing with the general public over the Internet is that there are some crazies out there, and they may have nothing better to do with their time than annoy you on eBay.

The changes, which include anonymous Detailed Seller Ratings, are a big step forward; they recognize that the person risking the most on eBay is the buyer; ultimately it's the buyer who sends the funds and risks receiving nothing, or something they didn't bargain for.

POSITIVE FEEDBACK
Though there's much to say on the subject of dealing with negative feedback, it's worth remembering that part of being a good eBay trader is the accumulation of positive feedback from different eBay users in order to aggregate a good overall score. A better score will enable you to deal with more eBay users.

Good communication and prompt payment or delivery are the main sources of positive eBay feedback. If in your communication or item description you under-promise, and then, in reality, over-deliver (for example, claiming you deliver in a week, but you actually turn around delivery in three days), you will make people happy. If, in addition, you contact the other eBay user on completion of the transaction and remind them to leave you feedback, having given them a positive feedback score, then you are more than likely to receive positive feedback in kind. Success on eBay can be as much about good social skills as good business skills.

WHEN TRANSACTIONS GO BAD

Overall, trading on eBay is about as safe as buying something from a stall at your local market. eBay provides a range of services to help you resolve disputes, and the vast majority of transactions go by without a hitch. However, when eBay transactions go wrong, they can do so spectacularly. The fact that most items are bought by mail order is a significant complicating factor, as is the fact that many people on eBay are enthusiastic amateurs, rather than professional businesspeople.

TAKING THE RISK

Although there are risks associated with eBay transactions, and though you may prefer to reduce those risks by dealing only with PowerSellers or those eBay users with huge feedback ratings, it's best for the eBay community as a whole to give people the benefit of the doubt. There are ways of dealing with failed transactions and, assuming that the other person is in the UK, normal trading laws govern the sale. Although some eBay users are unreliable, it is better to play the game rather than miss out on good deals 'just in case'.

Conversely, when buying something from an eBay user with a low feedback rating, you should consider the value of the transaction. Could you afford to lose this money? Although you might, ultimately, be able to recover the funds or replace a faulty item bought at that price, would it be worth the hassle?

Generally speaking, the average eBay user should expect to have some sort of problem with an eBay transaction around 5% of the time, usually with low-value items where the seller isn't making enough of a profit to be able to do much to rectify any problems that occur.

▲ If your item arrives looking like this, negative feedback might be in order, but try to resolve the situation amicably first

NOT RECEIVING THE GOODS

Sometimes eBay items do not arrive. In this situation, the first thing to do is check that the seller has received the funds and ask them for the date when the item was sent. If the seller has proof of mailing, then they should be able to chase the matter up with the post office. If they've sent the item via Special Delivery, it's possible to track the item through the post office's system.

In order to bring costs down, many items are sent via normal mail. This makes them difficult to track and they may end up permanently lost in the mail. Given that many eBay sellers are selling unique items, possibly from their own personal house clearance, the chances of getting a replacement for that exact item are low.

If you're concerned about the possibility of the item being lost in the mail, ask whether the seller is prepared to add postal insurance to their delivery service, which should offer some guarantee of arrival or a refund if the item is lost.

BUYER COMPLAINING OF NON-RECEIPT

When considering how a seller might respond to your complaint about non-receipt of an item, think how you

A Tale Of Two Problems

In one eBay transaction, a particular seller had specified that they would only deal with damaged goods if the buyer paid postal insurance. The item in question, a CD, was shipped without its jewel case in a padded envelope. It arrived at the buyer's snapped in two. The buyer complained and was told that nothing could be done. This resulted in a heated e-mail exchange, with various insults traded, and negative feedback. All that fuss over a £5 CD.

In a different eBay transaction, the seller had specified a refund or replacement on computer hard disk sales. One of the hard disks, retailing for about £40, was found to be faulty, so was duly returned and a replacement was received a day or so later. This too was found to be faulty. The seller again agreed to replace it and sent another through. This third disk was also faulty. The buyer complained again to the seller, who offered a refund, concerned that perhaps something about the buyer's usage of the disks was the problem. Eventually, the seller was persuaded to send another disk, which worked perfectly. Positive feedback all around. Cooperation really works.

would react if one of your buyers contacted you, claiming they haven't received the goods. On one hand, it's quite possible that the postal system has failed, or that you incorrectly addressed the package. On the other hand, there are going to be some people who receive their items perfectly, and then contact you complaining of non-receipt in an attempt to get a refund on top of the goods.

You have to take the buyer's claims at face value. Therefore, it's recommended that for any item of value, you use Royal Mail's special delivery service or an equivalent (even getting a simple certificate of posting for low-value items). Postal or courier tracking on an item, and the insurance to replace it if it's lost, is a good way to resolve any complaints. For items worth more money than you can afford to lose, consider tracking and insurance to be an absolute must.

RECEIVING DAMAGED GOODS

If an item arrives damaged or faulty, it's easier to convince a seller that there's a problem. You can take digital photographs or even return the item to them. It's important that you're fully aware of the seller's returns policy before you agree to bid on the item. Most sellers will expect you to pay for the return postage. Some sellers may stipulate that they will only deal with damaged items in situations where postal insurance has been bought. In any case, the first thing to do is contact the seller, explain the problem and ask them what they can do.

NOT RECEIVING PAYMENT

It's best not to send an item to your buyer until their payment has already cleared. Receiving a check is all very well, but checks can easily bounce. PayPal, despite charging a transaction fee for sellers, is an instant method of payment and it also simplifies things greatly.

If you haven't received any form of payment, you can prompt the other user with an eBay invoice, for which there's a link on the e-mail confirming the sale. After that, you can contact them directly, perhaps offering them an alternative means of payment (PayPal, check, money order, bank transfer and so on).

If you've sent the item out before cleared payment, or if a check bounces, then you're in a very weak negotiating position. Don't do this; it's really not worth the stress. If you've sent the item on trust and have received no payment, then you can send an invoice to the buyer's delivery address and could, ultimately, proceed to the small claims court. This is much better avoided by withholding the item until cleared funds are received. The overwhelming majority of buyers will have no problem with you doing so. If a buyer is putting pressure on you to deliver before you receive the check, consider it a warning sign; there's seldom a good reason for this sort of behavior.

NEGOTIATING WITH THE OTHER PERSON

eBay users are, in general, reasonable people who are worried about their feedback rating. Putting aside all the things that can go wrong, people generally go onto eBay to trade honestly, rather than con each other. Wherever there has been a problem, the best step to take first is to contact the other user and discuss it. You shouldn't storm in with threats about negative feedback, because although it means something, it's also a fairly limited 'punishment'. If you're polite and reasonable with the other person, there's a high chance you'll be able to come to an agreement over how to solve the problems blighting a transaction.

EBAY COMPLAINTS PROCEDURE

If negotiation fails, then eBay has a Dispute Console. You can use this to ask eBay to step in to help resolve the problem. eBay will not refund your money. Indeed, the worst eBay can do to a buyer or seller is suspend their account until they have either resolved the problem or, more likely, set up a new account in a different name and continued trading regardless.

In some cases, the threat of an account suspension, or even the more official nature of disputes taken up through eBay's Dispute Console, will break a stalemate in negotiations, so it's worth

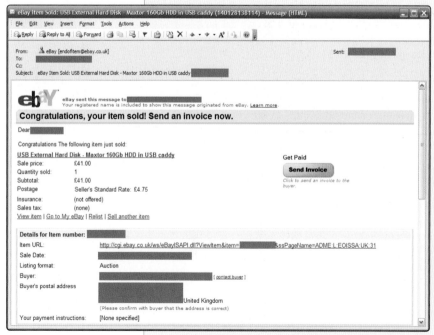

▲ You should keep careful records of your transactions, and make sure the other party has a copy too

THE PHOTO GUIDE YOU CAN TAKE ANYWHERE

ON SALE NOW!

following this course of action if you can't resolve things amicably directly with the other person.

PAYPAL PROTECTION

PayPal was acquired by eBay in order to provide financial services for its customers. Along with the ability to manage credit cards and virtual funds in multiple currencies, protecting those vital personal details, rather than revealing them to the other person, PayPal also provides insurance on every purchase you make. This insurance will cover you up to 100% of the value of an item that never arrives, or arrives but proves to be significantly different from the item description. Given that this is an insurance policy, however, PayPal will be as keen to follow the small print of the original item description as the seller was.

It is certainly confidence inspiring to think that if an expensive item does not arrive, there's the possibility of PayPal refunding its worth. PayPal's service extends to sellers as well, offering insurance against chargebacks. A chargeback is when someone asks their credit card company to reverse a transaction for some reason. If this were to happen against an eBay sale you were involved with, you would be obliged to return the funds. However, PayPal insures you against this.

Overall, using PayPal is a good way to protect your interests on eBay, even though its disputes team and complaints process can be quite hard work.

CREDIT CARD PROTECTION

Many credit cards offer protection against fraudulent transactions. If you've bought something and paid by credit card, and this includes your credit card being debited by PayPal for an auction item, you can contact your credit card company for its assistance in reversing a transaction, or at least putting pressure on the merchant to resolve the matter. At the very least, it may put a hold on the transaction so you neither have to pay it off, nor pay any interest on it until the matter is resolved.

THE LAW

If you've paid for services and they haven't been provided, or if the items sent to you are counterfeit or unfit for purpose, then you have the support of UK law. This is more complicated when dealing with overseas eBay users. Within the UK though, you can contact your lawyer, Citizen's Advice Bureau, local Trading Standards office, or even the police, in order to get help dealing with your problem.

In particular, if you've been provided with counterfeit goods, your complaint to the authorities may help them to deal with an organised counterfeiting group.

Caveat Emptor

The eBay item description will show you what you might be getting should you choose to bid. It can be an excellent sales pitch. However, it also represents a contract between the seller and buyer. Read the description in its entirety and do not bid if you're uncertain about exactly what is being sold. Ask questions of the seller before bidding if you're still not sure. A small phrase in the description might well be used retrospectively to justify why the item turns out to be something other than expected. Likewise, a few words in the seller's returns policy might make it difficult to get any after-sales service if something goes wrong.

Although you have statutory rights dealing with traders in the UK, bear in mind that not all eBay traders are based in the UK (this may be in the small print), and it may simply not be worth your while to pursue a claim.

The 'Resolved' Dispute

A particular eBay purchase of some apparently end-of-line DVDs with boxes missing resulted in the delivery of some illegal DVD copies. The buyer contacted the Resolution Center. The Resolution Center went through its procedure until the seller terminated their eBay account.

At this point, the dispute was marked as resolved. There was nothing further that eBay would do. The buyer could have taken the matter further with external agencies, including FACT (the Federation Against Copyright Theft), but seemingly thought it not worth the effort for the few pounds that the item cost.

THE REALITY

Thankfully, trading on eBay seldom results in a complaint, claim, or lawsuit. The reason eBay works as well as it does is that there are huge numbers of honest people out there. Likewise, selling on eBay is a relatively straightforward process, especially if you go into it with the right attitude.

You need to recognize the difference between an eBay PowerSeller, from whom you might expect the same guarantee of service as many dedicated online stores (and many PowerSellers have their own sites outside of eBay as well), and an individual trader, who won't be selling on eBay full time, so might need longer to complete the transaction, and is less able to provide after-sales support. eBay is as its best when buyers and sellers work together to make the transactions succeed.

Ten eBay Con Tricks To Watch Out For

What are the most common tricks used by the less scrupulous eBayers, and how can you go about protecting yourself?

1 PHOTOS OR HOW-TO GUIDES

A quick look at the description suggests that you will be buying the item in the picture. Watch out for the small print, though. People commonly sell a picture of or a document about an item, rather than the item itself. The listing may have the same title as others for that item, perhaps with a clone of the item description used in the other auctions. Copy-cat item descriptions do not bode well for the seller.

Some listings suggest you can buy something that will help you get the item you want cheaply. Perhaps they're offering a 'trade secrets' book or CD, which claims to tell you how to get the item at a heavily discounted price - that's after first forking out for the guide, which in turn may simply state something completely obvious.

2 COUNTERFEIT GOODS

Although eBay is proactive about removing fake items from its listings, there's good business in the quick sale of fake designer items, even at a fraction of their high-street price. When buying branded goods, be sure to identify the seller and read their feedback carefully. There are also legal clones of popular items. Beware of descriptions with 'like' in them. The item may well be similar to the real thing, but may be a generic brand, not worth as much as you paid.

3 ILLEGAL IMPORTS

Because eBay is an international marketplace, you can deal with traders from anywhere in the world. It doesn't follow that listings on the UK site come from UK sellers only. If the item you're buying is usually subject to import duty, you should check that the seller is going to pay this tax. If they're not paying to export the item to the UK, it's possible that you'll end up having to pay duty before Customs & Excise will release the item. This is something that eBay will not protect against.

▲ That new chart album might not be such a good deal

4 PRE-BROKEN ITEMS

An old-fashioned auctioneering con is to sell items 'as seen'. This can be used by an unscrupulous seller as a way of selling items that are already broken. Alternatively, if the seller stipulates that they will not be held responsible for breakages during delivery, they could send an already broken item and claim it broke in transit. Watch out for small print in the item description and returns policy. Even an item that claims to be broken may not be much of a deal; the words 'ideal for spares or repair' may actually mean 'totally destroyed and ideal for the bin'.

5 CD-R VERSIONS

With several major retail sites selling brand new chart CDs at around £7, it's fair to say they can't be bought much more cheaply. Older albums may well come out cheaper, sold second-hand, or from surplus stock. However, if you're buying a new album at too cheap a price, be cautious. Some people are happy to buy illegal -copies of CDs, or CD-Rs with MP3 versions of several albums on. These are an infringement of copyright, and no money goes to the artist.

6 MASSIVE STOCK NEW SHOP

A seller with little to no selling history and a huge stock of items might be a genuine person doing a life-laundry. Alternatively, they may be trying to close a large number of bogus deals before being discovered. A bogus seller is unlikely to have as random an assortment of different items as a genuine first-timer with a bunch of their possessions to sell.

7 FAKE MEMORABILIA

Buying memorabilia is always a risky business. How can you be sure that this really is the towel that Amy Winehouse wiped herself on at Glastonbury 2008? Do your research. For instance, with a signed item, try to find out how it was acquired by the seller. Can you see a picture of the signature? Does it match another example of a signed item by the same celebrity? Memorabilia can be cherished greatly, but is far too easy to fake.

8 FAKE RATINGS

You have chosen to deal with a particular seller because they have a 100% positive rating with several happy buyers. Are you sure that these are genuine buyers? Have you looked at what they bought? It's not very difficult to set up several fake eBay accounts and use them to buy very cheap eBay items that were listed by another fake eBay account, thus building up a ratings portfolio paid for with a few hundred eBay listing fees.

This sounds like a lot of effort to go to, but if the seller is selling something expensive, like jewellery or large electrical items, it may be worth building up a fake profile in order to get away with a few bogus sales before cessation of trading. If you're buying something that costs more than a few pounds, perhaps look at the items and other eBay users listed on the seller's feedback profile. It's harder to fake a lot of genuine satisfied customers, buying the same item as you, who have been eBay users for years.

9 THE IMPOSSIBLE TO GET ITEM

A lot of people use eBay to buy something that's not available elsewhere. If you're looking for something that everyone is trying to buy, where genuine stocks are in short supply, the chances are that you'll risk rubbing shoulders with some dodgy sellers. Whether it's the latest videogames console, or tickets to a sold-out music festival, the season's hot properties are going to appear on eBay, and not all of the listings are going to be genuine. Even with the genuine article, the chances are that you might be dealing with a trader who's bought from the limited stock in order to tout the item at an inflated price to make a profit. It is up to you whether you wish to line this person's pockets.

If you're buying sold-out festival tickets, you're advised to check whether those tickets are genuinely transferable. Go to the festival's website and find out about the security measures. Many festivals have learned from the over-touting of Glastonbury tickets in previous years and now have strict policies regarding ticket transfers.

10 TOO GOOD TO BE TRUE

There are some excellent deals to be had on eBay, but the fundamental concepts of trading still apply to eBay sellers. In other words, although you can get a huge discount buying something directly from an eBay seller, who may be running without the overheads of a larger business, they still have to source the goods from somewhere and pay something similar to the usual trade price. If anything is discounted too much, or seems to be too good a deal, you need to question exactly why. How sure can you be that you're buying what you expect? How sure can you be that the goods are legitimate?

If something looks too good to be true...

11 THE JOKE ITEM/DO NOT USE EBAY WHILE DRUNK!

At number 11 in the list of ten, this is definitely the joker in the pack. Sometimes people make bizarre things and put them on eBay. Sometimes, in the spirit of adventure, or under the influence of alcohol, some items seem like a good purchase. A joke item may have been listed on eBay to make people laugh and raise a couple of pounds. A serious item, like, say, a wheelchair, may also seem like a hilarious purchase when you're drunk. Beware the joke item; it will only seem like a good idea until it arrives. Strangely, the novelty wears off and you're left with the eBay equivalent of a hangover.

Dishonourable Mentions

Don't forget to avoid:

- DVDs with the same name as a famous film, but which happen to be the non-famous film-adaptation of the story.
- Revenge items - the disgruntled husband trying to sell his estranged wife by putting her personal details on eBay. Don't ring her; for all you know, the whole thing is a scam. Anyway, someone else probably beat you to asking her out.
- Dodgy photos. Don't look in the reflections in photos of furniture or ceramics; some men forget to wear clothes while photographing their items.
- The 'question about your eBay item' scam. Spam e-mails, possibly snuck through eBay's system, inviting you to look at particular eBay items you've never heard of. If you wanted to look at an eBay item, you'd search for it. ·

micro mart SAVE 24%
SUBSCRIPTION FORM

☐ **YES!** Please start my subscription to Micro Mart.

☐ OR I am an existing subscriber, please extend my subscription to Micro Mart with this offer.

COMPLETE YOUR DETAILS

Mr/Mrs/Ms _____ Forename _____

Surname _____

Address _____

_____

_____ Postcode _____

Daytime phone _____ Year of birth _____

Mobile phone _____

Email _____

SELECT YOUR PAYMENT METHOD

1 ☐ **Direct Debit Payment** only £19.75 every 13 issues – **Save 24%** on the shop price – UK Only

Dennis **Instruction to your Bank or Building Society to pay by Direct Debit** ●**DIRECT Debit**

Please complete and send to: Freepost RLZS-ETGT-BCZR, Dennis Publishing Ltd, 800 Guillat Ave, Kent Science Park, Sittingbourne ME9 8GU
Name and full postal address of your Bank or Building Society

To the manager: Bank name _____

Address _____

_____

_____ Postcode _____

Account in the name(s) of _____

Branch sort code ☐☐ ☐☐ ☐☐

Bank/Building Society account number ☐☐☐☐☐☐☐☐

Originator's Identification Number

7	2	4	6	8	0

Ref no. to be completed by Dennis Publishing

Instructions to your bank or Building Society
Please pay Dennis Publishing Ltd. Direct Debits from the account detailed in this instruction subject to the safeguards assured by the Direct Debit Guarantee. I understand that this instruction may remain with Dennis Publishing Ltd and, if so, details will be passed electronically to my Bank/Building Society.

Signature(s) _____

Date _____

Banks and building societies may not accept Direct Debit instructions for some types of account

2 ☐ **Cheque or Credit/Debit Card Payment** 26 issues for only £39.50 – **Save 24%** on the shop price

☐ I enclose a cheque made payable to Dennis Publishing Ltd.

☐ Please charge my: ☐ Visa ☐ MasterCard
☐ AMEX ☐ Debit/Maestro (Issue No. ☐)

CARD NO. ☐☐☐☐ ☐☐☐☐ ☐☐☐☐ ☐☐☐☐ ☐☐☐☐

START DATE ☐☐☐☐ EXPIRY DATE ☐☐☐☐

RETURN THIS ORDER FORM TO
**Freepost RLZS-ETGT-BCZR,
Micro Mart Subscriptions Dept, 800 Guillat Avenue,
Kent Science Park, Sittingbourne ME9 8GU**

(This address can be used on an envelope – no stamp required)

You will be able to view your subscription details online at **www.subsinfo.co.uk**

Offer Code: D1173

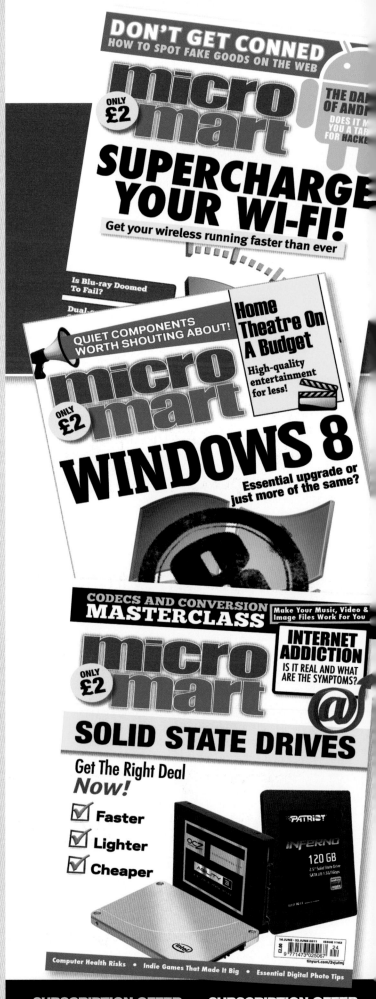

Case Study: **Console Passion**

Money for old rope? Maybe not but there is gold in some retro items....

Ones of the best ways to make money on eBay is to find a niche that interests you and sell items related to it. Not only does this allow you to create a identity for yourself, but it also means you will be dealing with like-minded people. You will be able to offer better service, because you will be in a better position to comment on the stock you have and such targeting also makes it easier to advertise - simply head for forums and websites dedicated to your niche and your shop should be off to a flying start.

Andy Brown is one such seller. He sells old videogames to a growing band of fans of all things retro. His stock consists of old Sega Mega Drives and Super Nintendos, Atari Lynxes and Game Boys. Indeed, if it was made in the 1980s and 1990s, then his company, Console Passion, will sell it. And such is Andy's passion for retro games, his knowledge is second to none, meaning he can also offer superlative customer service.

He started on eBay in 2001. He used Yahoo! Auctions as well, a free service that later closed. When Andy began, he wasn't sure how popular eBay would be and he entered the market purely because he was enthusiastic. "I didn't start out with any intentions of making money or running a business to be honest; I was a collector of videogames and eBay was a good place to find games I didn't own and an even better place to sell off my duplicates," he said.

Indeed, it is always advisable to test the market you are about to enter. This gives you a good opportunity to find out how much items tend to go for and what the competition is like. Your aim is to entice customers with better service and products than your competitors

and you can't do that if you work in isolation. And many of the best sellers were strong and frequent buyers.

"At first, any money I made just went into buying more games," said Andy. "After a while I figured I could do both and started making a small amount each month."

Console Passion has an eBay shop (**stores.ebay. co.uk/Console-Passion-Retro-Games**) as well as a stand-alone store (**www.consolepassion.co.uk**), but it was eBay that underpinned business in the earlier days and he loved the whole experience. "In the early days it really was a community. With no eBay shops, almost everything on the site was auction only and you could bag yourself a bargain if you were lucky. It was exciting too. Before sniping tools existed, people would wait until the last seconds to place manual bids. Sometimes if you were after something particularly rare, the adrenaline could really get pumping! Then there were the bidding wars: sellers would sometimes get an unexpectedly high price for an item if two buyers battled to outbid each other!"

But times have changed and Andy admits to having a love-hate relationship with the site. Things altered when eBay took a greater corporate approach, he said, with bedroom sellers being pushed aside in favour of large volume sellers. "There was a shift in emphasis from auctions to eBay shops, possibly in an attempt to compete with Amazon Marketplace. Awash with ever changing rules, regulations and seemingly perpetual price increases, eBay became a sad shadow of its former self in my opinion."

And yet he continues with his eBay business, because it's hard to ignore such a massive marketplace. With eBay, it's possible to reach the volume of buyers that a

Getting The Look Right

Andy gives us his essential tips for getting your listings looking perfect:

• Good pictures are essential - I can't understand why people list things without a picture. I never buy an item unless I can see a picture.
• The more details in the description, the better - I think some people are afraid of including too much information in case it puts buyers off. If I read a description that tells me the exact condition of an

item, I know I'm not in for any nasty surprises when it arrives so I'm more likely to buy.
• Use a common set of colours, fonts and themes across all your listings.
• Use your company logo if you have one - branding is just as important on eBay as it would be in any other marketplace.
• The 'Powerseller' and 'Top Rated Seller' logos instill confidence into buyers so use them. Have a returns policy and clear terms and conditions too.

stand-alone site without proper marketing would fail to reach. Although Andy stopped using eBay for a while because his own website was doing really well, he has recently become more forgiving and now his wife runs the eBay side of the business to sell off website duplicates, lesser value and lower grade items. It's a practice many companies are now taking.

One of the benefits of this is that you're able to sell surplus items that may otherwise not get attention on your own website while bringing your business to the attention of eBayers. They may like a product you're selling on eBay and decide to head to your stand-alone website to see what else you have. This is particularly important for niche sellers.

"Without a doubt, eBay is a great place to find all forms of weird and wonderful stuff," said Andy. "Toys, comics, video games, trading cards, antiques and the likes all have a big presence on eBay. It's almost contrary to the real-life marketplace, because these 'niche' categories are actually some of the biggest on eBay - I believe the 'collectibles' category has more items in it than any other."

For those just starting out, Andy says the support eBay brings is invaluable and he advises people to use the auction site to build a reputation, going it alone later. "For someone starting out in the marketplace, it's an ideal place to begin, and there's plenty of support out there to get you on your feet," he said. "It's then a good place to court new customers for any business. Every sale I make on eBay is a potential new customer to my website, so I make sure they're aware that my site exists by including marketing material when I post out the sold item."

Not that his misgivings have completely gone away. He would love a strong rival to eBay. If nothing else, it would give the site some extra competition. "I'm aware of a few smaller alternatives, but listings are sparse and buyers even more limited," he said. "It's a catch 22 situation, though: without buyers, sellers are unlikely to start listing on another online auction tool, and without the listings, buyers aren't going to start making that transition to an alternative. Unfortunately,

▲ The team behind Console Passion

unless a big Internet name puts its weight behind a well designed substitute, eBay will continue to monopolise. I'd love to see a new auction site that had all the old eBay values. Maybe I should start a Twitter campaign for Google Auctions?"

▲ Andy is as passionate about games as his customers

▲ Console Passion has its own stand-alone store

▲ eBay allows Andy to sell off surplus stock

Chapter 4
Advanced Selling

Setting Up An eBay shop

If you have lots of regular stock to sell, then you may want to consider setting up your own shop. We look at getting a store up and running

After you've dipped your toes into the eBay waters, you'll have gained a good feel for the buying and selling process. However, if you want to take your selling to higher level, then it's worth setting up an eBay shop.

By doing so, you're not limited to one-off auctions or short-term advertisements of your goods. You will be able to get yourself noticed, work on a larger scale and sell to your heart's content. In this chapter, we're going to explain what a shop actually is, and how it will benefit you, the eBay seller. We'll explore just how you go about setting up your shop and, more importantly, whether or not it's worth doing.

OPEN ALL HOURS

Using eBay to sell the odd item is a great way to make some extra cash, but if you're planning on using eBay to make a living, then you'll need a good way to make your auctions stand out from the crowd, and make a name for yourself in the eBay community. Selling items and providing a great service is a good way of doing this, but feedback alone won't get your merchandise the coverage you need.

One of the most effective methods to get this wide coverage and high profile is to set up an eBay shop, granting access to a whole heap of benefits. If all goes well, you'll shift more stock than ever before - a fact that eBay is proud to state, with a claim that "75% of eBay Shops sellers surveyed said that opening an eBay shop increased their sales."

An eBay shop is your own personal virtual storefront on the eBay site. Whereas selling individual items with a normal eBay auction account lets you put items up for sale that can then be searched for among all other items currently listed on the site, having a shop means

you have your very own marketplace. In this shop you can list and sell as many items as you like, with no one else's listings cluttering up the place.

The shop comes with your own customised header (shop name and/or logo), as well as your own search feature (to search through all of the items you sell), promotional sections and even the option to include a newsletter, among many other things. This all adds up to your own personalised area of commerce, and is a fantastic way to get your business up and running. You can enjoy some of the benefits of a bricks and mortar business, without the overheads. There's no shop floor to rent, and no staff or utility bills to pay - just the monthly subscription.

REQUIREMENTS

Before you consider setting up your own shop you'll need to meet the minimum demands laid down by eBay. You obviously need to be a registered eBay user, so if you've never sold anything on eBay before, you'll be unable to jump right in and set up shop. You'll also need to ensure that your PayPal account is linked to your eBay account, too. To run a featured shop you also need to be a registered business seller on eBay and maintain a 12-month average detailed sellers ratings score of 4.4 or above in each of the four areas that eBay users score. Those running Anchor shops must have an average score of 4.6 across the four areas, too..

EBAY SHOP FEATURES

The additional features available to eBay shop owners are many and varied. Some are basic extensions of current eBay features, and others are in-depth options geared towards larger-scale e-commerce. Let's look at some of the benefits you can expect.

To start with, your shop will be enveloped in your own store branding and will have a custom web address. This includes your own shop header featuring your own design and logos. Although the full eBay header still remains at the top for users on the Basic package (with the header being greatly reduced for Featured and Anchored shops), your own identity is still clear.

In the header, you can also enter your shop description. This includes your eBay rating, along with a description of your shop and the types of items you sell. By entering keywords into the shop description that accurately describe your shop, people looking for the types of goods you sell will find you far easier.

▲ You should take time to customise the e-mail that bidders will receive if they win your auction

▲ Using the List View option means you can display more products on screen at once

The Basic package used to be limited when it came to the header, and you could only select from available templates. Now, just as with the Featured or Anchored packages, you're able to fully customise your header (with HTML), forming a truly unique banner that can be used not only on your shop, but in other advertising too. This banner can include links to self-hosted pictures, text, and details of highlighted items and offers.

It's also possible to create and customise your own store-front pages. This grants your shop even more distinction. These pages, like the header, are created using HTML, so if you have the skills, you can let your imagination run wild, or you could pay someone to design it for you. Depending on the package you choose, you're limited to a number of custom pages, with those opting for the Basic subscription having the ability to make use of up to five custom pages in their shop.

TAGS

This customised content is all handled via the HTML builder tool eBay supplies, as well as some useful wizards. To help users get the most out of this user-defined content, eBay has also created special tags which, when combined with the right HTML code, can quickly add useful information to your shop.

These tags include {eBayUserID}, which will display your eBay User ID, along with your feedback score (including any relevant icons), {eBayFeedback}, which can display detailed feedback information in various configurations, and {StoreItemShowcase}, which is a very useful bit of code that, when used with your own settings, displays some of the items you're selling in your promotional boxes.

These tags eliminate the need to type out whole reams of code, and let users of all HTML abilities build their stores with ease. However, eBay has restricted the use of some shop tags (specifically the item specific shops tags) in the eBay Shops header. Using these restricted shops tags in the header will result in the shop tag appearing as text and eBay asks people not to use {eBayStoresItemList}, {eBayStoresItemShowcase}, eBayStoresItem}, {eBayStoresItemDetail} and {eBayPromo}.

eBay Shop Insertion Fees For Buy It Now Listings (Three, Five, Seven, Ten, 30 Days)

Insertion Price	Basic Shop	Featured Shop	Anchor Shop
All categories (excluding media - generally books, comics, magazines, DVDs, film and TV, games, music)	£0.20	£0.05	£0.00
Media products	£0.10	£0.05	£0.00

eBay Shop Listings Final Value Fees For Buy It Now Listings (Private Sellers)

Final Sale Price (Excluding Technology And Media)	Final Value Fee
Item not sold	No fee
£0.99 to £49.99	10% of the amount of the final selling price up to £40
£50 to £599.99	10% of the amount of the final selling price up to £40
£600 or more	10% of the amount of the final selling price up to £40

eBay Shop Listings Final Value Fees For Buy It Now Listings (Business Sellers)

Category	Final Value Fee
Item not sold (irrespective of category)	No fee
Technology (including computing, consumer electronics and mobile phones)	3% of final value
Parts (vehicle parts and accessories)	8% of final value
Media (including books, comics, magazines, DVDs, music and video games)	9% of final value
Collectables (including antiques, coins, sports memorabilia, stamps and art)	10% of final value
Clothing, shoes and accessories (also includes jewellery and watches)	12% of final value
Mobile phones with contract	No fee
Property	No fee
All other categories (except vehicles)	10% of final value

For a listing of these useful tags, along with the available settings to be used with them, visit **pages.ebay.co.uk/help/sell/stores-tags.html**.

SEARCH AND CATEGORIES

Along with the personalised header and custom page design, you'll get some staple additions, such as your own search and category boxes. Using the categories system, you can split the items you want to sell into different sections. For example, you could have a clothes section, a section for electronic goods, and a special section for collector's items.

You can have up to 300 categories at once, and all your categories can be changed and updated when you like. Changing names will not affect the item listings found within. You can also use subcategories too, further enhancing your browsing functions.

For people wishing to sell a lot of merchandise, this use of categories is a bonus, and enables the quick and easy browsing of your items. Couple this with the search facility, and all your items will be within easy reach.

Several promotion boxes are available to all subscription types. These are used to highlight different items being sold on special offer, or just to announce new stock, complete with links that take the customer to the item's own page.

Of course, no shop is complete without the main gallery page, where customers can scroll through the items on sale, and the main portion of your shop is taken up by this window.

That's the basic visual make-up of an eBay shop, but that's not all. As with the rest of eBay, when an item is clicked by a user, the product is opened up in a listing frame, which contains all the information associated with the item, along with a larger picture. This function is expanded in an eBay shop, and you have access to a custom listing frame. This is a special frame that allows customised headers and sidebars, thus giving you your own listing windows for your products. Not only does this look more professional, but it's also a great way to advertise your shop, because you have effectively branded your item, which can be discovered by any eBay user, whether they're in your shop or not.

▲ Increase your shop's profile with the 'Email Marketing' tool

SHOP INVENTORY

You will, no doubt, already be familiar with eBay's two main methods of selling items: auction style and fixed price. However, when you open an eBay shop you'll have access to a third sale type: Shop Inventory.

This is a special sale-type that lists items at a set price with no bidding. The fee structure for the listings is different to normal options, however. Up-front fee listings are lower, costing you less to place items on sale, but the final value fees if a sale is successful are higher. Your listings have an unlimited duration, as you can choose whether you want a listing to end after 30 days or continue beyond that.

There's also the option of a Good Till Cancelled (GTC) listing. This is a special option, which lets you list an item and have it automatically renewed every 30 days (as long as stock is available, and assuming your listing fits criteria). This renewal will occur every month, until you decide to cancel it (with each 30-day cycle incurring a new listing charge).

MARKETING TOOLS

No self-respecting shop owner would go into business and simply wait for customers to come rolling in. If people don't know your shop exists, they're not likely to visit. This is where the eBay Shops marketing features come into play.

Along with your shop, you'll have access to a range of marketing tools, designed to help you get noticed. One of the most useful is the e-mail marketing tool. Using this you can fire off e-mails to potential and existing customers, advertising new items or special offers.

As with most of the shop design process, you set up these e-mails using a step-by-step wizard in which you select the e-mail design and content. You can even include item galleries that users can click on to visit the shop. Feedback can be included, giving your customers peace of mind from the off.

As well as the e-mail service, eBay Shops lets you create promotional flyers that can be posted or packaged with items you sell. You'll also have access to a custom listing frame, and listing feeds (such as RSS). Shop comparisons are also an option, making your listings available to third-party search engines and product-comparison sites.

A range of item-based promotional functions are featured too, letting you cross-promote stock, advertise top picks, and point users to similar items. You can even customise the e-mail footers and invoices with your own logos. All this marketing muscle should be a very welcome aid for anyone trying to increase their sales.

IS IT WORTH IT?

Setting up an eBay shop certainly sounds like a good idea on paper, but will setting up your own shop help increase your sales? Can the extra costs be justified?

How To... Set Up Custom Pages

While the standard eBay pages aren't bad, if you really want to look professional, you'll want to add some extra personality. Here's how:

1 Custom Pages can be used to give your shop a more personalised look. Creating one is easy. Select the Custom Pages link from the Shop Manager menu and you'll see this screen. Select the layout from the range of templates, and click 'Continue' to go the next step.

2 Now you can tweak and refine your page. You'll need to give the page a title, and you can then start to add in the required text. At various points in this section you can also use eBay's HTML Builder, to further customise your page.

3 Custom pages also let you employ promotion boxes for various uses, such as advertising new items, or linking to other sections of the shop. You can also design your own promo boxes if you wish.

4 You can now add some more custom text to the page (again, with the help of the HTML Builder, if needed), and you can specify the item display type. To emphasise your items, you can also opt to hide the left-hand navigation bar, giving prime real-estate solely to your stock.

Would some users be better off staying with one-off auctions? The only people who can really answer these questions are actual shop owners.

Given the amount of extra coverage and space an eBay shop provides, it's no surprise that many shop owners are glad they decided to set one up. Cathy Grant, owner of Aromabar (**stores.ebay.co.uk/Aromabar**) is very happy with her featured eBay shop but would like more power and custom control. "I'm happy with my eBay store on the whole but would prefer to have more free, easy-to-use tools provided by eBay to allow me to make the design and layout better, as I feel it could look more professional."

Like many eBay shop owners, Cathy runs her eBay shop in parallel to her own website, and sees distinct benefits in running a stand-alone site: "I've made more profit on sales through my own site due to no fees. I paid a total of £40 for my site template with hosting and have done all the hard work myself." So eBay shops may be easy to set up, but having your own site is still the way to go for many users.

Other eBay shop owners don't necessarily open a shop for the profits alone, and instead use it as a glorified advert for their real shop. Peter, who used to run Genki Video Games as an eBay store, is one example. He appreciates the extra coverage that an

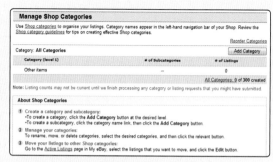

▲ Sort your goods out with the shop categories

▲ Creating promotional displays

▲ The shop summary page

▲ Keywords help potential customers find you

eBay shop grants, but doesn't welcome the additional costs. At the time, he said that "The main reason we use eBay is to try to get some additional coverage for our website. To be honest, I'm not sure we even break even once the listing fee, subscription fee, percentage of sale fee and PayPal fee is taken," he said.

Having a store doesn't guarantee extra visits either. "We do use auctions, but only to get attention for our store, as it seems surfers on eBay are far more drawn to auctions."

It's clear that having an eBay shop can be beneficial to setting up a business online, if only for the expanded audience and the extra advertising it generates. The costs are scalable, thanks to the three subscription options, and as long as you have the stock to keep your shop up and running, you'll have a constant outlet for your merchandise that gives you access to a range of extra features not as readily available to many stand-alone web stores.

But many eBay shops have come and gone and many people have become disillusioned with the service. Julie Stamp ran Lolli Dollies on eBay but has since closed it in favour of a stand-alone store. "For me, one of the drawbacks of running an eBay shop is that customers seem to think you're there to answer any enquiries they have, in my case with regards to doll collecting or a doll already in their collection, rather than sticking to questions about items in your eBay shop."

She said the amount of admin time and space required for packaging material is off-putting but the advantage is having your items sold to a worldwide customer base. "If you sell to a niche market, eBay is ideal, as it tends to be the first stop for collectors," she

said. "Search engine optimisation is a given with eBay, and listing items and uploading photos is easy."

Mark Withers, who used to actively sell pictures on eBay, now uses his stand-alone site **www.studioworx. co.uk**, but said, "What eBay does is help you build your own unique brand, and it's an easy point of contact and bookmark. You can organise products into custom categories, making it easier for the customer to find products. There's a buyer confidence with eBay, and while I don't actively sell on eBay any more, I do pursue other business interests associated with it, helping other sellers get started."

SHOP MAINTENANCE

When your shop is built, you can manage it from the Shop Management screen. You'll find a raft of options that cater for every facet of your new trading empire. A good place to start is by organising your stock.

Select Shop Categories from the left-hand menu and you'll be taken to the category screen. Click the 'Add Category' button to create your sections. Enter them into the boxes provided and then click 'Save'. Your categories will be added. You can add more if you like, and can also create subcategories.

Click the 'Promotion Boxes' link to customise these useful features and create more. You can move boxes around, change the box type, content text and name. You can view boxes by category and can edit, remove, or duplicate existing ones.

Just as with any website, search keywords are invaluable. Without them your shop would be very hard to find - not good for sales.

Subscription Types And Fees

BASIC SHOP
The starter pack of the shop system. This is the option for most users, and is great for first-time sellers or those who want to see if a shop is the right option for them before advancing further.

FEATURED SHOP
Has more options for tracking sales and performance, and has more advertising tools. Good for users who want to begin their business growth.

ANCHOR SHOP
The high-end option for advanced eBay sellers who need to get as much coverage as possible and who need to manage their business on a daily basis. Has the most advertising options.

eBay Shops Tariffs

	Basic	Featured	Anchor
Monthly subscription fee	£14.99	£49.99	£349.99
One-time set-up fee	£0	£0	£0
Sales management tools	N/A	£0 (Selling Manager Pro)	£0 (Selling Manager Pro)

Build Your Shop	Basic	Featured	Anchor
Shop home page and unlimited product pages	Yes	Yes	Yes
Custom pages	Five pages	Ten pages	15 pages
Custom web address	Yes	Yes	Yes
Promotion boxes	Yes	Yes	Yes
Shop categories	300	300	300
Custom shop header	Yes	Yes	Yes
eBay header reduction	No	Yes	Yes
Sales Management			
Free sales management tools	No	Selling Manager Pro	Selling Manager Pro
Vacation/holiday	Yes	Yes	Yes
Picture manager (hosting images)	1MB free	1MB free and reduced subscription fees	50MB free and reduced subscription fees

Promote Your Shop	Basic	Featured	Anchor
On eBay			
Increased Exposure On eBay			
Shops logo appears next to your shop name in listings	Yes	Yes	Yes
All listings include additional 'See All Items Listed in Your Shop' link	Yes	Yes	Yes
Listings displayed in eBay Shops gateway search and results browser	Yes	Yes	Yes
Shop name appears in 'Related Shops' search results	Occasionally	Sometimes	Frequently
Rotating promotional space on the eBay Shops gateway	None	Text link at centre of page	Shop logo at top of page
Cross-promotions	Yes	Yes	Yes
Custom listing frame	Yes	Yes	Yes
HTML builder	Yes	Yes	Yes
Off eBay			
E-mail marketing	1,000 e-mails per month	2,500 e-mails per month	5,000 e-mails per month
Promotional flyers	Yes	Yes	Yes
Shop-branded business materials	Yes	Yes	Yes
Search engine keyword management	Yes	Yes	Yes
Listing feeds	Yes	Yes	Yes
Track Your Success			
Traffic reports	Yes	Yes (advanced info)	Yes (advanced info)

How To... Set Up An eBay Shop

If you're serious about selling on eBay, and want to shift a large quantity of goods, then you may want to consider setting up your very own eBay shop. It takes a little bit more work to get going, compared to setting up a normal eBay account, but it stands a real chance of getting noticed and bringing in more business for you. Also, more and more buyers are used to the idea of buying direct from an eBay shop, rather than going through the traditional bidding process. So if you want to get cracking, here's what you need to do. Just follow this step-by-step guide...

1 The first thing you need to do is to select the subscription level you require. Obviously, you pay more for the advanced services, but for now, the Basic package will suffice. If you feel you need the extra features at a later date, you can always upgrade easily enough. For now, choose 'Basic Shop' and then click 'Continue'. You'll be offered some free extras on the next page. There's no harm in taking them.

2 As you'd expect, you'll need to read through a user agreement before you can proceed. Although you may skip this for most products, it's worth having a good read through, as it's a business you're setting up, not just a software package. Accept and then click 'Subscribe' to fire up your account. Remember, you must keep your shop open for a minimum of 30 days and will be billed for a month even if you cancel within that period.

3 Now you've set up your shop account and you're ready to begin. You're now offered the chance to use the Quick Shop Setup. This process will build and design your shop in just a few minutes. However, you can also refine and enhance your shop at any time later.

4 The Quick Shop Setup screen. Here you lay the foundation of your shop. As you scroll down through the page, you build the various aspects of your shop, and can personalise the template to suit your preferences.

5 First up is the shop colour and theme. Click the 'Edit' link under the 'Shop colour and theme' section and you'll see a box containing the options that are available to you. Simply browse through these and click the radio button next to your selection. Click 'Save' when you're done.

6 Now you need to give your shop a description. This is the text that will appear in search results for eBay shops, next to the shop logo. You'll want to make this as welcoming and descriptive as possible, but keep it short. Buyers don't want to read an essay to find out what your shop is all about.

7 Next, decide how you want your items to be displayed to your customers. You can choose Picture Gallery or List view. Gallery is the most descriptive option, but List view lets you fit more on screen. You can also choose the order in which items will appear.

8 Promotion boxes are important, because they help to draw a shopper's attention to certain items. Here you can choose to have four promotion boxes, or none at all. Depending on how much stock you have, you may or may not need these now. You can change this at a later date, so don't worry too much about your choice at this point.

9 Listing frames can be customised by shop owners, and in the next step you choose the template you wish to make use of. Header & Navigation is the best template, as it's the most flexible, but you may want to opt for the other layouts.

10 With the basic building blocks of your shop complete, you can now preview it. Although it's going to look a little sparse at the moment, you can see the general layout and feel of it. And there you have it; your shop is created. However, there are far more options to play around with, so don't be afraid to experiment.

DID YOU KNOW?

A common eBay con is to buy a new gadget, and then recoup some of the money by selling the empty box on eBay, hoping buyers misread the auction and think they're bidding for the product itself rather than the packaging. It's especially common with newly released technology where demand outstrips supply, such as freshly launched games consoles or the mobile phones.

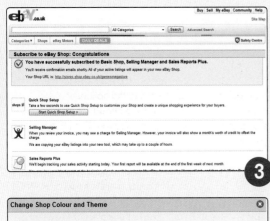

Subscribe to eBay Shop: Congratulations

✓ **You have successfully subscribed to Basic Shop, Selling Manager and Sales Reports Plus.**
You'll receive confirmation emails shortly. All of your active listings will appear in your new eBay Shop.
Your Shop URL is: http://stores.shop.ebay.co.uk/gamesmegastore

Quick Shop Setup
Take a few seconds to use Quick Shop Setup to customise your Shop and create a unique shopping experience for your buyers.

[Start Quick Shop Setup >]

Selling Manager
When you review your invoice, you may see a charge for Selling Manager. However, your invoice will also show a month's worth of credit to offset the charge.
We are copying your eBay listings into your new tool, which may take up to a couple of hours.

Sales Reports Plus
We'll begin tracking your sales activity starting today. Your first report will be available at the end of the first week of next month.

3

Quick Shop Setup

You have many options when customising your Shop. If you are short on time and want expert advice, we've preselected a few Shop features on this page that are popular with successful eBay Shop sellers.

You can do one of the following:
- Apply all of the recommended settings by clicking **Apply Settings**.
- Edit the recommended settings to suit your individual needs, and then click **Apply Settings**.
- You can always use Manage My Store (in My eBay) to make changes or further customize your Store using additional features not included in Quick Store Setup.

[Apply Settings]

Shop design

Shop colour and theme

Colour: Custom Selection
Theme: Classic Left
Edit

Preview settings

4

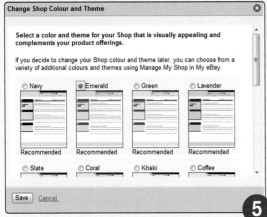

Change Shop Colour and Theme ⊗

Select a color and theme for your Shop that is visually appealing and complements your product offerings.

If you decide to change your Shop colour and theme later, you can choose from a variety of additional colours and themes using Manage My Shop in My eBay.

○ Navy   ⊙ Emerald   ○ Green   ○ Lavender

Recommended   Recommended   Recommended   Recommended

○ Slate   ○ Coral   ○ Khaki   ○ Coffee

[Save] Cancel

5

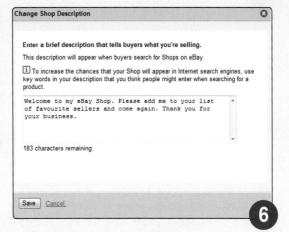

Change Shop Description ⊗

Enter a brief description that tells buyers what you're selling.

This description will appear when buyers search for Shops on eBay.

ⓘ To increase the chances that your Shop will appear in Internet search engines, use key words in your description that you think people might enter when searching for a product.

Welcome to my eBay Shop. Please add me to your list of favourite sellers and come again. Thank you for your business.

183 characters remaining.

[Save] Cancel

6

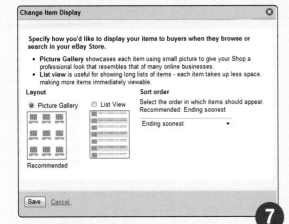

Change Item Display ⊗

Specify how you'd like to display your items to buyers when they browse or search in your eBay Store.

- **Picture Gallery** showcases each item using small picture to give your Shop a professional look that resembles that of many online businesses.
- **List view** is useful for showing long lists of items - each item takes up less space, making more items immediately viewable.

Layout
⊙ Picture Gallery   ○ List View

Sort order
Select the order in which items should appear.
Recommended: Ending soonest

[Ending soonest ▾]

Recommended

[Save] Cancel

7

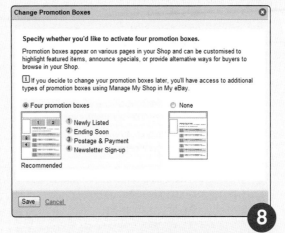

Change Promotion Boxes ⊗

Specify whether you'd like to activate four promotion boxes.

Promotion boxes appear on various pages in your Shop and can be customised to highlight featured items, announce specials, or provide alternative ways for buyers to browse in your Shop.

ⓘ If you decide to change your promotion boxes later, you'll have access to additional types of promotion boxes using Manage My Shop in My eBay.

⊙ Four promotion boxes   ○ None

1 Newly Listed
2 Ending Soon
3 Postage & Payment
4 Newsletter Sign-up

Recommended

[Save] Cancel

8

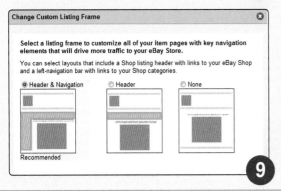

Change Custom Listing Frame ⊗

Select a listing frame to customize all of your item pages with key navigation elements that will drive more traffic to your eBay Store.

You can select layouts that include a Shop listing header with links to your eBay Shop and a left-navigation bar with links to your Shop categories.

⊙ Header & Navigation   ○ Header   ○ None

Recommended

9

Games Megastore
Maintained by: thecrookslegacy (195 ★)
Welcome to my eBay Shop. Please add me to your list of favourite sellers and come again. Thank you for your business.

Shop search
[Search]
☐ in titles & description

0 results found in all categories
ⓘ This Shop currently has 0 listings. You can come back later or check other Shops.

View: All Items

Display
» Hide gallery view
» View new listed

Postage & Payment
Payment must be made immediately. Game will be posted when payment clears. I have a reputation for very speedy delivery and will ensure this item is in the post the day after the auction ends and the payment has been made. I accept PayPal. Happy bidding.

Store Newsletter!

10

Increasing Your Share Of eBay Sales

So you're up and selling on the eBay site, but what's the best way to sell more items?

With an established, organised eBay shop, you're well situated to grow your business. And the most obvious way to do that is to offer more items for sale. By expanding your selection of merchandise and adding new categories of goods, you can drive your small shop toward the medium or high sales leagues.

But is that always a good idea? Are there any pitfalls to avoid? And is there help available to aid in expanding your shop listings?

THE PROS

Exposure: The main advantage of listing lots of items is the increased exposure it grants. The wider the range of products you have on offer, the greater the chance of catching a potential buyer's attention.

For example, you may enjoy a thriving business in men's ties, with your best-selling item being 100% silk styles, although in limited colour choices and a few traditional patterns. Anyone searching for 'ties', or 'silk', or even 'menswear' or 'men's accessories' is likely to find you. However, run out of your leading product one month, and sales slump, leaving you struggling to recover in

following months. If you add socks, belts and wallets to your inventory, you'll reach a much wider audience seeking those items. When they click into your shop, they'll see your popular silk-tie line and may add to their sock order. Even if they only buy socks, you're still ahead. A new customer has put that all-important, albeit virtual, first foot through your door.

Discounts: Widen the variety of items in your shop through wholesale purchases with the same supplier, and you'll likely be entitled to volume discounts. Check your supplier's discount schedules and ask about lower rates to evaluate new merchandise in addition to your usual orders, and watch for any special offer items you can audition. Deeply discounted sale items added to your shop listings will earn you maximum extra profits with minimal risk.

THE CONS

Space: More inventory requires more space. If you're selling 'virtual' goods (electronic books and the like) or services, floor space isn't a consideration. For anything else, you'll need room to store your inventory until it's sold. If your current shop is under-utilising existing space, you'll be able to stock more items without worry. But if you're already encroaching into non-work areas, and the dining room table, chairs and half a settee are overflowing with items, space - or the lack of it - is a high priority.

Capital: More items in your inventory requires more money. The more items you offer for sale, the more you'll pay or owe your suppliers. Also, more fees will be due to eBay. Increasing stock is always a gamble; you'll have the potential to sell and earn more, but it's never guaranteed.

Expanding listings in a shop that's already floundering may doom it to failure. You could easily over-extend yourself financially, and the damage may be difficult to recover from.

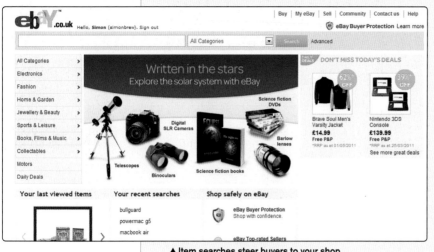

▲ Item searches steer buyers to your shop

Workload: The main goal of more stock is, ultimately, more sales. However, with it comes an increase in the time and effort required to reach that end.

Any successful business needs a fair bit of work in pre-sales areas like marketing and post-sales labours like bookkeeping and banking - all the while keeping an eye on everything else in between. Adding many listings to a flourishing small business may be the act that ruins it, with too much time taken from family or personal pleasures and the added stresses of bigger business worries.

THE BALANCE

It looks as though the cons outweigh the pros. Surely there's a happy medium, or no one would start or grow a business.

The key is in balance, finding ways to recognise and minimise the downsides. And the best way to prevent problems is with planning.

Measuring Up: When you opened your eBay shop you probably thought about how and where you would store things. Now, in considering listing even more things, you need to take a closer look at the space you have available. Will it be adequate for your needs? At what point will it become insufficient? Do you have family or friends nearby that can share for free or at low cost, clean, secure, always accessible space to store your stock? Would travelling there be more hassle than any added sales are worth?

Renting commercial, contracted space is a move that should only be considered by shops and sellers who've enjoyed substantial profits for well over a year or two. All others should be like goldfish, limiting their growth to the physical space they possess. Committing to a long-term expense in untested waters is a sink-or-swim affair, best avoided until it becomes the only option.

Controlling Cash: Everyone's familiar with the entrepreneurial edict 'It takes money to make money', and there's no arguing with that. There is great potential in offering more items to increase sales and profits, but how do you know just how big a leap to take into unknown territory? A good, established method is to stock about a month's worth of goods at a time. Research what amount of products similar eBay shops sell in a week and order roughly four times that much.

That gives you a few weeks grace period to reorder if sales are faster than you expected, while your out-of-pocket outlay is a maximum of a few weeks' worth of inventory if sales are sluggish.

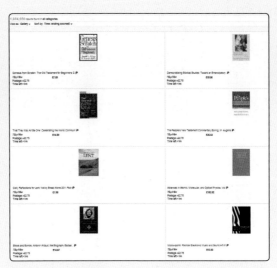

▲ Listing lots of items requires more pages, pictures and category classifications

For this to work, you need to be very familiar with your suppliers and know they're reliable and can supply stock quickly.

If your shop has never enjoyed brisk sales, and you suspect you'd do better selling entirely different items, replace your current items rather than add to unpopular products. Shove your slow-moving items into auctions to clear unwanted inventory and make room for new goods.

Be prepared for the added incidental expenses of per-item listing fees and extra packaging materials should your newly listed items prove popular. Be realistic, rather than begrudging, about fees. For many sellers, listing fees will be comparable to the cost of other advertising avenues such as Google AdWords. Consider the cost of listing fees a form of advertising investment and they become a much more tolerable business expense.

Taking Stock Of Yourself: When deciding if expanding your product line will be worth the added time and work, take a good look at yourself, as much as anywhere else. Are you the type who excels under stress? Or do you want a business that takes 40 hours per week of your time and not a minute more? Will adding 50 new items and the potential e-mail enquiries, order fulfilment, feedback activity, and possible complaints or returns for each, make you 50 times happier or 50 times more likely to hide away in a dark room with your regrets?

If you welcome the extra work, how much are you willing to do before needing to hire help? That could be the solution to reclaiming your leisure life, if you can trust someone else to do the work the way you want it done. If not, you'll be more

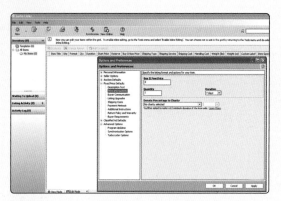

▲ A free multiple listings tool, Turbo Lister is available for Windows users

stressed than if you did it yourself in the 70th hour of the week.

Whether you decide to work alone, or with assistance, and in or out of 'normal' hours, there are programs and tools that can help.

TOOLS TO GROW ON
One of the advantages of building your business through an eBay shop is easy access to the seller tools eBay makes available.

When you first set up your shop, you probably used the Sell Your Item form to list each of your products. If you're adding many listings, that will quickly become a very frustrating and also time-consuming process.

Turbo Lister (**pages.ebay.co.uk/turbo_lister**) is a free Windows-only software application you can use to upload lots of listings all at the same time. You simply enter all the information for your items offline and then upload everything in one go. You can add thousands of items to your shop, previewing each of them before they're added. An online tour with step-by-step instructions is available, which will help you learn to use this customisable bulk-listing tool.

If you prefer to use your own inventory software, and you've been registered for 90 days or more and have at least 50 active listings per month for two months running, then you qualify for eBay's free File Exchange (**pages.ebay.co.uk/file_exchange**). It's a high-volume seller's tool for multiple listings from CSV (Comma Separated Values) files via Excel and other spreadsheet and database programs on all platforms.

Another free tool from eBay is Selling Manager (**pages.ebay.co.uk/selling_manager**). This tool is used online exclusively, so it's available to help sellers on all operating systems manage their listings and fees. The more listings you have, the more you'll need a tool of this type to keep track of what's pending, active and sold, generate feedback, and print invoices and labels. eBay identifies Selling Manager as a medium-volume tool and recommends Selling Manager Pro (**pages.ebay. co.uk/selling_manager_pro**), which automates some of the features and provides restock alerts to high-volume sellers, for £4.99 per month.

You can also use the eBay Seller Tools Finder (**pages.ebay.co.uk/seller_tools_finder**) to pick the right tool for the job based on the volume of sales you want to achieve in a month and what area you need help with - sales, shipping, repeat listings, and other categories.

Finally, eBay lists third-party software that can help with volume listings and the extra management they require.

You have an alternative choice in another free mega listing tool, an eBay-compatible program called The Poster Toaster (**www.brothersoft.com/ the-poster-toaster-65312.html**). It allows the creation of templates for categories of items you sell regularly and includes an image manager to automate FTP (File Transfer Protocol) uploads of item images. You can verify listings and fees before posting, and it accepts ads from Turbo Lister.

▲ File Exchange works with your existing software on any platform

▲ Use Selling Manager to keep track of more listings, fees and feedback - all for free

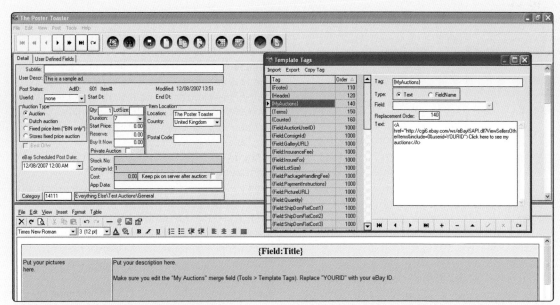

▲ The Poster Toaster is another free bulk-listing tool

A more fully featured option at a reasonable price is SDN Store, which you'll need to do a bit of searching to track down. It's an automated content-management system.

For a one-off fee, it enables you to build a shop-front website, complete with support for forums and e-mail, which you can integrate with an eBay shop. Mid- and high-volume sellers may benefit from the dual exposure, or use the eBay module on its own and synchronise it to their existing eBay shop. Both allow bulk listings you can verify before uploading.

Those are a few of the available tools to help list lots of items at a time and broaden your sales potential. New tools and options may be added, so check in the Solutions Directory under 'Listings Management' (**tinyurl.com/637y23**) for current information on companies, site (country) support, prices, and user ratings.

TO GROW OR NOT TO GROW

Put as much thought into each step you take in growing your shop as you did in deciding to sell in the first place. This should lead you down the road to success with a minimum of potholes along the way. Review your original research and revisit other eBay sellers' shops, auctions, and completed listings (**search-completed.ebay.co.uk**) to get the most up-to-date info before deciding to expand.

Remember, the larger the inventory the higher the risk, both to your finances and stress levels. Limit risk to a degree of loss you can recover from. Weigh up the risks, benefits, and work involved before you take each step in building your empire.

If a leap forward leaves you less than sure-footed, scale back, and reconsider your next growth spurt for another time. There's no rule that states you need to keep growing. Take small steps and you'll find the ideal shop inventory size for you.

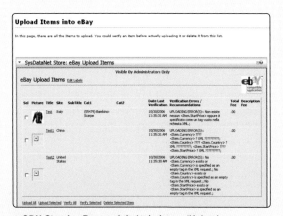

▲ Seller resources and tools are stored in eBay's Solutions Directory

▲ SDN Store's eBay module includes an 'Upload Items' tool

Keeping On Top Of Business

Building up sales is part of the challenge for the serious eBay user. However, it can be a stressful business, so be prepared

If you've been selling items on eBay for a while and want to ramp up the amount of goods you sell, then you'll need to become more organised. At the basic level, when you sell one or a handful of items, you have to list your goods, respond to queries, complete the sale, take payment and ship the goods. And all you need is the main eBay website, the My eBay account section, a consumer PayPal account and a cheap digital camera to photograph the goods with.

However, as the volume of products you sell on eBay increases, it will become clear very quickly that you need to keep a closer eye on a fair few other things. For example, how do you keep on top of money? Or of tracking payments? Of stock? Of postage? Of storage? Some people find the basic eBay sales tools aren't really up to the job of volume sales or, if you go a step further, running an eBay business. It is easy to very quickly get yourself into an administrative, organisational and logistical mess that will do nothing for your reputation, seller rating or finances.

As many of you will know, the popularity of eBay means it's an obvious business opportunity, and with the downturn in the economy leaving more people without steady employment, being able to make extra cash buying and selling will be welcomed. As anyone who's started a business will tell you, however, you do need to be aware of tax, accounting and legalities. If you end up selling online in order to subsidise your income, then such regular activity will mean you may come to the attention of the Inland Revenue.

Within three months of starting your business, you need to contact the Inland Revenue (it also has a handy guide to getting things off the ground at **www.hmrc.gov.uk/startingup/index.htm**) and decide whether or not you're going to be self-employed or a limited company. You will also want to set up a bank account separate from your personal one in order to keep a better check on your finances.

We're not going to delve too deeply in the accounting side of running a company, because it could fill an entire book in itself. There are, however, computer programs available that can help you to manage an increased customer base and ensure that your cash flow is properly accounted for.

PAYMENTS

Most eBay users who move up a scale into volume selling may struggle to keep a check on payments, however. It's easy to lose track of payments and work out when an item is ready to ship. Some people may pay by PayPal immediately, while others may opt for a cheque that takes a week to arrive. All the while, you need to keep on top of this and ensure orders don't get missed or that items aren't shipped before a payment has cleared.

Before we look at how to do this, let's look at the core parts of a transaction. This way it's easier to work out what kind of applications or services you'll need to help you out, and you can develop systems to help you keep on top of things.

The basics of an eBay transaction from start to finish roughly goes like this:

- Identify product to sell
- Write product description
- Determine starting price (along with reserve price or Buy It Now pricing, if applicable)
- Source/take photography
- Determine postal costs
- Assemble/publish auction page
- Respond to pre-sales queries
- Conclude sale
- Generate invoice for winning bidder
- Send reminders as necessary
- Collect payment via electronic payment service or physical payment method (cheque, postal order, cash, etc.)
- Dispatch goods
- Leave and receive feedback

The basic start-to-finish process can become more complicated by multiple-item sales to the same buyer, requests for combined or overseas

▲ Selling Manager is a free tool

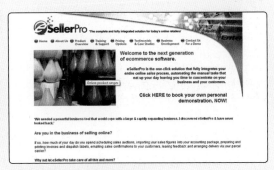

▲ eSellerPro isn't restricted to eBay

postage quotes, items returned as faulty, items not received at all, requests to collect items in person and requests to pay by other means (cheque, cash, postal orders, other electronic payment services). So if someone is going to sell in volume on eBay, they need tools and software in place to manage and automate as much of the process as possible. The option that many eBay home and small businesses opt for is the web-based all-in-one eBay management system.

SINGLE MANAGEMENT SYSTEMS

As you start to sell in volume, you begin to realise that the workload becomes so vast that without software to help you, it's likely you will struggle. But before you take the plunge, you need to know what you'll need the software for; if you are struggling to keep track of your items, unsure who should be sent what or whether a bidder has paid or not, then you will require an auction management package.

These programs act like a big toolbox, offering you everything you need to get your listings up and running, keeping a check of the stock that you have and aiding you with labelling your items, working out payments and allowing you to work with e-mail templates, which come in handy when dealing with your buyers.

You could start with eBay's own Turbo Lister, a package that lets you upload in bulk. What it doesn't do, though, is allow you to get a grip on payment management, and that's where the free eBay tool Selling Manager comes in.

Working online, it allows for better listings management. It lets you track your shipping, payment and feedback status more easily than within eBay itself but it doesn't allow you to create listings (although you can relist sold and unsold items). So anyone using Selling Manager would probably want to use Turbo Lister alongside it, allowing the former to manage the listings created by the latter.

By using Selling Manager you will also be able to cut down on the amount of time you spend sending e-mails, since it has customisable templates that you can use. The program also allows for the printing of smart-looking labels and invoices, and it even lets you tap in a selection of feedback comments that you'll be able to quickly add to buyers' accounts, thereby greatly reducing the time needed to type them in one by one.

If you're serious about your business, you may want to try eBay's Selling Manager Pro, which costs £4.99 a month. It allows you to create listings and it also has facilities for automatic listing and relisting, automated payment and shipping status. Usefully, you can create monthly profit and loss reports, discover your products' success ratio and average selling price and download your sales history as a .csv file.

THIRD-PARTY HELP

Of course, you don't have to use eBay's own auction management tools. Depending on the extent to which you want to grow your eBay activities, you can choose a third-party tool. eSellerPro (**www.esellerpro.com**) has many fans and it not only allows you to work with eBay, but it also integrates with sites such as Amazon, and it comes with a complete stock management system that even covers ordering from suppliers. It has designs that can be used for the website too.

Marketplaces (**www.channeladvisor.co.uk/marketplaces**) is the most popular single solution for managing an entire eBay business, but it can be

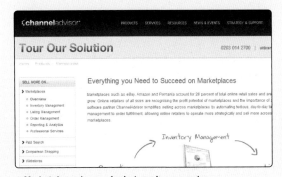

▲ Marketplaces is popular but can be expensive

expensive and it's really aimed at heavy auction business. It makes it easier to deal with bulk purchases, with the software allowing you to take full advantage of eBay, delivering a level of operational automation, and helping you sell more. It claims to lower costs and enhance customer service, in short making dealing with bulk items easier for the seller.

One of the benefits of Marketplaces is being able to manage an entire eBay transaction from start to finish. It can handle the initial creation and uploading of an auction item, including creating pages in advance and presetting future start times for auctions, thus automating the replenishment of active auctions. Marketplaces can also host product images (you get between 100MB and 500MB of space), dispensing with the need for a separate image-hosting service such as Flickr, or even paying eBay to use images in an auction. While the auction is running, it can help you keep track of the number of watchers, the number of visitors to each auction page, the number of bids in a single view and it can automate most communications with the buyer.

Aside from automating the eBay sales process, Marketplaces also provides tools for postage management and integrates it with PayPal for payment collection. The problem is that it's geared up more for heavy business. If you're after a simpler system of keeping track of eBay's comings and goings, you may well want something else.

NetSuite (**www.netsuite.com/portal/industries/ ecommerce/ebay-integration.shtml**) is a popular hosted business application suite. It is designed for small businesses, and integrates with eBay as one of several ways to sell goods. It offers many of the same features as Marketplaces, such as

integration with postal services, and payment management, and can combine an existing web-based shop (created and hosted in NetSuite) with eBay auctions. Therefore, the items a seller has listed on eBay can be taken from an existing online store, and auctions shown in the same store. This is useful if you're using eBay for fixed-price Buy It Now sales rather than traditional auctions.

STORAGE

As your business grows, so too will the space you need to keep the items you're selling. And once you've taken up the garage, shed and children's bedrooms, you may be forced to look elsewhere in order to keep your stock in one place and your family from screaming at you.

Companies such as Safestore Self Storage (**www. safestore.co.uk**) have premises all across Britain. Annoyingly, there are no prices on the Safestore website, but many customers comment on its low cost, and how much you will pay is determined by the space you will need. There are many similar storage companies across the country, however, so it's worth doing a search online for a solution that suits you.

One thing worth factoring in, whether at home or in a storage facility, is a small area dedicated to packing and shipping. When you put an item up for sale, make sure it's located within your storage area, to prevent you having to search around for it. Indeed, it's important to organise your items well, and if you stack them, you can optimise your space.

Use plastic bags to help prevent items from developing smells or becoming musty. Bags also ensure items don't rub together and cause damage. Label each item and place them in boxes that are labelled alphabetically, which means you can get at them with greater ease and, if possible, buy transparent boxes so you can easily keep an eye on stock levels and know exactly what's in each container. If you develop good storage habits, you'll save lots of time.

An alternative to storage that's worth exploring is drop shipping. Essentially, this will mean the goods that you sell aren't kept in stock by you. Your orders are transferred to a manufacturer or a wholesaler, which then dispatches the item directly to the customer on your behalf. You take the difference in price between the amount you've sold at and the wholesale cost.

Some research online is needed, and you also need to understand the potential pitfalls (if an item isn't in stock at the warehouse, you'll be one receiving the hassle from a customer, and it becomes your job to find out if enough stock is available and that the price hasn't changed).

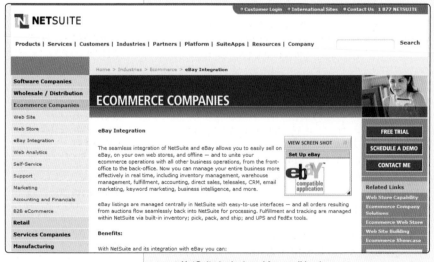

▲ NetSuite is designed for small businesses

▲ Self storage is an option worth thinking about

LOGISTICS AND SHIPPING

Depending on the size of your item, you may opt to use the standard postal service or you might decide to try out a courier. Using Royal Mail for postage has got much easier for the eBay seller, because you can now buy postage online and print it yourself (**tinyurl.com/38ebzk**). Online prepaid postage is the closest thing to having your own franking machine, without the costs and complexity of actually owning one. It also means that postage can be applied in the seller's own time, with the prepaid, pre-labelled packages dropped off, rather than the user having to queue to weigh and pay for postage for each individual item. For example, the cost of a first class stamp via home printing is exactly the same as a traditional stamp (£0.46), so online stamps are cheaper than a franking machine as well.

Royal Mail can also supply a post office box (PO Box) for your incoming mail in the same way as commercial services like Mail Boxes Etc. A Royal Mail PO Box costs £95 a year or £60 for six months, and is usually hosted at a local sorting office, or a large main post office. A seller can either collect the mail themselves or, for an additional fee, have it delivered with the regular post. Either option means a seller doesn't have to reveal their address to strangers, and can handle returns and payment by post.

Two essential purchases you'll need to make are a set of scales and a tape measure. With Royal Mail postal prices (**tinyurl.com/postprice**) now based on size as well as weight, it's important these metrics can be measured accurately, so that the correct postage is applied. Failure to apply the right postage will result in the buyer being hit with a surcharge from the postman before they can receive the goods.

High-street shipping specialists such as Mail Boxes Etc (**www.mbe.com**) have branches all over the UK and can offer specialist services to eBay sellers trying to tackle posting and package management. As well as providing packaging supplies and space to package goods, stores such as these can also help with the weighing and

▲ Print your own stamps from the Royal Mail website

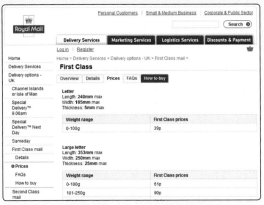

▲ There's a range of options available from Royal Mail

pricing of packages (particularly heavy and awkward-shaped goods) for conventional posting via Royal Mail (**www.royalmail.com**) or its parcel arm ParcelForce (**www.parcelforce.com**). In addition, these stores can tackle the more complex task of sending goods via a courier company such as FedEx (**www.fedex.com/gb**), UPS (**www.ups. com/content/gb/en/index/jsx**) or DHL (**www.dhl. co.uk**) on a per-item basis, without the seller having to set up their own account with the courier company. These stores can also provide a seller with a mailbox to receive incoming mail such as cheque payments, if they don't want the hassle or potential risk of distributing their home address to unknown customers.

Some buyers, particularly overseas customers, will prefer the security of a branded and traceable courier service delivering their goods purchased from an unknown seller. Courier companies can also offer competitive prices for international insured shipping compared to traditional postal services such as Royal Mail. It's worth checking out their prices, at least.

Also, they provide an important alternative to bypass delays caused by strikes, national holidays and the restrictive opening hours of a post office.

Keeping On Top Of Communications

Bad communication as a seller can potentially cause a lot of problems. How do you make sure this doesn't happen to you?

If there's one thing the Internet has done for mankind, it's aid communication. Whether we're letting people know what we were up to last night on Facebook or Twitter, or filing a quick e-mail to the boss to inform them of the progress of a project, keeping folk in the loop and divulging snippets of information has been made much easier with a keyboard at our fingertips.

So why do so many eBayers go wrong when it comes to communications? Bad communication is at the heart of most disputes, which means it's vital that you keep people up to date when they're buying your items on eBay. If you keep people informed at every opportunity, they're not only far less likely to leave you negative feedback, but they may well be encouraged to buy something else from you in the future, which is great if you decide to move up the ladder of eBay selling and shift items in greater volume.

STARTING POINT

Communication starts from the moment you begin to create your eBay listing. It's important that your descriptions are incredibly clear, because you're trying to give people a feel for an item without them actually being able to get their hands on it before they make a purchase. Go to Amazon.co.uk, Play.com or any number of other top websites and see how they produce listings but essentially give as much information as possible. Indeed, why not go the whole hog; if something needs instructions, maybe put those up as part of your listings so that buyers will be able to see just what they need to do after they make their purchases. Less is not more in the case of eBay, but lay out your listing so that it doesn't overwhelm.

Secondly, make sure everything that's included in your package is listed and, if something that a buyer will believe to be in the box is missing, let them know at this stage so you don't encounter problems later

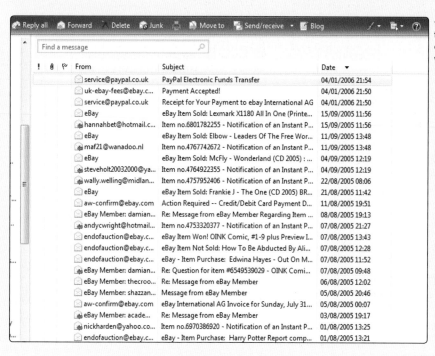

◀ Make sure you keep on top of your e-mails, otherwise you could end up with some unhappy buyers

on. And do make this information prominent; if, for example, you're selling a computer and you're not shipping it with a mouse, keyboard or monitor, it would be good for your reputation and prove less hassle in the long run to make this absolutely clear up front.

Also, it goes without saying that you will pack that listing with good-quality images and state very clearly exactly how long a buyer will expect to have to wait to receive the item you're selling. The clearer you are about this right from the start, the greater the chance of avoiding any hassle from somebody who believed you would be shipping the item that very same day. Add in a returns policy that's properly spelled out, and a buyer will be less inclined to take issue further down the line should a problem become apparent.

While your listing is running its course, you may receive countless messages from potential buyers asking questions about your item (although a good FAQ, an About Me page and a solid description should limit the numbers). Questions that go unanswered will result in customers taking their bids elsewhere, because they'll see you as unreliable, perhaps rude and disorganised.

It is vital that you answer every query politely, courteously and with as much information as you can. Don't lie - be honest if you're not sure about something - and answer as quickly as possible. You may have bad news or you may need time to find an answer, but by letting people know straight away, you'll reap the rewards. Even an immediate and simple "I'm not sure - let me find out and I'll get back to you asap" is better than not replying or taking days

to do so. Above all, be friendly. People are more likely to buy something from you if you come across as being pleasant.

AFTER SALES

Communication, however, must continue when somebody actually makes a purchase. This is the stage where many eBay sellers fall short. Countless buyers can tell you about sellers who take your money and then cut off communication, leaving you wondering what's happening with your purchase until the moment it suddenly arrives on your doorstep.

This points to one of the biggest problems eBay users face: staying on top of the barrage of messages associated with trading. Even someone selling the occasional item will quickly find that a single act of selling on eBay can generate an enormous amount of e-mail.

To put the volume of mail generated by a single item into perspective, here's what a seller can expect to see arrive in their inbox. There are confirmations of a listing, daily updates on the progress of the auction item or multiple items, questions from potential buyers, replies to those queries, confirmation of the final selling price or confirmation that the item didn't sell, any reminders sent to the buyer seeking payment, PayPal payment confirmation, and the invoice from eBay requesting payment for the initial listing. It can, at first glance, be overwhelming but, as with most things, some common sense and good organisation really pays off.

Many eBay sellers swear by Google Mail (**gmail. com**), with many opting for it because of the large

▲ ReplyManager can take some of the hard work out of communicating with your customers

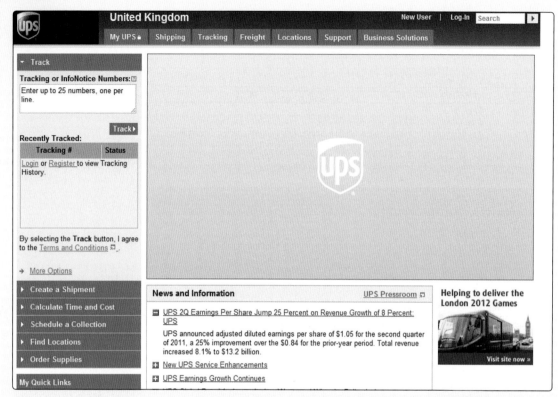

▲ If you have a tracking number for an item, make sure you pass it to your customer, so they can track their purchase

storage space (more than 7GB), good anti-spam features and a powerful search which, as Google itself claims, means you never have to delete anything to stay on top of your e-mail.

Of course, you can use other e-mail providers such as Hotmail (**hotmail.co.uk**) or Yahoo! (**mail.yahoo. com**). And if you're serious about selling, why not try Reply Manager (**replymanager.com**), which is free to try for 15 days and is a web-based e-mail management tool? It will send automatic replies to customer inquiries as well as organise your inbound e-mails, working with accounts such as Google Mail and Yahoo!. It can be expensive, however, with prices starting at $50 a month (roughly £30) and for that you only get 50MB of storage. There's also a one-off fee of $150 to get you started.

No matter what system you choose, it's how you use it that matters. We've already stated the importance of responding; if you send people e-mails and never get a reply, odds are you will feel quite disgruntled and so will your customers. You need to be proactive too; if you have an item ready to ship but you're having a problem getting it to the Post Office within the promised time, let your customer know. If you've sold an item that you don't have available at that time, then give them an estimated time of arrival. Don't leave them hanging and wondering where their item is.

Indeed, if you use a courier to ship an item and are able to get a tracking number, let your customer

know what it is. This way they can quickly find out when their package is set to arrive, and it takes away some of the pressure on you.

Of course, you don't want to ship out an item until it has been paid for, so if a buyer is late with his or her payment, then contact them, politely asking if they still intend to pay. If you don't hear back, write again, asking if they would like to mutually cancel the transaction. If they do, then you can file an Unpaid Item Dispute (UID) with eBay and receive a refund on your fees. Sometimes you won't get a reply from the buyer at all, in which case you can go ahead and file the UID, but don't file one without having tried to contact the buyer first, because that could lead to negative feedback.

Sometimes it pays to be generous, however, especially if you're serious about setting up an eBay business. A small card apologising for a late delivery or a simple, inexpensive gift thrown in to make up for a delay can go a long way to appeasing an otherwise annoyed customer. If you have other stock, you could think about throwing in a discount on their next purchase. This will encourage them to buy something else from you, and it also shows them the value of their custom.

One thing you also want to do is offer good after-sales service. People want to feel secure in the knowledge that, even after they've received an item, they can still go back to you if they have a problem, so

▲ Consider sending surveys to your buyers to gauge their satisfaction with your service

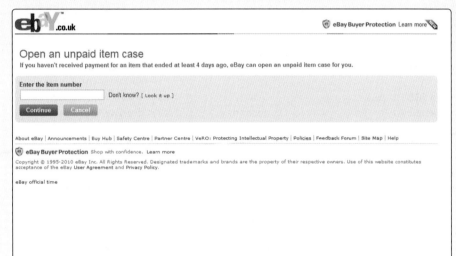

◀ If a buyer doesn't pay you, then you can open a dispute with eBay, but make sure you try to contact the other party first to get their side of the story

have a set of cards or letters printed that include your telephone number or e-mail address, and include them with every order. Make them as personal as possible so that buyers will feel they're dealing with a real person, and include on these cards or letters a pleasant note asking them to get in touch without hesitation if they have an issue. This shows that communication is both ways, and will hopefully prevent a buyer from posting a negative comment without having contacted you first.

Indeed, you may want to actively encourage buyers to post feedback. One good thing about this is that when a buyer leaves positive feedback, you can effectively tick off that particular transaction. Feedback also allows you to improve; you may even want to go beyond eBay and send buyers a survey (try

SurveyMonkey.com). This will inspire confidence and trust in you from purchasers, since they will see you as someone that's keen to improve their service. If you place a link to the survey on your eBay listing page, you'll be able to hammer that message home right from the start.

FEEDBACK

Finally, hang fire on leaving feedback. Although you're unable to post negative feedback against poor buyers, you can withhold positives. Therefore, wait until you get positive feedback. Most buyers will want to boost their feedback numbers, so will be more inclined to try to get good feedback from you by posting a positive account of your transaction rather than risk not getting any feedback from you at all.

Making Extra Money

There are ways to squeeze every penny out of an eBay transaction. However, some of them are rightly frowned upon

When you're selling items online, the aim is to make as much money as possible. Luckily, there are many ways in which you can maximise your revenue using a few neat tricks. However, beware, not all of them are entirely fair, and you run a serious risk of receiving potentially damaging negative feedback.

POSTAGE FEES

While searching for items on eBay, you might notice how much the costs of postage often differ widely, even if identical products are being sold. It's a fair bet that the more expensive postage fees include extra revenue for the seller. Although eBay policy states sellers may charge reasonable postage and packaging charges to cover the costs of posting, packaging, and handling, many people add on a little more and pocket the difference.

That's because the term 'handling' is vague and open to interpretation, so those who appear to charge more than others can justify it by calling the extra cost a 'handling charge'. The key is not to get carried away; charge too much and you will inevitably attract negative feedback. Also, if the buyer reports you, further action could be taken by eBay, with your account put in jeopardy. It's really about what you can get away with, but it's essential to have morals in a community-based site on which feedback is everything. Otherwise it can badly backfire on you (see **pages.ebay.co.uk/help/policies/listing-shipping.html**).

It's worth noting that you're also banned from listing postage, packaging and handling charges as a percentage of the final sale price. This is for obvious reasons. If an item sells unexpectedly for £100 and you were charging 10% for postage, then you would pick up an extra £10. If it sold for £20, you would receive an extra £2. The actual cost of sending the parcel would remain the same, however, so you would, in effect, be ripping off your customer on goods that sold for higher prices.

For fixed-cost sales, there are sellers who try to be a little cleverer. They use a low price for their item and then use the postage fees to make up for it. For example, you may see a memory stick retailing for £1 and decide, because it's so inexpensive, it's worth getting. Only when you read the listing properly do you see the postage costs are £10, yet the seller has achieved the aim of at least getting you to look at the listing. Of course, with postage fees now listed alongside the cost of an item, it's becoming easier to spot this 'scam'.

eBay did for a while make it compulsory for you to offer free shipping on a selection of categories. This was not a popular move among sellers, but in 39 categories, they had no choice. However, after a backlash from users, it subsequently revised this policy in 2010 to apply maximum shipping costs instead. This applies on certain, but not all product lines. You are still able to charge extra for premium postage services, such as guaranteed delivery or extra insurance.

POSTAGE COSTS

There is nothing wrong in trying to cut costs when posting items, however. One top tip is to keep any padded envelopes or boxes that you may come across. You can reuse these to send items of your own, not only saving you the cost of buying a new padded envelope or box but also helping to save the environment. All you need to do is pop a fresh label over the old one. Even if you've torn open a padded envelope in the excitement of getting your hands on

▲ Some sellers set high postage prices to get more money

▲ Be wary of trying to inflate insurance prices

Get ideas about pricing by searching completed listings.

| Online Auction | **Fixed Price** |

* Buy It Now price (see listing fees) ⓘ

£ 50.00

Best Offer ⓘ

☑ Allow buyers to send you their Best Offers for your

Respond to offers automatically

☐ Automatically accept offers of at least   £

   If the buyer has specified additional terms, you will

☐ Automatically decline offers lower than   £

▲ By using the Buy It Now option, you can decide on an actual price and boost your profit

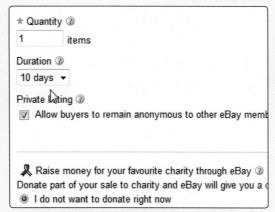

* Quantity ⓘ

1   items

Duration ⓘ

10 days ▾

Private listing ⓘ

☑ Allow buyers to remain anonymous to other eBay memb

🎗 Raise money for your favourite charity through eBay ⓘ
Donate part of your sale to charity and eBay will give you a
◉ I do not want to donate right now

▲ Changing the duration of your auction can impact on your sales and the amount you can earn

the goodies inside, you could place it inside a normal envelope and still save cash. Do buyers mind? Not at all; the main point is their purchases arrive in one piece and few care about the funny-looking wrapper.

INSURANCE

Another way sellers have been known in the past to make money is by upping the insurance cost by a small amount. This is forbidden by eBay, which says sellers offering insurance may only charge the actual fee for insurance. No additional amount may be added, such as 'self-insurance', and sellers who don't use a licensed third-party insurance company may not ask buyers to purchase insurance. It's easy for buyers to check if the insurance charge is over the top, so if you're selling, you need to be aware of that.

PENALTIES

If eBay feels you have breached its policy, it can take a range of actions, including cancelling your listing, limiting your account privileges, suspending your account, forcing you to forfeit your eBay fees and stripping you of PowerSeller status, if applicable.

SECOND CHANCE OFFERS

When an auction ends, you can offer non-winning bidders the chance to buy your item. Of course, you will need to have more stock of the item in question, and it must be exactly the same product as the one you have just sold.

It works by allowing sellers to make an offer to a non-winning bidder under certain conditions. The offer contains a Buy It Now price equal to the non-winning bidder's bid amount. You can offer the second chance immediately after a listing ends and for 60 days afterwards.

Second Chance Offers can be sent for a one-, three- or seven-day duration. They come in handy if your winning bidder fails to pay you or if your reserve

price has not been met. In the latter scenario, you may decide that a non-winning bidder's offer is acceptable. The price at which you can offer your product is equal to their last-showing bid amount.

By offering a second chance, you can increase your revenue without all the hassle of going through the whole eBay process again. If you have multiple stock of an item, this is a great way to offload it, and because there are no fees associated with making a Second Chance Offer, you're saving money too. All you have to do is pay the final value fee when the offer is accepted.

Some sellers try to make offers via the Ask Question facility, which sends an e-mail to a buyer with the subject line 'Question from eBay Member'. This is outlawed by eBay, because it's not a legitimate way to offer a second chance, and if you use it, you can be banned. The transaction will certainly not be supported by eBay.

Feedback can still be placed with Second Chance Offers, so you still need to take the utmost care when dealing with your buyer, otherwise you may receive a negative in the process.

BUY IT NOW

Offering a Buy It Now means you're in control of the price. It's the best way to maximise profits in the shortest possible time. However, set the price too high and you won't sell; you need to look at other listings for an indication of how much your item is going for and set it accordingly.

Buy It Now options can also run alongside an auction to give a buyer the chance to snap up the item without bidding. As soon as a bid is made, the option is removed. If it's a Reserve Price Auction, the option disappears as soon as the reserve is met.

What's good about Buy It Now is that it helps you to use some neat advertising tricks. The whole Buy It Now concept creates a sense of urgency, so why not build on that by creating added impetus to buy your product? It's far more popular than running a straight auction on eBay now.

One way of adding urgency is to add a subtitle to your listing. In this subtitle you can add some pushy statements such as 'Buy now while stocks last', 'Buy now or lose it forever', or 'Only two in stock - buy now'. Then in the listing itself, continue to push the urgent line without being rude or over the top. You want to create a feeling that the buyer shouldn't wait, just in case someone else comes in, without alienating that person with over-the-top claims.

You're appealing to impulse buyers, and you can speed up your profit-making. Rather than wait for a seven-day auction to end, you could, if your product and selling approach is right, sell items every day.

So to maximise the amount of money you can make from your sale, you have to be canny. Don't list a videogame such as Grand Theft Auto IV as 'Buy now - only two in stock' because there are so many copies of this title being sold elsewhere that you'll simply end up losing credibility. If your price is competitive, however, you could perhaps write 'Last chance to buy at this price'.

Similarly, there's no point in putting a DVD on eBay with a starting price of 99p and a Buy It Now of £50. That £50 is more than you would expect to pay in a high-street shop. What you need to do is pitch the Buy It Now so that it attracts an inpatient buyer and doesn't encourage someone to bid just to get rid of the option.

DIFFERENT-LENGTH LISTINGS
By opting for a ten-day option and paying the small additional listing costs, it means that your item can be on eBay for a longer period of time, therefore increasing the likelihood of it being seen. Although most bids come in the dying moments of an auction, it doesn't hurt to have the item on display for a few days longer.

For Buy It Now options, you may find a shorter time frame is better; after all, you'll be looking for a speedier sale and you'll want it to be shown on the front page of the listings as soon as possible. A

three- or five-day option could be ideal, but you should gauge this according to how popular you feel your item will be and how many other listings of a similar nature are out there.

USE ABBREVIATIONS IN TITLE
You're only given a limited number of characters in an eBay title, so you need to make good use of the space available. Using abbreviations is one effective way of doing so. Useful ones include BNIB (Brand New, In Box), NBW (Never Been Worn), NR (No Reserve). The eBay savvy will notice them and be more likely to be drawn in. See **pages.ebay.com/help/account/acronyms.html** for a good list.

SHOPS
Having a shop can also maximise your profits, particularly if you use effective links in your listings. You could pop a product into auction for ten days and also make it available from your eBay shop. All you need to do then is place a link saying 'Click here to buy this item now from my shop'.

This also drives traffic to your shop. If they decide they don't want the item any more, they may be persuaded to have a quick browse around your store and pick up something else.

GENERATING SALES
What if you're able to get hold of lots of stock, yet a buyer has ended up on your listing and then realised your product is not the perfect match for their requirements? Simple. Just ask buyers to contact you through your About Me page with their requirements. Promise them you will have a look around for the right product to suit their needs.

Beware of trying to conduct sales outside of the eBay service, however. Although you save on listing and final value fees, you can incur the auction house's wrath if the buyer reports you.

CREATE A BIDDING WAR
There's nothing more exciting than watching two or three people battling it out for your item, pushing the

▲ By having a sense of urgency, you can push people into buying

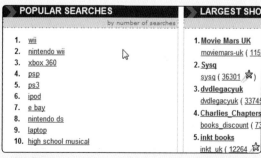

▲ eBay Pulse is the place to go to see the trends, including top keywords

price skywards. All you need are a couple of enthusiasts and your bank balance will start to look much healthier.

One thing you could do is bundle two items together. For example, you may have a mint condition Superman comic and a signed Star Wars photograph. Even better, you could pop unrelated items into one lot - a Shakespeare book with an old Beano, maybe. Now what you have done is made your listing attractive to two different types of buyer. Pop a listing under 'books', for instance, and create another under 'comics' and you're further widening the scope. If your items are desirable enough, you may get one person dying to get hold of your Shakespeare book and another itching for the comic. They'll battle it out, raising your price. This won't work if one item is so common that no one will bother bidding anyway. Also, by its nature, it's a risky strategy.

USE KEYWORDS

Using popular keywords is a great way to ensure that people are being drawn to your listings. This can also create a bidding war or may simply result in a quicker sale.

The eBay Pulse pages are a perfect source of keywords. See what the most common search terms are and pop them in (without losing the gist of what your product is all about, of course). You can find eBay Pulse at **pulse.ebay.co.uk**.

OFFER FREEBIES

You need to make your listing more attractive to potential buyers than the competition. So you could offer full after-sales support, have free postage (which you may be able to absorb into a Buy It Now price), and add extra bits and bobs into the package that add value to the overall sale (a nice box or a free badge, for example).

Offer free gifts and bonuses to attract interest away from people selling similar items. For example, offer

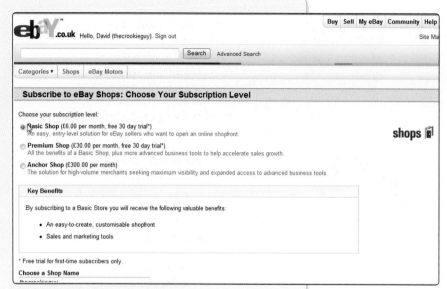

▲ Put your goods on sale in an eBay Shop

three cufflinks where most offer two (emphasise these things get damaged, lost, stolen); ship items postage free; add complementary items such as a matching tie pin (free or otherwise) with cufflinks, free presentation boxes with every batch of wholesale necklaces, and so on. If you make your free gift even more valuable than the actual product for sale, you can not only create a bidding war, but offload less saleable products.

You just need to make sure that the bonus is available to the buyer no matter what the outcome of the auction and that, if using Multiple Item Listings, the bonus will be sent out to all winners.

BIDDING ON YOUR OWN ITEM

Artificially inflating the price by bidding on your own item or getting friends and family to bid is morally wrong, but it does happen. Such shill bidding is forbidden on eBay and it's not something we would ever recommend.

▲ Allowing as many payment options as possible can increase the chance of a sale

▲ Using abbreviations such as BNIB (Brand New, In Box) can save space in your title

DID YOU KNOW?

'Mystery' auctions, where buyers bid for a sealed box containing a mystery item, or an envelope stuffed with an unspecified amount of cash, are often fraudulent. Because there are no checks on these type of auctions, sellers can manipulate the results according to the final price. It's been estimated that on average, a 'winner' in an envelope auction only receives 20% to 30% of his or her outlay.

Chapter 5
Buying Through eBay

Finding Your Dream Item On eBay

Let's take a look at eBay from a buyer's perspective now. What should you do if you're looking to pick up a bargain or two?

To bag an eBay bargain, you first have to find it. The ubiquitous eBay 'Search' box can yield an impractically long and unfocused list of results. Filtering out inappropriate auctions - and sellers - is essential to good eBaying...

SEARCHING BY TITLE AND DESCRIPTION

By default, eBay searches only in the short title description of auction items. Therefore, if the search word you enter only exists in the description of an auction, that auction will not appear in your search results - and it could, of course, be just the item you're looking for.

However, you can click on Advanced Search at the top of the screen, and then you can tick the 'Include title and description' box and repeat the search.

With descriptions included, search results may multiply alarmingly, frequently on account of sellers who practice keyword spamming (we'll be talking about that a little later) in their listings.

You can narrow down your search by adding extra keywords (such as 'walnut cupboard' instead of 'cupboard'), but this may remove as many interesting and valid auctions as 'spam' auctions. A better approach is to use the search commands that eBay provides in its search facility.

USING CATEGORIES

One obvious way to streamline bloated search-results is to select an appropriate category from the drop-down menu next to the search box, at the top of your results page.

Unfortunately, many eBay listings remain miscategorised; a very rare and sought-after DVD, for instance, may end up being put in Entertainment Memorabilia instead of the DVD category. Adding extra categories to an auction listing costs the seller more, so they may not bother to do so. The item might also comprise part of a lot of diverse items, or be miscategorised by mistake, so you should use this feature with care.

LOCAL VERSUS GLOBAL

More than 150 countries participate in eBay, but search results from ebay.co.uk will not automatically include listings from non-UK auctions (unless the sellers have specifically included the UK as a target market for their item).

There are good reasons to begin your search 'locally': items won may arrive quicker, affordable courier services are available for larger items and you may be able to pay for your win by cheque, postal order or Nochex as well as PayPal. You can also search for items within a certain distance from where you live, which means you can pick them up in person if the seller agrees.

However, the UK is a relatively small marketplace, with a price levy often reflected in eBay auctions, and associated postal costs that can often dwarf overseas shipping tariffs for smaller items. Even with international shipping, your item may be available cheaper abroad, or may never have been available here (such as rare editions in the fields of music, movies, books and magazines).

▲ Searching in the description can reward you with more results   ▲ The categories can help narrow down results

BIDDING ON ITEMS FROM NON-UK SELLERS

You can include worldwide sellers in your eBay searches, but there are special considerations to take into account when bidding on non-UK auctions.

Delivery: Will the seller deliver to the United Kingdom? Check the item's 'Postage and packaging' section; if you can click on 'United Kingdom' in the drop-down list, the seller will ship here and has provided a price. If not, check the listing itself; it may provide information as to where the seller is willing to ship their item. Otherwise, you can use the 'Ask a question' link to ask about the possibility and cost of shipping to the UK.

Payment: If the seller doesn't accept or you don't use PayPal, how can an item you've won be paid for? Wire transfer services such as Western Union and Moneygram are not permitted at eBay, while international money orders can be costly and might not be acceptable to the seller in question. Sending currency-exchanged cash in the post is against eBay regulations, and is unwise anyway, because it leaves you with no redress in disputes over payment and

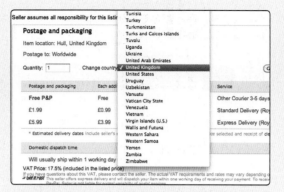

▲ Remember to check the shipping costs if buying from abroad

delivery. Shortly, we'll see how to limit worldwide eBay search results to sellers that accept PayPal.

The Language Barrier: eBay will warn you if you're sending a question to a seller from a non-English-speaking part of eBay. Unless you speak the seller's language, try to keep all communications brief; the responsibility rests with you if you fall foul of terms, conditions or information that were explained in a listing (or correspondence) you couldn't understand.

eBay Search Commands

Aim	Method	Example
Exclude several keywords from a search	Put a minus sign after your keyword and then a list of comma-separated words in brackets. There must be no space after each comma OR Add each excluded word after your search term preceded by a dash (-) There must be a space between each 'excluded' term and no space between the dash and the word it is excluding	Genesis -(sega,bible,trek,manga,snorkel) OR Genesis -sega -bible -trek -manga -snorkel
Find an exact phrase	Put the words in full quotes (")	"New Order"
Find at least one of two (or more) words	Group the comma-separated words in parentheses (no spaces after the comma)	(hammer,nails,screwdriver) Will return search results containing any of the above words.
Find auctions containing words that begin with a certain sequence of letters	Append an asterisk (*) to the search-term	record* Will find auctions containing 'record', 'records', 'recorder', 'recording', etc.
Find auctions with a specific spelling of a search term	Enclose the word in quotations (")	"record" Will exclude auctions containing 'records' in title or description.
Find two (or more) words without 'auto-expanding' search results	Enclose a possible category word in quotations (")	If one of your keywords is recognised by eBay as pertaining to an eBay category, your search may be 'automatically expanded' to search for the remaining words in that category. For example, the search 'Bruce Willis DVD' may 'auto-include' irrelevant results in the DVD category that contain 'Bruce' or 'Willis' - e.g. Bruce Almighty. The search 'Bruce Willis "DVD"' will only return pertinent results that actually contain the word 'DVD'.

▲ Seek out misspelled bargains at fatfingers.co.uk

Online translation services such as Babelfish (**babelfish.yahoo.com**) and Google Translate (**translate.google.com**) can help when dealing with foreign sellers, but they don't cover all possible languages. They're also best used for short and simple phrases, because they often produce muddled results that could make matters worse.

Mindful of these caveats, foreign-language eBay auctions can be a good opportunity to find sought-after items with fewer competing bidders: simply run your translated keyword through an online translation service and do a 'rest of the world' search.

TYPO BARGAINS

Sometimes sellers mistype (or just don't know how to spell) a word when placing a listing on eBay; the resultant 'nonsense' word (for example, 'cuboard' instead of 'cupboard') will probably never end up in a bidding war - or even in search results. You can take advantage of the low visibility of auctions such as this by hunting out typos and misspelt words when searching for items.

Many sites offer eBay typo searches, where you can search eBay directly for a wide range of possible misspellings. Two of the most popular are **www.fatfingers.co.uk** and **www.typozay.co.uk** (which even offers search plug-ins for users of the Firefox web browser). Check out the reviews from page 146 for more examples.

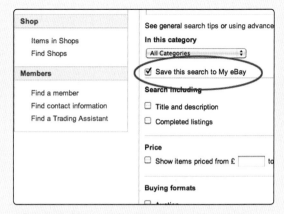

▲ Saved searches remember all your custom search options, and results can be e-mailed to you daily

ADVANCED SEARCH

Power bidders and buyers belong on the 'Advanced Search' page, where you can broaden your search results to include sellers worldwide, and specify many other options to focus your search and zero in on a potential bargain.

To get started, click on the 'Advanced Search' link to the right of the search box at the top of your results, or go to **search.ebay.co.uk**.

SEARCH COMMANDS

At the top of Advanced Search, you can apply some of the search commands that we came across earlier without needing to use any of the special formatting (see 'eBay Search Commands' table).

View Ended Auctions: The 'completed listings' checkbox enables you to search for auctions that have finished. This is a useful indicator of prices you can expect to pay for items you're currently seeking. It's also a good way to locate sellers who are suitable for you but may not currently be offering any items.

▲ The 'Advanced Search' link

▲ Apply search commands naturally

✓ Dispatches items quickly

✓ Has earned a track record of excellent service

Save this seller

See other items

Visit shop:

Registered as a Business Seller

▲ You can add sellers to your favourites list

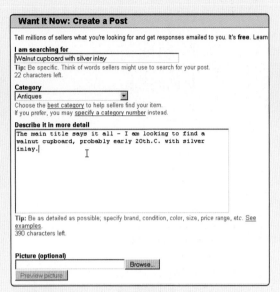

Want It Now: Create a Post

Tell millions of sellers what you're looking for and get responses emailed to you. It's **free**. Learn

I am searching for

Walnut cupboard with silver inlay

Tip: Be specific. Think of words sellers might use to search for your post.
22 characters left.

Category

Antiques

Choose the best category to help sellers find your item.
If you prefer, you may specify a category number instead.

Describe it in more detail

The main title says it all – I am looking to find a walnut cupboard, probably early 20th.C. with silver inlay.

Tip: Be as detailed as possible; specify brand, condition, color, size, price range, etc. See examples.
390 characters left.

Picture (optional)

Browse...

Preview picture

▲ **Want It Now** enables you to tell sellers exactly what you're looking for

▲ (Top) Search the whole world if you like
▲ (Bottom) Find a local bargain on eBay with Advanced Search

Save The Search: Saved searches are a useful way of repeating an advanced search at a later date. You can save your custom search by ticking the 'Save this search to My eBay' option in Advanced Search, or with the 'Save this search' link near the top of your results.

Saved searches have their own section in My eBay, and you can subscribe to them, receiving the initial ten results from any saved search by daily e-mail.

Specify A Price Range: In the 'Items Priced' boxes you can place minimum and maximum prices for item listings.

The 'minimum price' option is particularly useful for excluding the thousands of worthless 'one cent' auctions that some unscrupulous sellers employ to boost their own reputations.

Specify Sellers: If you're looking for items from a particular eBay seller, you can type in their eBay User ID here (you'll need to know exactly what it is). You can also use the 'Exclude' option in the drop-down box to make sure that a particular seller's items don't appear in your results. Currently, you can only 'blacklist' one seller per search in this way.

If you've built up a list of favourite sellers (see 'Other search methods'), you can also specify to search their auctions only.

Include The World!: Here, finally, we can search beyond the UK by selecting 'Worldwide' from the drop-down list in the 'Location' section. .

The 'Items located in' section lets you specify a geographical location for the item. You can choose any country that eBay deals with from the drop-down list, but this is most useful when seeking UK-based items.

If you want to include foreign listings from only those sellers who explicitly ship to the UK, leave the

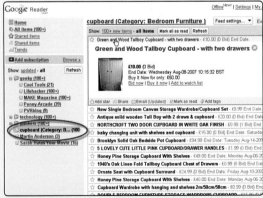

▲ Check out the latest listings via Google Reader or any RSS aggregator
◀ Look for this icon to add an RSS feed for a search

◀▲ Customising your search

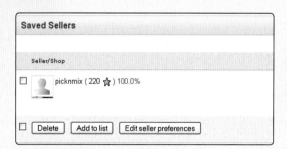

▲ Your Saved Sellers list

▲ Custom search options will narrow down results

'Items available to' drop-down list at 'United Kingdom', but be aware that you exclude many UK-friendly foreign sellers by doing so.

OTHER OPTIONS IN ADVANCED SEARCH
- Find PayPal-listed items only.
- Find Buy It Now items only (no bidding necessary).
- Find items that are located near you (the United Kingdom version - you gave eBay your postcode when you signed up).
- Find items with free postage and packaging.
- Find items that have a minimum and/or maximum number of existing bids.

THE SIDEBAR
eBay displays a yellow Search Options sidebar to the left of search results; here you can toggle advanced options and further refine your search. You can customise the sidebar to include only the parts of Advanced Search that you want to use regularly by clicking the 'Customise' link.

TRACK LISTINGS VIA RSS
You can subscribe to an RSS feed for any search, and keep track of new listings via Google Reader, Live Bookmarks in Firefox, the RSS features in Internet Explorer or any other RSS aggregator. You can set a feed to be updated as often as you like; it's a good way

to keep on top of new Buy It Now offers, which can close within minutes of first being listed.

OTHER SEARCH METHODS
Want It Now: At **pages.ebay.co.uk/wantitnow** you can let eBay sellers know about items you're looking for, and optionally post a picture as a guideline.

Favourite Sellers: You can add any seller or eBay shop to your Favourite Sellers list simply by clicking the 'Add to favourite sellers' link in their profile. eBay can optionally send you regular e-mails with new listings from your favourite sellers, who also have their own page in My eBay where you can find them again easily and even add notes about them.

Seller Communication: Whether you've won or lost an auction at eBay, why not get in touch with the seller and let them know if you're looking for something specific? Serious sellers will be glad to have a ready-made potential buyer for new listings.

IS IT CHEAPER ELSEWHERE?
Check the regular commercial outlets for your item before going to eBay. Are you sure that special edition DVD you're after isn't also available on Play or Amazon, but brand new and cheaper than the lowest eBay price?

▲ The feedback system has been a vital part of eBay's success

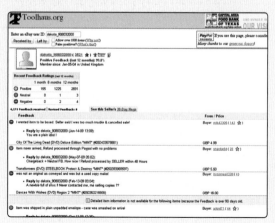

▲ Check out all of a seller's negative feedback at a glance at Toolhaus.org

CHECKING SELLER FEEDBACK BEFORE BIDDING

Every time an item sells, people have the chance to leave feedback about a seller. Feedback can be positive, negative or neutral, and can also be withdrawn by mutual agreement. We've covered it in more depth elsewhere in this guide. The total number of items sold and bought by the seller is displayed in brackets next to their name in the item's listing - click on it to go to their Feedback Profile.

The Positive Feedback percentage is the seller's reputation. If it's below 98%, then it's worth considering whether you want to do business with them. However, this is modified by how many total sales and purchases are represented. You can check for both positive and negative feedback up to 12 months, or you can also input the user's ID at www.toolhaus.org to see a full listing of their negatives.

QUALITY OF FEEDBACK

Check one or two of the 'View Item' links in the seller's Feedback Profile. Many eBayers boost their reputation by buying 'one cent' lots that automatically grant positive feedback; such auctions are selling good reputation in volume. Certain sellers also manage to maintain more than one eBay account with the intention of 'selling' feedback to themselves. This trick is easy to spot with a little investigation of a Feedback Profile: look for numerous low-value items from the same seller, often digital goods such as 'guides' in PDF and Microsoft Word format. Some of these practices have been clamped down on by eBay, however.

CHANGED IDENTITY

eBay users can change their User ID, and if your seller has done this, then a symbol will appear next to their name.

Feedback is carried over from the old ID, but an auction where the seller is in the process of switching identity could mean that they're trying to start over at eBay. Why? Tucked away in the 'View more options'

drop-down menu in the Feedback Profile screen is the 'View ID History' option, which will quickly reveal any identity changes.

THE REAL DEAL

There is no pervasively useful method to identify fake goods across all listings in eBay, since signs of bad faith vary greatly across types of items. However, here are some considerations:

- If it's too good to be true, then it probably isn't true, particularly for Buy It Now items. Maybe a cuckolded wife really is selling her husband's Porsche for a dollar, but avoid items listed at significantly below market value.

- Does the listing have a generic picture that you've seen before? eBay supplies stock images for DVDs, CDs and certain other types of listings to sellers, but a 'domestic' picture of the item listed is a more encouraging sign, although it's not an infallible mark of authenticity.

- Does the listing explicitly state what the item is? You could be bidding on the very picture you're examining, rather than the item it displays! The devil is in the details, and nothing protects you better than a careful reading of the listing.

Boosting profits by overcharging for postage is known as 'scalping', and the 'Postage and packaging' section in each item listing should state clearly what you'll pay to have the item sent to you. If it doesn't, check the listing, and use the 'Ask a question' link to ascertain exact postal charges if necessary. If the seller is vague in response, pin them down, and if they won't specify an exact cost, don't bid.

Use the 'Customise view' link in your search results to add 'Shipping costs' to your search results (although they should be displayed by default). While not all items will be able to display their cost in the shipping costs column, it will help you eliminate most scalpers at a glance.

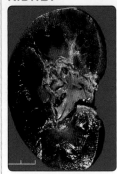
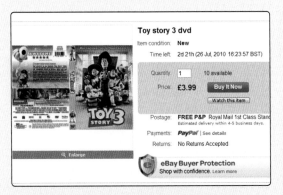

▲ At the time, Toy Story 3 was barely into cinemas. Pirated goods like this are likely to be poor quality

Member quick links

Contact member

View items for sale

View seller's shop

View ID history

Add to favourite sellers

View eBay My World

▲ Check the ID History of an eBayer to see how many times they've changed their name

Smart Bidding And Good Buying

When and how you bid on an item can make all the difference. We look at how you can increase your chances

So you've found your item; now it's time to bid and win it. However, there are some tricks to master before the item is in your hands and all parties are leaving positive feedback for each other.

SNIPING

Waiting until the last few minutes - or seconds - of an auction to place your bid is known as 'sniping'. Last-minute bidding gives your rivals no chance to bid higher, but this technique cannot defeat a bidder whose secret top-bid is higher than yours. The best way to ensure a win is to bid as much as you're willing to pay for the item. If you lose, it will usually be by a much higher margin than it appears, as eBay augments bids in small increments, and all top-bids are secret until outbid. The top-bid of a winner is known only to them.

ODD BIDS

Most eBayers place bids in rounded-off amounts, but sometimes you really can win an auction by a margin of a few pennies, so make your bids in odd amounts such as £11.67 or £7.89.

SILENT RUNNING

The more attention an auction receives, the more likely a costly bidding war is - great for the seller, not so great for you. A listing has three possible 'attracting forces': a bidder, a hit counter (if the seller has put one in the listing) and the number of

people who add the listing to their 'watch' list in order to monitor the auction's progress.

The hit counter is usually visible to all, but only the seller knows how many people are 'watching' the item; if sufficient 'watchers' gather, the seller may be encouraged to augment the listing and attempt to attract further buyers. The only safe way to track a listing without hiking up the hit counter or adding to the number of 'watchers', is to chase it through the ever-shifting pages of the search results through which you found the item in the first place. If you bookmark the listing and check it regularly, your own 'hit' is counted once a day.

However, nothing can turn an unnoticed listing into a frantic bidding war more effectively than when it's bid on very early in its run. Many eBayers search for items based on the existing number of bids, so even if you're not planning to 'snipe', don't bid on an item too early.

EBAY FEVER

When an item you've been seeking for years suddenly shows up on eBay, it's surprisingly easy to ignore all preceding advice and get caught up in the excitement. If you bid (or buy) recklessly, you can end up with an overseas item that you're unable to pay for due to the seller's payment methods or for other practical reasons. The only recourse then is to contact the seller via the 'Ask a question' link, explain what happened, and offer to pay the cost of a relisting. The seller remains entitled to wait 30 days and open a dispute for non-payment, so examine alternative payment methods if possible and keep it courteous, since the fault is with you.

Retracting a bid is rarely permitted, and you're only usually allowed to withdraw substantially mistyped amounts bid (i.e. entering £1,010 instead of £10.10). A bid on eBay is a binding contract. For an overview of eBay's policy, see **pages.ebay.co.uk/ help/buy/bid-retract.html**.

CORRESPONDING VIA EBAY

Corresponding with sellers outside of the eBay messaging system is ill-advised; if all your

Find answers from rain-bows4u

Childrens Remote control Dinosaur
Item number: 320736899629
Price: £0.99
Time left: 35m 34s

Select a topic
○ Details about the item (1)
○ Postage (3)
○ Combined postage (0)
○ Pay for the item (1)
○ Returns (1)
○ Other (0)

We'll look for an answer for you

About eBay | Announcements | Buy Hub | Safety Centre | Partner Centre | VeRO: Protecting Intellectual Property | Policies | Feedback Forum | Site Map | Help | eBay official

eBay Buyer Protection Shop with confidence. Learn more
Copyright © 1995-2011 eBay Inc. All Rights Reserved. Designated trademarks and brands are the property of their respective owners. Use of this website constitutes acceptance
Privacy Policy.

▲ **Choose the right option when corresponding with sellers**

Congratulations You committed to buy the following item:

THE ENTITY (1981) Uncut | +Extras | Anchor Bay | R1 DVD

Sale price:	£8.99
Quantity:	1
Subtotal:	£8.99
Postage	Royal Mail 1st Class £2.00 Standard:
	Royal Mail Airmail £3.00 (Small Packets):
Insurance:	(not offered)

View item | Go to My eBay

Get Your Item

Pay Now

Click to confirm postage, get total price and arrange payment.

▲ eBay's 'Pay Now' button

correspondence remains within eBay, you have a clear history to present in the event of dispute arbitration. Take it to e-mail, and you're on your own. The 'Ask a question' message form has a tick-box that lets you choose to hide your e-mail address from the recipient. This is the easiest way to keep your messages in eBay itself.

The form also has four options in a drop-down list to indicate whether your enquiry concerns payment, combined shipping for multiple items, shipping, or is a general enquiry. Since you have to choose one of these options to send a message, choose the right one; a busy seller may respond more quickly if you do so.

SIDE-STEPPING EBAY

Do not approach sellers with offers outside eBay's listings system. It's against the rules, and auctions can only be ended early in unusual circumstances. If you're interested in buying similar items 'off-site' from the seller in future, they may be interested in dealing with you, but they can't cancel an auction in progress, can't privately offer you the safeguards that eBay does, and would probably prefer to see someone as enthusiastic as you bidding hard against others users in a regular eBay auction!

DUPLICATE BIDDING

Do not place bids on multiple listings of the same item in the hope of winning one of them. If you win them all, you'll have to pay for them all.

UNWELCOME BIDS

Do you qualify to bid for an item? If you can't meet the seller's terms for a listing, they have the power to cancel your bid and bring down penalties on you from eBay administration. These can include account suspension and loss of PowerSeller status.

Sellers can refuse bids from buyers on their 'blocked bidder' list, and for many other reasons. As long as these are clearly stated in the listing itself, you'll have to respect them. Sellers may choose to 'ban' bidders who:

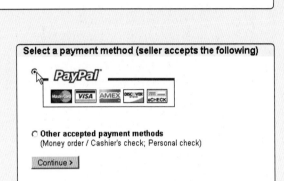

Select a payment method (seller accepts the following)

PayPal
MasterCard VISA AMEX DISCOVER eCHECK

○ **Other accepted payment methods**
(Money order / Cashier's check; Personal check)

Continue >

About eBay | Announcements | Security Center | Policies | Site Map | Help

▲ Select a method of payment from those available

- Have negative feedback comments.
- Have a 'non-domestic' shipping address.
- Have received Unpaid Item Strikes in an after-sales dispute.
- Don't have a PayPal account (although this doesn't oblige the seller to use PayPal as the payment method for their listing).

'Malicious buying' is deemed by eBay to occur when a buyer:

- Bids far beyond an item's value to 'prevent' serious bids and block the sale.
- Bids on multiple items from one seller with no real intent to buy.
- Bids on a seller's item after being placed on their 'blocked bidder' list.

Review payment details

Seller:	⚡ Power Seller 🗐			
Item Title		Qty.	Price	Subtotal
THE ENTITY (1981) Uncut	+Extras	Anchor Bay	R1 DVD (280128288110)		1	£8.99	£8.99

Payment Instructions
PAYMENT METHODS FOR UK BUYERS - Credit/Debit Card, Personal Cheque, Postal Order & Bank Transfer. PAYMENT METHODS FOR BUYERS OUTSIDE THE UK - Credit Cards, International Bank Transfer, International Money Orders/Bank Drafts provided they are made out in Sterling (GBP) & Moneybookers.

Postage and packing via Royal Mail 1st Class Standard:	£2.00
Postal insurance:(not offered)	--
Seller discounts (-) or charges (+):	2
Seller Total:	£12.99

recalculate

Questions about the total? Request total from seller

▲ Add the correct postage, if it's not already included in the total

PAYING FOR YOUR WIN

When you finally win an auction listing, you will receive two notification e-mails from eBay: one to confirm your win, and one soliciting payment on behalf of the seller. Both will contain a big 'Pay Now' button, as will the item listing and the 'Won' page in My eBay.

Press it, and you'll be asked to select a method of payment (the methods available will be in accordance with those of the original listing).

You'll be asked to confirm shipping details and to add postage to the invoice if this hasn't automatically been done. Take care to input the correct postage. Postage is usually charged in the seller's native currency, but you may need to translate the agreed postage amount in order to input it (try the Universal Currency Converter at **www.xe.com/ucc**). You can also add an optional note to the seller at this point, and change the

shipping address by selecting another from your eBay Saved Addresses or adding a new one.

PAYING DIRECT FROM PAYPAL

In certain circumstances - usually when you've arranged unusual terms with a foreign seller - you may find that your only options for inputting postage are inappropriate drop-down lists of 'domestic' packing rates. In this case, you'll need to contact the seller and ask them to change the automated payment procedure from their end. If this proves problematic, and PayPal is acceptable to your seller, you can still use PayPal's Send Money feature to conclude the auction, without losing the security of an eBay acknowledgement that you've paid for your win. However, you'll need the seller's e-mail address. The process is as follows:

- Log into your PayPal account and click the 'Send Money' tab.
- Click on 'eBay item' in the 'For...?' section and type your eBay User ID and the auction number.
- Enter the seller's e-mail address in the 'To' field, or, if you've previously dealt with the seller, select it from the drop-down list underneath.
- Enter the winning amount including postage, click 'Continue, and then confirm on the next page. The item will be acknowledged as 'paid' in My eBay.

PAYING WITHOUT PAYPAL

PayPal is an eBay subsidiary company, and using it to pay for an eBay win means that you're covered for the full transaction price plus original shipping charges through the PayPal Buyer Protection Program (see 'Damage Limitation'). Since no other eBay payment method carries this kind of guarantee, PayPal is arguably the best choice to complete auctions, and eBay is at times borderline insistent that you use it.

However, PayPal has many detractors, and if you need to complete a deal by other means, the options allowed (but not necessarily endorsed) by eBay are:

- **Personal cheque:** Convenient, can be stopped if necessary (for varying fees) and is traceable.
- **Credit/debit card:** The seller may have their own checkout system, integrated (often poorly) into eBay's own payment procedures. Credit card payments additionally have varying - and limited - liability insurance for physical items. Be sure that your auction payment is acknowledged by eBay afterwards, as this fails to happen more often through bad coding than ill intent.
- **Postal orders:** Convenient, but almost as transparent as cash.

▲ Pay for your win directly from the PayPal site

▲ Check all the details again before finalising the payment

- **Bank transfer:** A favourite in European transactions, but involves sharing banking information with a third party. Refunds can be very problematic.
- **Banker's draft:** For higher value items; fees for issue may exceed the item's value.
- **E-cheque:** Slightly faster clearing than physical cheques, but if you're able to send one, you might as well use PayPal.
- **Escrow:** Only practical for higher amounts. Both parties have to be happy with the transaction before money is released - www.escrow.com.
- **Cash:** Caveat emptor - if you must use it, send the package well wrapped (with opaque lining) and by a method whereby the receiver must sign for it.

INTERNATIONAL MONEY ORDERS

Some transnational banks used to make international money orders a relatively easy option. These days, the term has little meaning, and generally sellers are actually talking about cheques from international banks that are to be specified in the seller's native currency (usually dollars). Such services are far too expensive to be practical for small wins.

LEAVING FEEDBACK

Many sections of My eBay will ask you to leave feedback on transacted auctions (and the seller will remind you if no one else does!). eBay is regularly reviewing its feedback policy, and it's covered in more detail elsewhere in this book.

DAMAGE LIMITATION

If you don't receive your item, or the item is significantly different from its listing description, contact the seller about the matter in the first instance. An amicable solution is often possible, retaining goodwill and avoiding bad feedback for the seller.

One of the top causes of disputes is non-delivery, usually due to items being lost or stolen in the post. The only way to avoid this is to have them sent insured at greater expense, thus protecting both buyer and seller. Unfortunately, this can negate the 'bargain' value of eBay and, in practice, an enormous number of eBay items are consigned to the basic postal system (often of more than one country) every day. Nonetheless, verify the address used and date of actual posting from the seller, and ensure that adequate time has been allowed for the item to arrive.

For items covered by PayPal's Buyer Protection Program, the advantage is with the buyer if an uninsured item doesn't arrive or doesn't match its

listing description; you can open a dispute from My eBay within ten to 60 days of payment.

As ever, maintain any correspondence via eBay rather than e-mail. The seller has ten days to respond, but if no satisfactory agreement is reached, you can elevate your dispute to a claim. The seller's account may be limited or even suspended if a claim is granted, and funds are usually recovered and then credited back to your PayPal account.

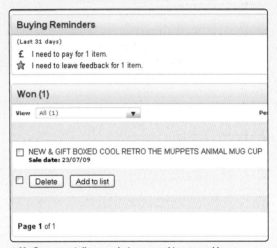

▲ My Summary tells you what you need to pay and leave feedback for

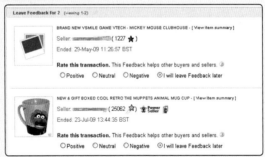

▲ Feedback allows you to rate and comment on other eBayers, either positively or negatively

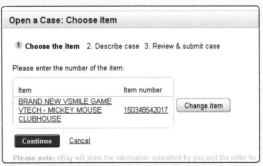

▲ If the seller won't help you, you can open a dispute about your missing or misdescribed item

Combining Purchases From One Seller

If you're buying several items from the same seller, you could save a bundle on postage costs. Here's how

Should you purchase more than one item from a single trader, you may find that you can combine said purchases into one shipment, thus saving yourself a few pounds in the process - at least in theory! There are various different approaches to doing this, but in all likelihood, eBay auctions that offer discounts on shipping for multiple items will continue to require a measure of personal correspondence between buyer and seller, and this is easy enough with the 'Ask a question' link. Simply select 'Question about combined shipping for multiple items' from the drop-down list and make your enquiry.

NO 'SHOPPING BASKET'

The problems begin to surface when the seller attempts to automate the process or let eBay do it on their behalf, and this is particularly true with North American sellers, who have the widest range of postage-calculating tools built into their listing templates. Many of these tools can auto-calculate combined shipping to the UK, usually via the UPS shipping service, but all of them require deviations from standard eBay practice regarding paying for items. As things stand, Bay has no ubiquitous 'shopping basket' - a la Amazon - and when you win an item or 'Commit To Buy' it, there is no consideration given for other items that you might have bought or wish to buy from the same seller.

However, while it's currently therefore impossible to combine purchases in one basket, eBay is at last experimenting with a basket system. There's no date as yet for when it plans to fully roll this out, however.

CUSTOM SOLUTIONS

Many PowerSellers invest in software solutions that provide a 'shopping basket' for you behind the scenes; when eBay informs them of a new sale of one of their items, they will invite you to pay for the item, but inform you that you may take advantage of shipping discounts for multiple items purchased. Committing to further items from that seller will add your deliveries to the seller's own Amazon-style list, with combined shipping calculated, and the final payment procedure may take place via eBay checkout (if the seller has integrated their system directly into it) or at the seller's site (if the seller has their own checkout software).

Sellers who offer such services will usually also mention them in their listings, along with (often tedious) instructions on how to proceed in order to not lose the combined shipping. Read and follow these carefully, because they vary widely from seller to seller.

Any custom checkout should send eBay an acknowledgement of payment for all your items automatically, but make sure this is done shortly after payment for your multiple items, and contact the seller otherwise.

COMBINED SHIPPING - GUIDELINES

If you intend to take advantage of any combined shipping deals a seller is offering, do not pay for any single item from them until you have 'claimed' all the items from their listings or store that you intend to buy (to 'claim' means to secure an item by either winning it in an auction or pressing 'Commit To Buy' on a Buy It Now listing).

- Read carefully what terms the seller is offering on combined postage for an item you intend to buy - if any automatic postage calculations should fall short after you've won or committed to buy the

▲ The best bet is always to ask the seller first

- We ship to Europe, Asia and Australia.
- Payment for all items must be made within 10 Days
- Payment **must** be made through eBay checkout
- To combine Postage & Packing rates, please wait for all auctions to close before going through checkout (one time).
- eBay checkout will automatically calculate the proper postage for each additional item.
- *Please visit our EBAY SHOP, where we carry all 250,000+ titles at even lower prices!!!*

▲ Check the seller's listings to see if they give details about combining postage

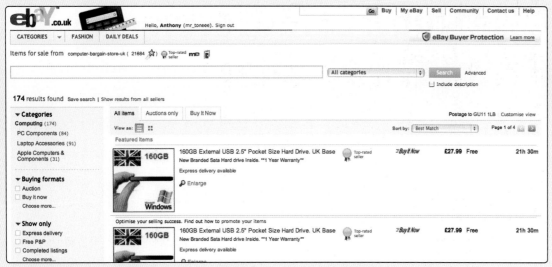

▲ Several items all from one seller, but what's the best way to buy more than one of them?

item, the seller will have to honour the postage that they offered - by other means if necessary - and you're likely to win any eventual dispute on the matter.

- Ensure that shipping terms are consistent across all the same-seller listings that you intend to bid on or buy. Calculate the combined postage based on the listing's stated rates and 'claim' your items. If you're bidding on multiple or sequential auctions and hoping to combine postage on successive wins, be aware that the first item won is payable within 30 days of a winning bid or a commitment to buy.

- You're likely to receive more than one (usually automated) e-mail from eBay requesting payment for each item as you win (or Commit To Buy) it. If you do so before all the items are 'in the basket', you risk losing some or all of your combined shipping discount.

- When all your items are claimed, check out the most recent automated e-mail from the seller for details of how to combine shipping. If the calculation is to be done through eBay Checkout itself, make sure that eBay's combined estimate corresponds with the seller's advertised deal. Verify also that the rates are appropriately UK or international, depending on the seller's location.

PAYPAL ITEMS FROM DIFFERENT SELLERS

Be careful not to confuse combined shipping with combined payment. If you've won several eBay items from different sellers, but haven't paid yet, you can click the 'Pay For All PayPal Items' link in My eBay.

Any items not listed with PayPal won't be included in the combined payment. If there are multiple items in the list from one seller from whom you wish to obtain a shipping discount, remove them from the list before making your combined payment; they will need to be dealt with separately.

▲ 'Pay For All PayPal Items' is not the same as a combined order

Case Study: **Carousel Pig**

For Alison McKinley, eBay is a hugely important part of her business - selling soft toys...

For those who already own a physical, high-street store, an eBay shop is a perfect accompaniment. And so it has proved for Alison McKinley who is now in her 15th year of trading and continues to pull in hundreds of orders each year on the popular auction site.

The 54-year-old felt trade in her store, Carousel Pig, in Wiveliscombe, a small town in Somerset was starting to tail away, so she began to look around for fresh outlets to sell her Jellycat toys, Russ bears and jewellery. And it was then that she turned to eBay - never looking back since.

"The shop had reached a plateau," she said. "Village life began to change as more women went out to work and youngsters left for larger towns. More people buying online was taking its toll, so I thought if you can't beat them.. Well, all businesses have to evolve if you want to survive, don't they?"

At first, Alison saw her eBay shop as a means of selling older and discontinued items as well as excess stock from her retail store, but as sales boomed, she began to list current stock as well, particularly the items that are easy to post and cheap to send abroad.

"I often have to buy in larger quantities than I really need," she said. "And via eBay, I can reach customers that I would otherwise never have had."

The major sellers are Jellycats. "I've been selling them from their outset several years ago," Alison said. "So I really know the product."

Jellycats are designer-led soft that which appeal to all age ranges, with adults often buying for themselves. According to those in the know, they appeal to mid-range buyers looking for well-designed, high-quality pieces; Americans apparently love them and the Japanese can be quite fond. With eBay being worldwide, it means Alison can sell her products across the globe.

So far, her feedback has been good, with just one negative. "I get paranoid about feedback," she said. "With so much fraud around, I'm sure many customers will only buy after checking out feedback first."

She certainly understands the importance of keeping customers happy. Alison has been self-employed since she was in her 20s and has worked in many jobs, from selling antiques to a freelance graphic designer.

"I enjoy the inevitable risks and feast or famine lifestyle that self-employment has brought. I would hate life to be predictable," she laughs.

Not that this career path has done her any harm at all. She currently lives in a 16th century house, built for the Bishop of Bath, just around the corner from her shop.

And she also has a great family life, having been married for 34 years to husband Mac, who sells taxidermy props for television, films and collectors. He works from home so is able to help out with postage - and cooking the evening meal.

Alison, meanwhile, beavers away on eBay, although she does have time to play with her two grandchildren, aged seven and five, chat to her children and look after her dog, cats and chickens. It helps that she now has two able assistants.

"It was certainly well worth setting up the shop," she said. "The costs were negligible - I already had the stock, so apart from the costs of setting up an eBay store of £6 a month and investing in wholesale quantities of jiffy bags, there wasn't much to fork out."

▲ eBay is a vital part of Alison's business

▲ Many of Carousel Pig's customers are based abroad

So it's time to close the retail shop, then? "Not at all. Having a retail store keeps you in touch with the latest products, gives you a chance to test-drive them and helps you keep a finger on the pulse of what customers are looking for."

Alison's online online shop now represents an integral part of her business. She always adds the eBay store domain and that of her traditional website (**www.carouselpig.co.uk**) to any local newspaper advertising.

"I set up the traditional website because Pilgrim no longer allows its bona fide retailers to sell its jewellery on eBay," she said.

Alison is not looking to stand still, though. She's planning to convert a spare room at home into an eBay office. "It'll stop my husband from falling over Jellycats and it should stop fights over the PC."

But does she need a cure for her addiction to work? "Well, eBay pays for my exotic taste in holidays, so it's not all bad. It's just very easy to become addicted, so I have to curtail it sometimes."

Top Tips From Alison

1. Be committed, professional and realistic about the time you will have to spend if you want to be successful - no pain no gain!
2. Post items and answer e-mails asap - I always send a 'thank you for payment' e-mail and include an invoice with the parcel.
3. Invest in a set of postal scales to be accurate and avoid costly mistakes - don't overcharge on postage, but make sure you don't lose out either.
4. Be totally honest in your listings and dealings and organise your listings with the help of eBay's Selling Manager - a free service.
5. Keep your cool! - you will undoubtedly encounter some very difficult customers (most are lovely).

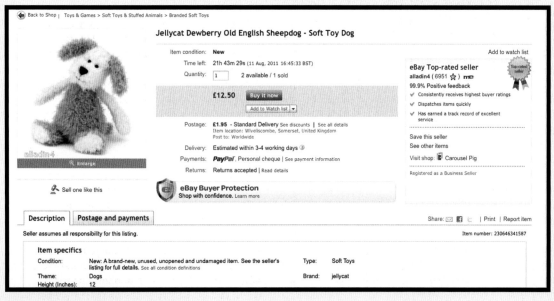

▲ Jellycat toys are particularly popular items

Chapter 6
PayPal

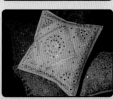

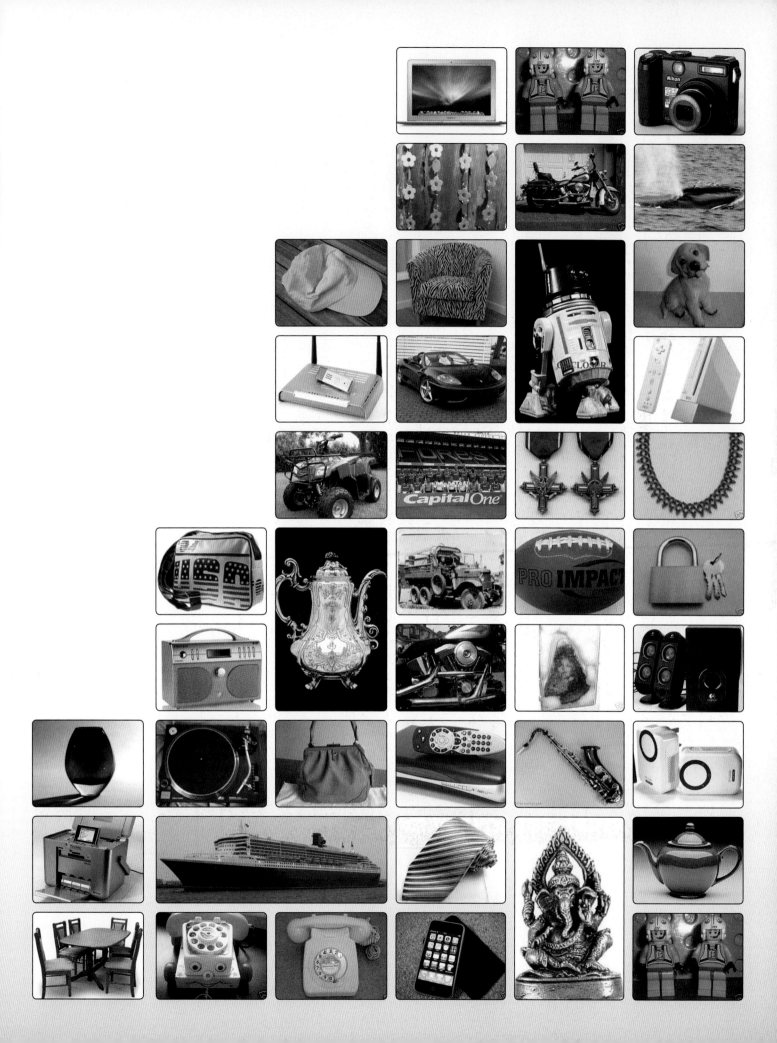

What Is PayPal?

It's now an essential part of the eBay experience, so here's your crash course on what this payment system is all about

You'll have seen PayPal mentioned many times throughout this guide, but what exactly is it, and how does it work? Well, while PayPal isn't really a bank, you won't go far wrong if you think of your PayPal account as being like a bank account. Ordinarily, you can't use it to set up direct debits for your energy bills, though; almost all your transactions will be manual and one time only. PayPal is also entirely virtual: you can't nip to your local branch on a Saturday morning to make a deposit or withdrawal. Everything occurs over the Internet.

On eBay, a PayPal account is vital. About 90% of all eBay sales are concluded with PayPal, and worldwide there are over 244 million accounts. For buyers, PayPal is simply the most convenient way to pay (although hardly the cheapest). For sellers, allowing PayPal as a payment method is pretty much compulsory (you can only get away with not offering it on items listed in property, services, or eBay Motors).

One of PayPal's big advantages over traditional payment methods is its speed. You can pay for an item via your PayPal balance or a credit or debit card (and, with some caveats, direct from your bank account), and in most cases the seller receives the money instantly. Neither party has to mess about with cheques, waiting for them to clear. For the seller, it's like having a professional merchant system, the sort of thing used by large retailers.

Another big advantage is security. When you buy something off eBay, you're usually dealing with strangers or unknown businesses. Only a fool wouldn't be cautious about handing over debit- or credit-card information. With PayPal, though, there are no worries. You see, PayPal acts as an

intermediary, a broker, so you don't actually pay the seller directly. Your financial details are locked up safe in your PayPal account, and the seller never sees them.

HOW IT WORKS

As a buyer, having just won an auction, you're given several opportunities to pay. First, you'll see a big Pay Now button at the top of your browser window. Second, there'll be a new entry, and a 'Pay now' link, in the Won section of your Activity tab in the all-seeing eye that is My eBay. Third, you'll receive an eBay-generated e-mail, with a win confirmation and an invoice. There will be a Pay Now button, too. You might receive an e-mail directly from the seller as well.

Whichever path you take, you'll soon enough find yourself at the screen where you need to choose your payment method. PayPal is usually the default, but if the seller also takes cheques and so on, there'll be an option for 'Other accepted payment methods'. Taking the PayPal route, just type in your PayPal password (your PayPal e-mail address will normally already be displayed) and click 'Log in'.

PayPal and eBay are parts of the same organisation, so naturally they're very tightly integrated. The beauty of this is that the PayPal payment process occurs within eBay itself; you won't get whisked away to the actual PayPal website. What you'll see now is the review screen. If your PayPal account has sufficient funds in it, payment will be sourced entirely from your balance. However, if there's not enough (or none at all), the amount not covered (or, where your balance is £0, the full cost)

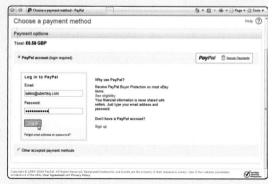

▲ If you haven't yet signed up, what are you waiting for?

▲ Around 90% of all eBay purchases are paid for with PayPal

▲ After a win, click the Pay Now button in the browser window...

▲...or click the Pay now link in My eBay...

will be sourced from your bank account or credit or debit card (depending on what you've got registered). If you want to change anything here, just click 'More funding options'.

As a seller, having just achieved a spectacular price for your first-edition copy of Gulliver's Travels, the PayPal process is even simpler. Basically, you don't need to lift a finger. When the buyer makes payment, you'll receive confirmation by e-mail. If you then log into your account, you'll find the money ready and waiting. A receipt is e-mailed to the buyer automatically, but in the name of good feedback and communication, you'd do well to also send a personal thank you.

Tip: Be aware that a payment made from your bank account - an e-cheque - will usually take between seven and nine days to clear. Don't expect despatch of your purchase until the money finally drops into the seller's PayPal account. You're much better using your PayPal balance or a credit or debit card.

ACCOUNT TYPES

Setting up PayPal is a subject covered in chapter two, but here it's worthwhile going into more detail about the different types of account. Basically, there are three main options: Personal, Premier, and Business (a Student account is also available). All of them are free, and there are no start-up costs or monthly administration fees.

▲ You can change the funding source that PayPal will use

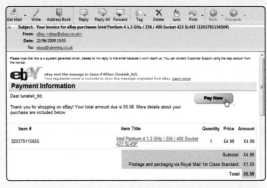

▲...or the Pay Now button in either of the sale-generated e-mails

A Personal account is intended for eBayers who are chiefly interested in buying. If you sell, any PayPal payments you receive must be funded from a PayPal balance or a bank account (although your buyers won't be aware of that). If someone pays for an item via a card - a scenario that'll happen sooner rather than later - your confirmation e-mail will inform you that you need to upgrade. Until you do, the money will remain unavailable, and if you haven't upgraded after 30 days, it'll be returned to the buyer.

You can upgrade at any time; after logging into your account, just click the Upgrade link at the top of the Overview page. If you intend to sell, however, you might as well forgo a Personal account altogether and just sign up for a Premier account. This will lift the limitation on card payments right from the start. Most people who begin as buyers quickly end up as sellers, so save yourself the hassle. Once the eBay bug bites, you'll want to start making some cash from all that stuff in your attic.

A Business account differs from a Premier account in that it can be held in the name of a company (Dealz4U Ltd, for example) - the other account types can only be held in the name of an individual. Transactions and e-mails will therefore look more professional. Furthermore, if you've got co-workers, they can be assigned different access rights. For instance, you might want someone to be able to view transactions but not spend or withdraw. To set

▲ There are three account types to choose from

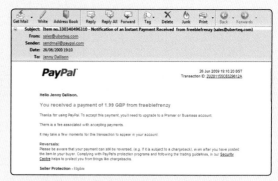

▲ A Personal account is great for buyers but not sellers

▲ If you've got a Business account, you can configure different access rights for different users

this up, go to your account's Overview page, click 'Profile', select 'Manage Users', then click 'Add User'. Choose a User ID and password, which will then be the co-worker's login (instead of the usual e-mail address and password), and tick the required rights.

Tip: Officially, you're allowed one Personal account and one Premier or Business account. In practice, though, there's no way for that restriction to be enforced, so you can actually set up as many accounts as you want or need. However, every account must have its own e-mail address and financial details. You can't register the same credit card to two different accounts, for example.

STANDARD FEES
They say it's better to give than to receive, and that's certainly true where PayPal's concerned. While sending money (to a seller, say) is free, getting paid (by a buyer, for instance) is anything but. There are nasty, nasty fees.

In most cases, the commission you pay to PayPal is 3.4% of the transaction amount plus an extra £0.20. For example, if a buyer pays you £100, you'll be charged £3.60 - that's £3.40 (3.4%) plus £0.20. In your PayPal account, you'll receive £96.40.

Matters are worse if the buyer pays in a currency other than British pounds. For that, there's a 2.5% conversion fee. Furthermore, if the buyer doesn't live

in the UK, there's a 0.5% cross-border fee. It all adds up! Imagine you've just sold an item to someone in the USA. Payment will be made in dollars. When the money hits your account, it'll be automatically converted into pounds (for PayPal's current exchange rates, visit **tinyurl.com/47rsl**). Your total commission will be a whopping 6.4%. And then there's the old £0.20 to be added on top. To check in advance what fees will be payable on any given transaction, have a look at PPCalc at **tinyurl.com/d5golw**.

Sadly, PayPal fees are levied in addition to eBay fees: you're charged twice. That's a situation that makes most eBay sellers quite, quite mad. After all, as PayPal and eBay are really one and the same, it's a case of double-dipping. Most categories on eBay attract a 10% selling fee, so when everything's combined (don't forget there are usually listing fees too), you're likely to be coughing up about 15% in commission - even more if the transaction involves an extra currency and a border crossing. Small wonder that Pierre Omidyar, eBay's founder, is one of the richest people in the world!

Tip: Don't try to reclaim your PayPal fees from buyers. It's against the rules. If you adorn your listings with something like 'PayPal payments incur a 3.5% charge', they're likely to get pulled, and for repeated offences your eBay account could be suspended. It's unfair, of course. Other outlets

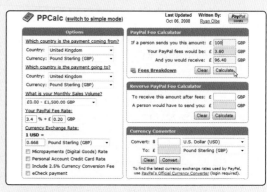

▲ For working out what it's all going to cost, try PPCalc, the online fee calculator

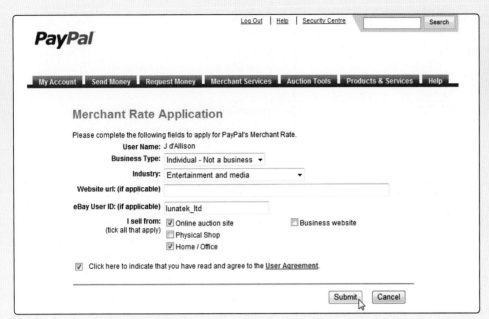

◀ Don't forget to apply for merchant commission rates as soon as you're eligible

regularly charge for using a credit card, so why can't eBay sellers charge for using PayPal?

MERCHANT FEES

As illustrated above, PayPal's standard commission rate is 3.4%. However, if you become a really successful seller and your monthly receipts exceed £1,500, you're entitled to a lower, merchant rate. The rate comes down as your income goes up. The full set of tariffs is shown below.

- £0 to £1,500 = 3.4% +20p
- £1,500.01 to £6,000 = 2.9% +20p
- £6,000.01 to £15,000 = 2.4% +20p
- £15,000.01 to £55,000 = 1.9% +20p
- £55,000.01 or more = 1.4% +20p

The rate for the current month is decided by your income for the previous month. For instance, if you have a great January and receive £7,000, your rate in February will be 2.4%. However, if February is terrible and you receive only £1,200, your rate in March will be 2.9%.

To be eligible for these lower rates, you must have held your PayPal account for at least 90 days. Also, you need to submit an application. Once this is accepted, you'll be moved up and down the tariffs automatically as appropriate. There's no need to reapply if you slip back to the standard 3.4% from time to time. Note that the rates aren't back-dated, however, so don't mess about; send in your application as soon as possible.

To do that, log into your account, click 'Fees' at the bottom of any page, click '1.4% to 3.4% + £0.20 GBP', then click 'Are you eligible for lower rates?'

Read through the introductory spiel and then click the 'Apply now' link. Finally, fill out the form, accept the user agreement, and click 'Submit'. Don't apply before your 90 days are up or before you've clocked up £1,500 or more in the previous month, because the application will be immediately refused (though you can reapply later, of course).

PERSONAL TRANSFERS

Not all PayPal receipts attract a fee. Personal transfers - payments between friends and family - can in fact be free. That's only true if they're funded from a PayPal balance or a bank account, though. If they're funded by a card, that old 3.4% commission applies (regardless of the sum involved).

To make such a transfer, click 'Send Money' at the top of any page and then select the Personal tab. Enter the amount to be sent and also the recipient's PayPal-linked e-mail address. Next, click 'Continue'. You'll now be shown a summary, and if there are any fees, this is where you'll need to decide who pays

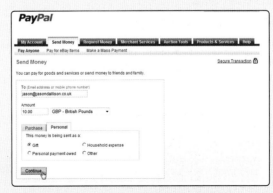

▲ Payments between friends and family are usually free

▲ Where have all the fees gone?

them - you or the recipient. Once you're all done, just click 'Send Money'.

ACCOUNT WITHDRAWALS

Often you'll want to spend your PayPal money right out of your PayPal account, particularly as an ever-increasing number of websites are offering PayPal as a payment method (it's not just an eBay thing). Just as often, though, you'll want to withdraw your PayPal money to your regular current- or savings account - especially as PayPal doesn't pay interest. Until recently, there was a £0.50 charge for withdrawing less than £50, but now there's no charge at all. So that's something. PayPal does reserve the right, however, to bill you £0.50 if your attempt to withdraw funds fails,.

To get the ball rolling, go to your account's Overview page, hover your mouse over the Withdraw menu, then select 'Transfer to Bank Account'. On the next screen, enter the amount to withdraw and also the bank account you want to withdraw it to (if you've

got more than one bank account registered). After clicking 'Continue', you'll get a confirmation screen. Click 'Submit' and you're done. Within a few seconds you'll also get a confirmation e-mail. Note that it'll take up to five working days for the money to arrive.

VERIFYING YOUR FINANCIAL DETAILS

When you first open your PayPal account, its status will be Unverified. This means that you've yet to establish ownership of the associated bank account - assuming you've registered one. If you haven't yet registered one (during the initial PayPal set-up, it's possible to get away with registering just a credit or debit card), you'll need to do so. On your account's Overview page, hover your mouse over the Profile menu and select 'Add or Remove Bank Account'.

But what's the big deal? Well, until you upgrade your status from Unverified to Verified, there'll be limits on the amount of money you can spend, receive, and withdraw. These are listed below.

- Sending limit per transaction = £900
- Sending limit per year = £1,000
- Withdrawal limit per month = £500
- Withdrawal limit per year = £650
- Receiving limit per year = £1,700

The limits are there so that PayPal can conform to EU anti-money-laundering laws. They also help to fight fraud. To see how much you've currently eaten into them, click the 'View limits' link on your account's Overview page.

To lift the limits, and thus become Verified, there are a couple of hoops you need to jump through first.

▶ Withdrawing your PayPal money to your regular bank account really couldn't be easier

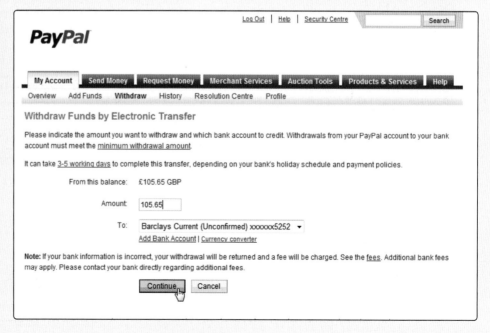

▲ Until you become Verified, your PayPal account will be somewhat limited

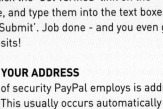

▲ Keep your eyes peeled for those two small sums deposited into your bank account

When you registered your bank account, PayPal will have dropped two small deposits into it, each less than £1. You'll need to wait between two and five days for these to appear; keep checking your statement online or use the mini-statement facility at your bank's cash machines. With the figures to hand, log into PayPal, click the 'Get verified' link on the Overview page, and type them into the text boxes. Finally, click 'Submit'. Job done - and you even get to keep the deposits!

CONFIRMING YOUR ADDRESS

Another form of security PayPal employs is address confirmation. This usually occurs automatically as soon as you register a credit or debit card. PayPal checks that the address you gave when setting up your account matches the one held by the card issuer. Unfortunately, if you've only registered a bank account (and have no card you can register), your address will probably remain forever Unconfirmed.

That could arouse suspicion. Imagine your PayPal login details have somehow been stolen. A fraudster could change your address, go on a spending spree, and attempt to clean you out. However, the supplied address would then show as Unconfirmed, and for many sellers that would be grounds enough to refuse shipment (and reverse payment). Indeed, if a seller ships an item to an address that isn't Confirmed, the transaction ceases to be eligible for Seller Protection. As a genuine buyer, you could find that no one will take your money!

All these security measures are, of course, designed to make PayPal safe. They also facilitate the aforementioned Seller Protection - and Buyer Protection too. Details on those areas are covered in chapter five, and for the latest policies and eligibility requirements, visit the PayPal Security Centre (**tinyurl.com/3abeq8k**). Is PayPal as perfect as it's cracked up to be, though? Is it 100% secure and problem-free? Well, you're about to find out...

▶ Does your address show as confirmed?

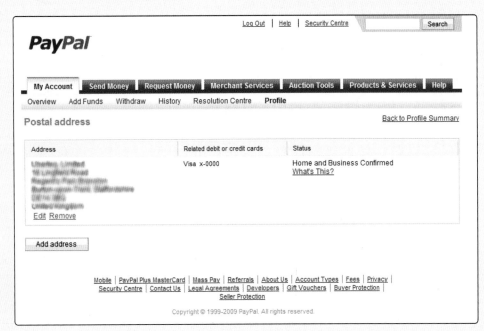

Problems With PayPal

It may be the most popular payment system on eBay, but don't be fooled by the hype; it's far from perfect...

PayPal has been with us for over ten years now, and as time has gone by, it has come to dominate online auction transactions the world over. These days, it's almost impossible to trade on eBay without holding such an account, thanks to the increasing tightening of eBay regulations in that area. But is it really all it's made out to be? Are there any chinks in its armour that you should be aware of?

Firstly, it would only be fair to point out that the vast majority of PayPal's millions of customers have never had a problem with the service. They find it both a convenient and reliable means for trading on eBay. For them, PayPal works exactly as it should, providing a means of transferring money from one account into another securely and without fuss. It's a free service for the buyer, and sellers don't mind paying a little bit extra in charges if it takes away the hassle of receiving payments.

However, the picture isn't quite as rosy as you might first think. There are countless horror stories of people having their accounts locked out, and being unable to access their money. Every day, millions of hoax e-mails get sent pretending to be from PayPal, and people have fallen for scams like this in the past. There are also plenty of users who feel hard done by when it comes to paying the charges set by both eBay and PayPal when selling an item. And, of course, there's the lack of choice presented to those consumers who wish to avoid the service altogether. They view PayPal's share of the market and lack of viable alternatives as being both anti-competitive and negative.

ACCOUNT FREEZES

It's important to remember that PayPal, despite handling some extremely large financial transactions, is not actually a bank. As such, it's not governed by the same rules and regulations that banks and similar organisations are. For this reason, it can attract money launderers and other criminal elements looking to transfer substantial sums of money without raising too many eyebrows. This was particularly rife in PayPal's early days, but since then, stricter security measures have been put in place, and there are now more regular audits and checks on people's accounts. The upshot of all this is that PayPal is now more a lot more careful and stringent with how it deals with potential cases.

One of the first things PayPal does when it notices discrepancies is to place a freeze on the account in question. This means that while an account is being investigated, all money is blocked from entering or leaving. In some cases, perfectly innocent people have had a lock placed on their account, and have had to wait months until the restriction was lifted and they could use their account again. As you can

▲ You can take a test on PayPal's website that helps you spot phishing e-mails

▲ PayPal's fees can soon add up, especially when you consider they come on top of the standard eBay charges

▲ PayPal has had its fair share of hackers and fraudsters over the years

imagine, this has left a fair few people unhappy, particularly as many of them rely on PayPal as a source of income.

The most practical advice here is to make sure that there's never a large sum of money resident in your PayPal account. It could be potentially disastrous if you can't get access to several thousand pounds, but not so if there's less money involved.

It's very rare for this to happen to anyone, but if you're worried that you may fall victim to this one day, the best thing to do is look at alternative payment systems to use instead. Unfortunately, for eBay users, however, they don't really have much choice in the matter.

It's notoriously easy to open a PayPal account, so it can be open to abuse, but just be careful with who you trade with, apply some common sense, and the problem can be minimised.

PHISHING AND HOAX E-MAILS

Hoax e-mails have been a problem that has plagued PayPal for a number of years now. If you ever receive a message purporting to be from PayPal, but something doesn't seem right (for example, you may be told that an item has been purchased from your account that you previously weren't aware of, or money has left your account that you didn't authorise), the safest thing to do is log into PayPal yourself to check. It always pays to be far too cautious than far too little. By clicking on the link in one of these hoax e-mails, you'll usually be redirected to

another website, which requests your bank details and other personal information. This is known as a phishing scam.

These e-mails look almost identical to official e-mails sent out by both PayPal and eBay, which can fool some people if they're not careful. The e-mail normally instructs the person to follow a link to a website, which again looks very similar to a legitimate site, whereupon they're asked to enter their bank details in order to verify the account.

It goes without saying that you shouldn't do this, because you're handing over all your personal information to a stranger. You should always be very wary when asked via e-mail to send any personal information. A little bit of common sense is required to spot these e-mails, but some scams are less obvious than others.

One of the biggest giveaways is the address in the browser. The link may say www.paypal.com, but when you click on it and actually visit the site, you'll find that you've been redirected somewhere else. It's best to always play safe.

If you're worried about falling victim to fraudsters and hackers, there are a few simple precautions that you can take in order to keep your account safe. These are all sensible procedures that you should follow for any online accounts involving finances or personal details.

Firstly, make sure you choose a good password that other people can't guess easily. Having your surname or part of your address as a password is a

MEMORABLE EBAY AUCTIONS

A MAMMOTH SKELETON

One of the five best-preserved prehistoric mammoth skeletons in the world sold on eBay for £61,000. It was 50,000 years old and weighed a massive 250,00kg.

▲ Phishing is one of the many scams PayPal users have to contend with

▲ Credit card fraud is one of the biggest problems facing the Internet today

risky move. Try to keep it as ambiguous as possible - nothing that a potential hacker will be able to easily guess. If you're worried that your details may still be in danger of falling into the wrong hands, then change it regularly.

Do not share your account details with anyone who isn't connected with PayPal itself. Certain hoax e-mails ask for this information, but you should always bypass these and log into your PayPal account by typing the web address in your browser. Never follow a link sent via e-mail, because this could be rerouted to another website.

When accessing your PayPal information, make sure the site is accessed through a secure connection. You can tell if it is by looking at the address bar. It should read 'https' rather than 'http' before the actual web address.

Keep on top of things too. Check your PayPal account regularly, in order to know exactly how much money is in there at any given time. It will show all your recent transactions, and if there's any unexpected activity on your account, you should be able to catch it as soon as possible.

DOUBLE CHARGES

PayPal sellers on eBay are hit with two sets of charges - something that has irked many users for some time now. When you decide to sell an item on eBay, you're charged an insertion fee, based on either the starting or reserve price. You may also be charged optional fees for various features that can be incorporated into the listing (such as a picture). The fees don't end there, though; when you make a sale, eBay then charges you a fee based on the final selling price. All well and good, but then if you make a sale using PayPal, you will also get charged an additional fee for the transaction (normally 3.4% plus £0.20). That's two sets of fees: one for eBay and the other for PayPal. This is particularly annoying when you consider that eBay owns PayPal, so you're pretty much paying the same company twice.

As a case in point, let's have a look at how much selling an item for £10 would cost you, with the list price starting at £0.01.

Item value: £10
eBay insertion fee: £0
eBay sale completion: £1
PayPal charge: £0.54
Total returned to you: £8.46

The more expensive the product, the more charges increase in value. For example:

Item value: £50
eBay insertion fee: £0
eBay sale completion: £5
PayPal charge: £1.90
Total returned to you: £43.10

Many sellers offset these fees by including them in the list price. The buyer will cover any charges in their purchase, as a consequence leaving the seller with more profit. As mentioned previously, you can

▲ PayPal and eBay - there's no escaping them!

use the online calculator at **www.ppcalc.com** to find out exactly how much charges will come to.

POOR CUSTOMER SERVICE

PayPal's customer service has also come under attack in some quarters, with the majority of complaints being centered around its support guarantee. Because PayPal doesn't operate under the same laws as a bank or financial organisation, many people are left disappointed when it comes to trying to claim money back. PayPal, it has be said, is almost a law unto itself.

If your claim is rejected by PayPal, and you feel that justice hasn't been done, apart from the police, there's nowhere else really that you can turn, short of something like the small claims court. It may offer guarantees, but these are only set by an extremely strict criteria that a seller must follow if they're to have any chance of winning their money back. Even then, if everything possible is done to follow the conditions set (all records and proof of postage have been kept, and the claim is within the period of response), PayPal can still decide to reject the claim.

Matters are only made worse with the lack of customer contact numbers on its website. If you wish to make a complaint, then you have to e-mail customer services and wait for a reply, which is hardly the swift response you need in a crisis.

So what can you do? If you're unhappy with your complaint to PayPal, you must obtain a letter from it that's known legally as a 'stalemate letter', confirming that there's a dispute. Once you receive that, you the have the right to complain to the Financial Ombudsman. A long, drawn out and rather painful process.

Like many things in life, PayPal is fine when it's working for you, but a complete pain when something goes wrong. Poor response times, unsatisfactory solutions and, most importantly, no way of legally challenging its decisions have resulted in some people losing a lot of money.

MARKET DOMINATION

PayPal has such a grip on eBay that buyers and sellers are almost forced to use it if they wish to trade. For more than two years now, it has been a compulsory ruling for new sellers on eBay's UK site to offer PayPal as a payment method in their listings. The rules are simple: if you don't use PayPal, you can't list your item. It argues that PayPal is the safest way of trading on the auction site, but this has still riled many people, who may have wished to avoid using it.

As it stands, the only category where PayPal isn't a must-have is in Motors, where by its very nature the

▲ It's hard to find any mention of rival payment services on eBay

collection and payment part of the transaction is normally dealt with in person.

The same ruling has been applied in other countries as well. That said, in Australia, eBay had to backtrack on its PayPal-only crusade. The ruling conflicted with the Australian Consumer Competition Commission, which forced eBay to delay making such widespread changes.

The PayPal-only plan effectively blocks other payment systems from use on eBay and, as such, many rival services are missing out on their share of any profits to be made. Buyers too, who may not wish to use PayPal, are equally left with no alternative options. Unfortunately, with eBay being as established as it is, there aren't many alternative auction sites to use either.

▲ In the early days, PayPal was no stranger to courts of law...

PayPal Alternatives

It's not just about PayPal when it comes to eBay. Here are some of the other web-based payment methods available

Without doubt PayPal is the king of web-based payment methods. Indeed, such is its dominance that you'd be forgiven for thinking it's the *only* web-based payment method, but it isn't - far from it. Of course, as an eBay seller, offering PayPal is in most cases compulsory. And as an eBay buyer, PayPal is both quick and convenient.

It's always good to have a back-up plan, though. As a seller, you'll sometimes encounter buyers for whom PayPal is a no-no. Maybe they've had their fingers burnt in the past. If you're able to offer an alternative, you could swing deals in your favour. And as a buyer, what if you get tangled up in a claim or dispute and your PayPal account becomes temporarily frozen? Being signed up with a different payment system could be a life-saver.

Generally, PayPal alternatives fall into two categories. First, there are those that eBay specifically permits: sellers are allowed to offer them. Second, there are those that eBay specifically forbids: sellers who offer them are likely get their listings pulled.

EBAY-COMPATIBLE PAYMENT SYSTEMS
The PayPal alternatives that eBay allows are sadly few and far between. Here's the list: Allpay.net, cash2india,

CertaPay, Checkfree.com, hyperwallet.com, Moneybookers.com, Nochex.com, Ozpay.biz, Paymate. com.au, Propay.com, XOOM. All but two can be discounted; they're either heavyweight merchant solutions or intended simply for person-to-person transfers. Some also unavailable in the UK. The only systems of interest are Moneybookers and Nochex.

MONEYBOOKERS
www.moneybookers.com
The Moneybookers website immediately inspires confidence. It's a very polished affair - more helpful and better organised than PayPal's. If there's safety in numbers, the 13 million account holders should inspire confidence too. Sure, 13 million is small potatoes compared to PayPal's 150 million, but it's a respectable figure nonetheless.

There are two types of account: Personal and Business. The nuts and bolts of the fee structure are shown below:

- Sending money = 1% (maximum £0.44)
- Receiving money = Free
- Funding = Free by bank transfer, cheque, Maestro, and Solo; 1.9% by credit card
- Withdrawals = £1.58 by bank transfer and credit card, £3.06 by cheque
- Currency conversions = 1.99%
- Border crossings = Free

Unlike PayPal, it's the buyer, not the seller, who gets stung for the fees. But just look at those fees; they're so

▲ Moneybookers: one of only a handful of PayPal alternatives

▲ Moneybookers' fees are generally very competitive

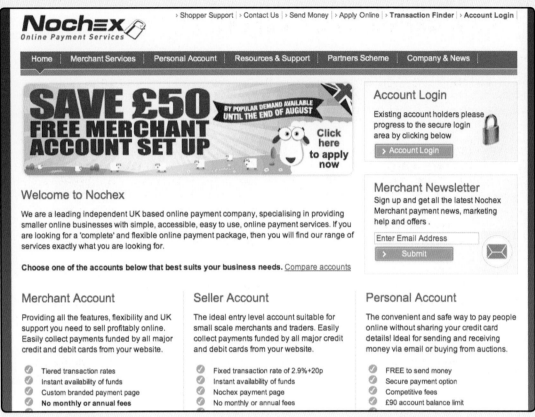

▲ Nochex: a worthy PayPal rival

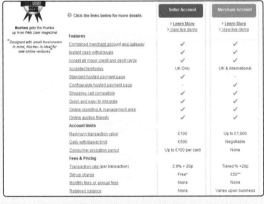

▲ The Nochex fee structure can be a little hard to understand

low they make PayPal look positively greedy. The snag, of course, is that buyers are never going to make payment via a service that charges them, not when they can use PayPal for free. Sellers can get round this, perhaps, by reducing the initial amount that buyers need to pay. The fees, once added on, will bring the total up to the full and proper purchase price.

Unfortunately, as a buyer, you have to fund your account in advance (the methods and fees for doing so are listed above). That means that if the cupboard's bare, you can't buy anything. With PayPal, of course, it's perfectly okay to keep your balance permanently at £0;

purchases just get charged directly to your bank account or credit or debit card. By comparison, then, the Moneybookers approach is a hassle.

Even so, Moneybookers is a worthy PayPal rival. In some ways it's superior - look at the options for withdrawals, for example. As a buyer, though, the choker is finding auctions that actually offer it. And as a seller, how do you persuade buyers away from PayPal? The chief issue there is that Moneybookers and eBay aren't integrated, so buyers will always have to visit the Moneybookers website and enter the transaction details themselves. First, they'll have to sign up for an account.

NOCHEX
www.nochex.com

Nochex, like Moneybookers, is based in the UK. Once again too, its website is polished and intuitive. There's no hint of how many account holders there are, but the company has had a presence on auction sites since 2001. Its name is also probably better known than Moneybookers'.

There are three account types: Personal, Seller, and Merchant. Broadly, these are aligned with PayPal's Personal, Premium, and Business accounts. The first of the bunch can be pretty much ignored, because it has some ludicrous restrictions. For example, you're not allowed to hold an account balance of more than £90 - a total deal-breaker for most people. All in all,

DID YOU KNOW?

PowerSellers are described by the auction house as "pillars of the eBay community", yet the BBC's Watchdog programme managed to buy a number of fake items from them. These included Prada shoes, Christian Dior bags and Adidas trainers.

the Seller account is the one for eBayers. The core features of this are:

- Sending money = Free
- Receiving money = 2.9% + £0.20 (regardless of your monthly receipts)
- Withdrawals = Free (£0.25 for less than £50)
- Maximum transaction value = £100
- Daily withdrawal limit = £500

An advantage over Moneybookers is that sellers pay the fees - just like PayPal. Also, there's no requirement for buyers to pre-fund their accounts - again, just like PayPal. One nasty downside to the service, though, is the maximum-transaction amount, which at a stroke renders Nochex unsuitable for sellers trading in items of high value. Also, the Seller account is UK-only; there's no facility to take payments from abroad or in foreign currencies.

You should be aware too that inactive accounts - those not used for six months or more - can be charged an administration fee of up to £5 per quarter (unless the balance is £0). Ouch.

Interestingly, and stealing a march on both Moneybookers and PayPal, buyers can make payment via Nochex even if they don't hold an account. However, such buyers can only spend up to £100 with any one card (in either a single transaction or several). Once that limit's reached, any further payments require a different card (with the same proviso). However, after 75 days from a card's first use, this restriction is lifted.

Like Moneybookers, Nochex is a worthy rival to the hugely dominant PayPal, and, like Moneybookers again,

it's managed to pick up a good reputation for customer service (PayPal could learn a thing or two there). Also, there are some great features, not least of which for low-volume sellers is the cracking 2.9% fee rate (compared to PayPal's 3.4%). As ever, though, the big downer is lack of eBay integration.

Of course, if you've got your own retail website outside of eBay, take a good look at the Nochex Merchant account. There's a £50 set-up fee, but it's definitely a big hitter - you even get a dedicated account manager. In terms of services, it's a system that operates in a similar fashion to Moneybookers' 'Gateway' affair.

NON-EBAY-COMPATIBLE PAYMENT SERVICES

Now it's time for the PayPal alternatives that eBay forbids. The list is long, but there's little point in printing it, because if a payment system isn't specifically permitted, you can assume it's banned.

Why would you need a payment system that isn't accepted on eBay, anyway? Well, as shown in Chapter 7, eBay isn't the only auction site in town. On these rival sites, PayPal doesn't have the same stranglehold. Being signed up to a PayPal alternative could be useful for buying and selling via classified ads as well, and also for sending monetary gifts to friends and family. Below is an overview of some of the better services.

PPPAY
www.pppay.com

According to eBay, it only permits payment systems that are safe, easy to use, and able to offer strong protection. However, like the other services detailed here, PPPay, a

▲ PPPay is popular on eBay rival eBid

UK company, meets every one of those requirements. For a start, it's the official payment method of eBay's increasingly popular rival eBid, and people are more than happy with the service there.

Could it be, then, that eBay's real reason for disliking PPPay is that it poses a serious threat to its own service, PayPal? Certainly the fees are competitive. There's a two-level scheme for receiving: payments from another PPPay account are free; payments via card attract a 3.3% commission. A slight downer is that sending or buying costs £0.49, and unfortunately there's also a 1% withdrawal fee (£0.75 minimum). Even so, use PPPay with confidence, especially as it's almost a must-join if you're planning to buy or sell on the UK's second most popular auction site (eBid).

NETELLER
www.neteller.com
Neteller might sound like a brand of chocolate spread, but there's definitely nothing nutty about it. As with PPPay, though, it's not clear why eBay feels justified in banning it - it's been around since 1999, has a solid UK foundation, and is even listed on the London Stock Exchange. It's true that Neteller is often the payment system of choice for funding accounts on gambling sites, so maybe it's felt this somehow tarnishes it.

Like Moneybookers, Neteller accounts have to be pre-funded. Doing that is free by bank transfer or debit card but 1.75% by credit card. Unlike Moneybookers, though, sending money costs nothing - in a more traditional manner, the recipient gets charged 1.9%. What really sets Neteller above the rest, however, is the Net+ debit card. You can use this to spend your account's funds at any online or high-street retailer that accepts MasterCard (no charge), and you can also use it for instant withdrawals at virtually any cash machine (£3 a time). It's a winning trick by any standard.

▲ Neteller's Net+ card is a serious incentive for signing up

GOOGLE CHECKOUT
checkout.google.com
When Checkout launched, it was regarded by many as a being full-on challenger to PayPal. However, in reality it's always been intended as a simple, competition-busting merchant process for online retailers looking for shopping-cart functionality. For example, there's no virtual bank account, so you can't store funds anywhere. All purchases must be done directly via card, and all receipts are deposited to your bank account.

Until February 2008, the fee for receiving was as low as mathematically possible: there wasn't one. Now, though, Checkout employs a tiered structure, with fees effectively identical to PayPal's. As a merchant system, though, it's got PayPal beat.

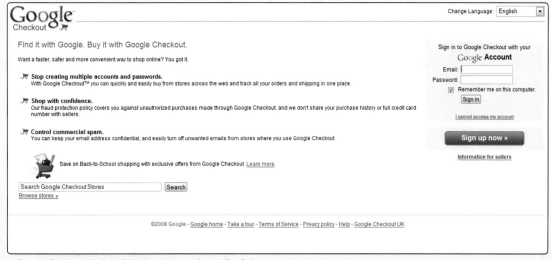

▲ Google Checkout isn't really in the same market as PayPal

MEMORABLE EBAY AUCTIONS

A HAUNTED PAINTING

'The Hands Resist Him' by Bill Stoneham came with a warning -when sold on eBay: "Do not bid on this painting if you are susceptible to stress-related disease, faint of heart or are unfamiliar with supernatural events." The painting, which the seller claimed to be haunted, sold for $1,025 on the back of the rather fanciful ghost story offered in the listing.

Chapter 7
eBay
Alternatives

Using PlayTrade

A comparably new service that's proving something of a rival to eBay and Amazon Marketplace...

One of the biggest online retailers in the UK is Play.com. Relatively recently, the firm launched its own attempt to muscle in on the likes of eBay and Amazon Marketplace in early 2007, entitled PlayTrade.

PlayTrade is a service through which sellers can put up items for sale at Play.com. A link to PlayTrade sellers then appears on virtually every item description page. This works in a similar manner to Amazon Marketplace, in that Play's own price for a product is prominently displayed, followed a little further down the screen by PlayTrade's best price.

The obvious limitation is that you can only sell items that Play.com itself stocks, and even then, you can't sell mobile content, clothing or accessories. A further restriction is that the sale of certain electronics and

gadgets is limited to what Play.com calls ProTraders. That said, there are still tens of thousands of products you can list as a standard user of PlayTrade. Furthermore, it also specifically allows you to list collectable versions of a product. Amazon Marketplace didn't use to do this, but has caught up since PlayTrade introduced the feature. As such, you can highlight a book signed by its author, or a very rare limited-edition DVD, for example.

PROS AND CONS

There are certain pros and cons to using the PlayTrade service, and the biggest advantage is price. Play.com charges a £0.50 fee per completed sale, and then a commission of 10% on the final item price (the

How To... Sell On PlayTrade

1 The first thing you need to do is find the item you want to sell. In our example, we've got a Tangled Blu-ray we'd like to list, so we choose the Sell Your Stuff option at the bottom of the screen.

2 This brings you to a search box. We choose DVD & Blu-ray from the drop-down menu, typed in 'Tangled', and hit 'Search'. If we had an ISBN, UPC or EAN number, then that could be entered directly.

3 Now you should be at this screen. We're selling the Double Play Edition (do make sure you choose the exact version of anything you're selling) Thus, all we need to do here is click on the 'Sell This Item' button to the right of it.

4 That brings you here, to a screen that looks very similar to its Amazon equivalent. Here, we fill in details regarding the condition of our item, and any extra information. Use the Comments box to elaborate regarding the item's condition, if necessary (particularly useful if it's a collectable item you're selling!), and you can select delivery region by scrolling to the bottom of the screen. Hit 'Continue'.

5 Now it's time to set a price. Remember, the amount has to include delivery costs! Use the Play.com price and the current lowest price on PlayTrade as a guideline. Go over those amounts too much, and you'll have little chance of attracting a sale.

exception to the rule is with tickets, where Play.com pockets 15% of the sale price, on top of the £0.50 completion fee). That's keenly competitive with its major rivals (especially eBay now), and may be tantalising enough to tempt a few sellers, who are fed up with the service that other e-tailers are offering. As with Amazon Marketplace, there's no listing fee, and you only pay a fee should you sell a product.

However, in line with Play.com's policy of offering free shipping across the board, the price that you sell your item for must include postage and packing, so an allowance needs to be made for that. It's a great feature for a buyer, but may prove a headache for a seller. Furthermore, compared to Amazon Marketplace and eBay, PlayTrade is a service that's still comparably in its infancy. Thus, its userbase is smaller, although that could, conversely, make it easier to be noticed. That said, PlayTrade has been growing at speed for the past three years, and this is less of a problem than it was.

Do note, however, that PlayTrade has slightly different delivery demands from the likes of Amazon. Firstly, there's the aforementioned inability to add a shipping charge. Secondly, Play.com requires you to post out

ProTrader

Sellers who intend to move a reasonable number of items through PlayTrade may want to consider the ProTrader option. ProTraders don't have to pay the £0.50 fee on each of their listings, instead paying a £19.99 monthly subscription. This makes it a worthwhile option for those selling more than 20 individual items.

Further benefits include being able to list more than 100 items at once, and the ability to list items in otherwise restricted categories. Furthermore, special volume selling tools are also made available.

However, not all applications to become a ProTrader are successful, as Play.com has extra security checks for those who apply.

your item within 24 hours of a sale taking place. That's a little quicker than the one to two days you're given by Amazon, and this needs to be taken into consideration.

Most other features are broadly in line with what you'd expect. Funds, for instance, are deposited in a PlayFunds account, which incurs a 5% transfer fee when you withdraw money. There's no fee if you use these funds as credit towards a Play.com purchase, however. PlayTrade also works on a similar feedback system to its rivals, where positive and negative scores can be applied.

6 Further down the same screen, here you need to state what country you'll be posting the item from (usually UK), how many you have to sell (one in our case) and an optional reference code. The latter would be useful if you have lots of listings to manage! All done? Hit 'Continue'. and move on.

7 At this stage, you'll either have to sign in if you haven't already, or create an account if you don't have one. Both are straightforward enough. You ultimately end up at the item confirmation screen where, if you're happy with everything, you can press the 'Confirm Listing' button. That's it!

MEMORABLE EBAY AUCTIONS

VIRGINITY

Several women have auctioned - or attempted to auction - their virginity on eBay. Bristol student Rosie Reid, 18, did so to help fund her course. The auction site withdrew the sale, but she continued on her own website. She eventually lost her virginity to a 44-year-old BT engineer for £8,400. When 22-year-old Los Angeles student Natalie Dylan launched a similar auction, eBay again pulled it. She eventually held her auction at a Nevada brothel. "We live in a capitalist society," she argued. "Why shouldn't I be allowed to capitalise on my virginity?"

Should You Use Amazon Instead?

eBay isn't the only place you can buy from, and there are a lot of good alternatives, including one very familiar name

If you dig out the list of the UK's 50 most popular online retailers, compiled by IMRG-Hitwise and published regularly, you'll discover that it managed to include the same company twice in its top ten released in July 2010. And no, this wasn't a mistake, or some kind of typo. Instead, this was testament to the global reach and power of one of e-tailing's biggest names.

Leading the chart, as it pretty much always does and has done since the list first came about, was Amazon.co.uk. It's held this position for some time, and sits ahead of the likes of Argos, Play.com and Tesco. But number four in the list is the firm's American arm, Amazon.com. Incredibly, it's actually gone up since last year, too, overtaking Tesco, which now sits in fifth. It's staggering to think that so many UK residents favour shopping at an American-based site - with high postage charges and customs fees to consider - over the thousands of UK alternatives. Such is the power of the Amazon name.

It's worth noting that said list excludes online auction houses, or else no doubt eBay would march straight into the top slot (or at least put up a mighty fight for it), but it does also highlight the fact that there's a potent alternative if you decide eBay is not for you.

THE AMAZON ROUTE

For many years now, Amazon has run its Marketplace service, which allows small traders to offer their products on the site. Marketplace's big advantage is that it potentially lists your price alongside Amazon's on the same single product screen. So should a buyer search for a paperback copy of Stieg Larsson's The Girl Who Played With Fire, the product screen offers the choice to pay Amazon's price, but underneath that is a box labeled 'More Buying Choices', listing the lowest available price from new and second-hand alternatives. Clicking on that box will bring up a list of sellers and the prices they're charging.

Inevitably, this makes the Amazon Marketplace service even more price-focused than eBay, and the lowest price nearly always wins here. Even if you're only a few pence over the current lowest price, yours inevitably won't be the listing that buyers will be clicking on, unless there's a distinct positive difference in the condition of your item. On the upside, it does get your listing on the world's biggest online retailer, and gives it surprising prominence too.

Yet there's a hefty downside: Amazon takes a sizeable amount of your purchase price as a result. Considering it handles the entire transaction for you - processing the credit card payment, generating a packing slip, providing e-mail communication - you

◀ Amazon Marketplace listings are increasingly popular

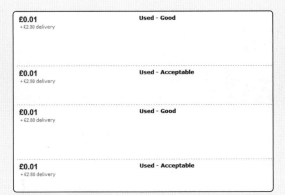

£0.01 +£2.80 delivery	Used – Good
£0.01 +£2.80 delivery	Used – Acceptable
£0.01 +£2.80 delivery	Used – Good
£0.01 +£2.80 delivery	Used – Acceptable

▲ Traders can sell books for just a penny, and make the money back on postage charges

◄ Here, Marketplace sellers are offering a music CD for over £3 less than the official Amazon download version costs!

get a bit more for your money. Amazon charges an £0.86 fee on completion of every purchase, in addition to 17.25% of the selling price (an amount that decreases to 11.5% if it's an item in the electronics or photo categories).

HARRY POTTER

Imagine you sold a copy of Harry Potter And The Deathly Hallows for £5. Out of that money, for starters, would come that £0.86 charge, so we're down to £4.14. Take away 17.25% of £5 as well, which knocks a further £0.86 out of your takings, and the money that you're credited with from the sale is £3.28.

Only it isn't, because on top of that - and this is a bonus - Amazon also allows you a generous domestic postage allowance, which varies depending on what item you're sending. You have no variance on postage costs, because Amazon rigidly applies a uniform amount, so for a DVD it's £1.26, while for a videogame £2.03 is allowed. Books have a generous £2.80 allowance, and what's more, Amazon doesn't support postage discounts for multiple purchase. So for two slim paperbacks, Amazon automatically charges your buyer two lots of £2.80. However, there's a slight hit here, as Amazon also charges an administration fee on said delivery charges. On books, the admin fee - which is in addition to the large slice that Amazon already takes - is £0.49, leaving the postage credit at £2.31.

Let's go back to our (VAT-exempt) Harry Potter book. When we left it, we had £3.28 of our £5 sale price left. When we add the £2.80 to it, Amazon is now giving us £6.08 for the sale, and is taking the aforementioned £0.49 administration charge off. The total to us, therefore, is £5.59, and Amazon transfers our money every fortnight directly into our bank account. If ever you wonder why Amazon sellers sell books for £0.01, it's down to the generosity of this postage allowance, presumably calculated with a good hardback in mind. A paperback book, in reality, would cost less than £0.50 to post. For certain items, then, the Amazon service is well worth using.

There's no listing fee, and your item remains on the site for 60 days. You pay nothing unless your items sells. For items that people go to Amazon for regularly - books and DVDs being prime examples - there's a hefty procession of potential customers likely to see your listing. If you're a Pro-Merchant seller (a status designed for those selling more than 30 items a month), then items stay on the site until sold.

However, there's a further fly in the ointment where Amazon is concerned: you can only place Marketplace listings alongside items that the site already sells. Therefore, if you have a DVD for sale that Amazon doesn't, you simply can't add it. Furthermore, if you have 50 copies of a new major book release coming in, you can't list them until it has been released; you won't be able to try to attract preorders, even if Amazon has a listing page up for the product concerned.

Selling Toys

Given the large number of individuals who look to sell toys and games in the run-up to Christmas, and presumably given the corresponding increase in fraudulent sellers at that time of year, Amazon places strict criteria in place for this category at certain points of the year.

Amazon generally stops accepting new sellers into the Toys & Games category from September of each year. Furthermore, for a seller to list toys or games between mid-November and early January, Amazon asks that they've shipped at least 25 orders using Marketplace, and that they have a defect rate of at most 1%. These are restrictions to the Toys & Games category only, and it means that sellers looking to do business in this sector at the most lucrative time of the year need to plan ahead to be able to do so. If you fail to do so, you won't be allowed to sell your wares.

How To... List An Item On Amazon Marketplace

Assuming you already have an account with Amazon - which you will have if you've ever bought anything from the site before - it's not too tricky to get yourself selling on Amazon Marketplace. Here's how:

1 Here, we're on an item page on the Amazon site. See that 'Have One To Sell?' option on the right of the screen? That's where we're going to start. Give it a click.

2 You need to choose what you want to sell. For this example, we're going to sell a copy of One Day by David Nicholls in paperback. You can head to a special 'Sell Your Stuff' page at https://www.amazon.co.uk/gp/seller/sell-your-stuff.html to do a search for your item. Then click on 'Sell Yours Here'.

3 With books, you can also search by the likes of ISBN number, but seeing as it's a very popular title we're selling, it's unsurprisingly popped up at the top of the list. We're selling the 2010 paperback edition, which is first in the list, so we're going to click the 'Sell Yours Here' button to the right of it.

4 Check that you've picked the right item, and then enter the condition of the item from the drop-down menu. Our One Day had never been read and was in very good condition,. So we're choosing 'Used - Very Good'.

5 On the same screen, there's the option to add extra comments to your listing. In the same way you would with an eBay listing, this is where you should declare anything particular about the product. How damaged is it? Is it signed? Is it shrink-wrapped? Here's the place to let people know.

6 Hit 'Continue' and then it's time to set your price. Amazon tells you its own price, and the cheapest alternative already available from Marketplace sellers.

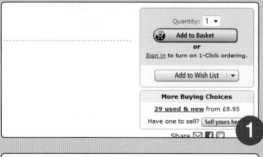

DID YOU KNOW?

There isn't much you can't sell on eBay, but some items are forbidden. These include plane tickets, alcohol, firearms, tobacco, credit cards, human body parts, lottery tickets, soiled underwear, drugs and lock-picking devices.

You can click on the list on the right to see if the low price is one seller or the general consensus, and then set your price accordingly. It's a good idea to at least undercut Amazon's price!

7 Scroll down the screen, and you then need to indicate how many copies you have to sell, where you're willing to ship to, and if you offer express delivery. We've only got one, and are only selling within the UK. And we've no express delivery, either. Once you've made your choices, click 'Continue'.

8 If you aren't already, you need to be logged in. First-time sellers now have to set up a selling account. If you haven't done this already, then you need to do so. If you have, then you'll end up at the confirmation screen.

9 That's it! Your listing is ready to go. Carefully check all the information that you're about to list, and hit the 'Submit Your Listing' button. You'll also find on this screen a breakdown of the fees and what Amazon will pay you if the item sells. Well done; you've listed your first item on Amazon!

Amazon used to try to compensate for this with its own Auctions and zShops services, but both of these seem to have been quietly closed down. The latter has migrated into the Marketplace services, while the former was simply unable to compete with the might of eBay. However, for the determined seller, there are still a couple of other tools at Amazon worth exploring.

AMAZON ADVANTAGE

Amazon Advantage is a scheme aimed at small publishers that are looking to get their products listed on the main Amazon site. It's available in the Books, Music and DVD & Video categories at Amazon, and allows you to manually add a new product into the site's catalogue, ready to be sold (although Amazon will review it before uploading it, a process that takes several working days).

Amazon Advantage is not a service that lends itself to someone clearing out the contents of their loft or garage, however, and is firmly targeted at those publishing their own works. That means certain requirements are in place. For instance, all books must have an ISBN number and scannable barcode, while a DVD must be shrink-wrapped and also fulfill the barcode criteria.

Furthermore, you have to formally apply for an account with the service, and pay an annual membership fee of £23.50. On top of that, you'll be expected to cover the cost of delivering your products to Amazon's warehouse, and of any returns to you.

Yet therein lies the key to Amazon Advantage. With Marketplace, you may be holding your stock in a spare room or in a cupboard (unless you have a business account and pay for Amazon to handle fulfilment for you), but with Amazon Advantage, everything's fulfilled by Amazon itself. So, should you be trying to publish a book, Amazon will initially take a copy off you, and if it sells, will order a few more. If sales continue to increase, more will be ordered. Amazon expects a (large) discount on the product you're looking to sell, so it can make its own mark-up on the product, yet Advantage remains a potent and useful way for smaller media producers to break onto the site.

For the buyer, the product will appear to be just another item shipped and sold by Amazon itself, and - assuming you take some time to get a strong description, and have good images - they're likely to be oblivious to the fact it's a small publisher behind it.

Seller Account

To set up an Amazon Seller account, you need a credit card, bank account, address and phone number ready. Amazon makes an automated phone call to you as part of the process, where you need to input a supplied PIN number. From there, you'll set up your financial information so Amazon can send you money from your sales.

Further Alternatives

Determined to find somewhere other than eBay or Amazon to do business? Here are some further options

According to some, it's the second most popular UK online auction site, but eBid nonetheless trails eBay by some way. However, unlike many of its other auction rivals, there's enough business done over on eBid to warrant at least taking a look. Certainly it manages to bring in a reasonable number of page views and item bids (it boasted over 2 million auctions when we were visiting), and it might be worth trying if you're struggling to find a niche on eBay.

Its big selling point is the fact that it doesn't take listing fees up front, instead charging you based on a final value fee, so there's no fee if you don't sell your item. Furthermore, you can pay a subscription, or a one-off charge, to quality for Seller+ status. The price for this ranges from £1.99 for a week, through to £74.99 for a lifetime. The big advantage is that you won't have to pay a final value fee ever again.

CQOUT (WWW.CQOUT.CO.UK)

CQOut - or Seek You Out - used to claim to be the UK's second largest marketplace, and it too is an online auction site that's existing in eBay's slipstream. It does boast a reasonable number of auctions, though, even though many of them appear to be Instant Buy auctions, eschewing bids in favour of an immediate outright sale.

When you sign up for selling, you're charged a £2 admin fee, and after that, there's no listing fee (unless

▲ Flogital is one man's hobby, but it's free to use

▲ CQOut is a popular alternative

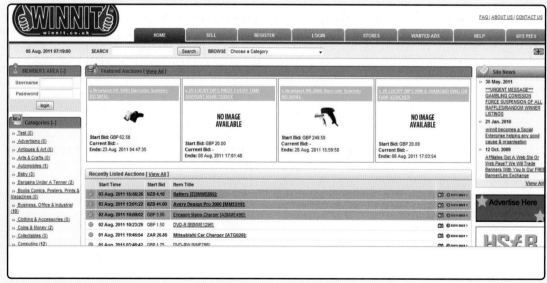

▲ Another alternative is Winnit

◀ Tazbar was successful for a while, but shut up shop in July 2009

you opt for extras such as second category listing or extra images), as CQOut charges a percentage of the item sale. It boasts too that its fees are less than eBay's, and presents a comparison on its site for your perusal.

CQOut has endured for many years, although it seems to offer little threat to eBay in the auction site business. Still, if you don't mind paying the initial administration fee, you might find you attract a new buyer or two by giving it a try (even if the business you get is likely to be moderate compared to eBay).

WINNIT (WWW.WINNIT.CO.UK)

Formerly known as Auctions-United, Winnit is a UK auction site that's again trying to move in on eBay's market. It charges a listing fee, starting at just a penny, as well as a final commission of 1% on listings. However, there doesn't seem to be much traffic at all heading towards the site, and lower footfall means less chance of a sale. One of the most popular areas of the site used to be its adult listings, but these appear to have been discontinued now. What that leaves behind, though, is pretty much an empty auction site, with little sign of much custom around.

FLOGITALL (WWW.FLOGITALL.COM)

FlogItAll appears to enjoy an even smaller audience than the sites already mentioned, but this one isn't the

Specialist

If you have a particular niche hobby, then it's always worth doing an Internet search to see if you can find a selling community specific to that interest. After all, while eBay brings in great quantities of buyers, there's little guarantee that it'll attract people specifically concerned with the type of items you're selling.

The same applies if you're buying; for instance, you'll find travel agents with auction modules as part of their service, offering late deals. It's an idea that's replicated in many sectors, so it's well worth hunting around.

work of an international conglomerate. Instead, it's one man's hobby, which he funds himself and, as such, it doesn't charge listing fees. It's entirely free to use.

YAHOO! AUCTIONS, QXL & TAZBAR

After many years of trying to unsuccessfully compete with eBay and Amazon, Yahoo! opted to 'retire' its US auction service in June 2007. In territories where Yahoo! Auctions is still popular - namely Hong Kong, Singapore and Taiwan - the service continues to exist, and thrive.

The British arm of Yahoo! Auctions was closed down even earlier, in 2002, with a holding page still in place that directs users to eBay in its place.

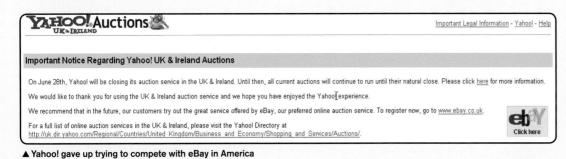

▲ Yahoo! gave up trying to compete with eBay in America

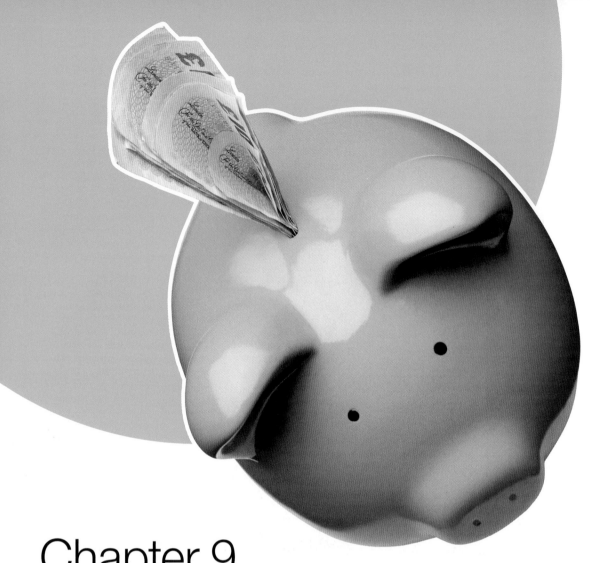

Chapter 9
Reviews
Directory

Reviews Directory

Over the following pages, we've tested a collection of products to help you with eBay, starting with buying & searching tools...

AUCTION AUTO BIDDER
www.auctionautobidder.com

★★★☆☆

$14.99
PC - Windows 98 or later

If you want to give people as little time as possible to beat your bid on eBay, then you want to be placing it as late as possible. That's a job that Auction Auto Bidder offers to take off your hands, among many other tasks. There's a lot packed in.

It's a collection of tools that allows you to watch, favourite and view certain listings, and you can also program the software to put in a late bit, in the same manner as sniping software. The package also includes a web browser, which it encourages you browse the web using. It's not compulsory, though.

It's a good collection of tools, here, and once you've tweaked the program so that it defaults to eBay's UK site, there's a good chance you'll find it all quite useful.

AUCTION INTELLIGENCE
www.auctionintelligence.com

★★☆☆☆

Free
Online service

Searching eBay is easy enough, but one thing you can't control is other people's typing or spelling abilities. For example, searching for 'PlayStation 3' will yield plenty of results, but you'll miss listings for such incorrect entries as 'Plastation' or 'Playtation', possibly losing out on some great bargains.

Auction Intelligence tries to address this problem, and using the service you can return incorrectly typed results for the item you're looking for. Simply type in the correct item name, and then click the search button, and you'll see a list of incorrectly typed entries and, hopefully, some good deals too.

A useful little tool, the service would score higher if it let you enter search criteria with more than one word, but it's still handy.

AUCTION LOTWATCH
www.auctionlotwatch.co.uk

★★★☆☆

Free
Online service

Saving precious time is paramount these days, and while some things can't be rushed, checking for the latest bargains on eBay needn't be a long and arduous task. In fact, you can search for items without even going to the website or downloading any new software.

A quick visit to Auction Lotwatch will grant you access to a speedy and easy search tool that can scour eBay, as well as a few other auction sites, in seconds, returning with a list of applicable items. Once the list has been retrieved, you can then view the items, prices and time left, and you can also click the direct link to the eBay page itself.

This is a great way to quickly view and compare auctions, and there's even an option to show common misspellings for the item you've searched for, so you can widen the search and include items you may usually miss due to typos.

As Auction Lotwatch is a website-based service, you don't need any extra software, and can access it from anywhere. But, although useful, the search results aren't as in depth as a dedicated program, and the difference between searching this way and using eBay itself isn't that great. However, if you want to compare auctions on eBay to similar additions on other auction sites, you should find this useful.

AUCTION REMIND
www.auctionremind.com

★★★☆☆

Free
Online service

If you fancy using your e-mail inbox to gather search results, Auction Remind may be for you. This is search automation of a different type. Register, then log in and launch a search and the service does the virtual legwork for you.

Whenever it turns up items that meet your criteria, it'll fire off an e-mail with the details.

The benefit of this is that you can retrieve finds from anywhere you can access your e-mail, and don't need to be at your own desk to learn of bargains. The downside, of course, is that you have to access your mail to receive results, but if you're an on-the-go type and frequently download e-mail anyway, this may suit.

The Auction Remind site states a very firm privacy policy but, nevertheless, a web-based disposable e-mail account may be in order. It also says you can cancel your account at any time, and it's an interesting free option to consider.

AUCTIONFINAL
www.auctionfinal.com

★★★☆☆

Free
Online service

Gazumping other eBay bidders at the last second is one of the best ways to get the items you desire on the world's biggest auction site, but this can be tricky at the best of times. Another way to get a good deal is to seek out auctions with no interest, and making a token bid before it closes.

AuctionFinal is an Internet tool that gives you this ability. Using the search engine provided on the site, you can choose any eBay site (from all the global eBay outlets), choose the time left before the auction finishes and select a specific category (including 'all'). The engine will then return a list of auctions matching your criteria that are about to close, giving you the chance to win auctions for next to nothing.

Results include item descriptions, end time, time left and the asking price, and you can click on any results to go straight to the eBay page.

This is a very useful tool for snooping out bargains but unfortunately, you can't manually type in actual product criteria, and can only search via eBay categories. Still, it's a handy trick to have up your sleeve, even with this limitation.

AUCTIONPIXIE SEARCH
www.auctionpixie.co.uk/search
★☆☆☆☆
Free
Online service

AuctionPixie produces a few eBay tools, and this particular app enables eBay browsers to search for misspelled items.

To use the tool, all you need to do is enter your search terms and click the Search button. AuctionPixie will then turn up any results for you. Options are very limited, with only the search box and a listing of recently searched for items.

Sadly, AuctionPixie just isn't very good, and several searches we ran turned up no results, despite

competing tools finding plenty. And the description for this tool still contains a typo, which doesn't instil confidence.

AUCTION SIDEBAR TOOL VERSION 2.91
www.auctionsidebar.com/download.htm
★★★★☆
Free
PC - Vista or Windows 7

Certainly one of the most visually pleasing eBay sidebars around, the Auction Sidebar Tool provides at-a-glance information about all of your current eBay bids, sales or watches. With product images, prices, number of bids and time left, this little tool can keep you on top of things at all times.

Also included is an eBay search bar, your own feedback and the ability to send notification pop-ups to you, making sure you're in the know. For more information, you can activate flyout windows simply by clicking on each item.

This is a very popular tool for eBay users, and deservedly so. It's small, easy to use and can provide all the info you need to stay on top of your account.

AUCTIONSLEUTH
www.auction-sleuth.com
★★★★☆
15-day free trial; $70 for lifetime licence
PC/Mac

Finding items interesting enough to part you from your cash can take a long time using eBay's standard search. Yes, it does the job, but it can be a laborious process at times. Luckily, AuctionSleuth can help improve this whole system.

The core of the program is made up of a powerful, user-

configured search engine. This allows custom searches throughout eBay based on the criteria you put in. This can be very specific, showing you results that meet your conditions to the letter, and you can also use the program to list auctions that are only a short time from ending, giving you a chance to jump in.

A very useful feature of AuctionSleuth is its ability to search for any new Buy It Now items that meet your criteria, and it includes being able to perform automatic refreshes at set times, so you can stay on top of new items without having to manually search for them.

Also included in the program is a fully integrated sniping tool. This isn't an online service, but runs from the installed program, and can make sure you're able to grab that last successful bid.

Other features include e-mail notifications, pop-up alerts, SMS text alerts and support for multiple users. And, as this isn't a pay per auction service, there are no extra bid costs, or winning auction fees.

This is a great tool that contains a wealth of valuable options and, for the relatively meagre price, it's certainly worth a punt.

AUCTIONSIEVE
www.auctionsieve.com
★★★☆☆
Free
PC/Mac

As the author of this tool states, searching eBay can be a very hit-and-miss affair, and also a time-consuming one. Finding the best items and weeding out those you're not interested in is a pain. With this program, you'll be able to filter the results, separating the wheat from the chaff.

To use the tool, you first need to build your preferences and individual searches. This is done by choosing categories to create

your 'sieves', and then using these to filter out the first level of unwanted items. You can then add 'catch words' to your searches to further trim down results to items that contain these words. To ditch items you're not interested in, you add words to the 'Trash Words' list, and any items that contain words in this list will be removed from your results.

This is a simple system, but one that, if handled correctly, can make finding items you're looking for much easier. However, it can also hint at sledgehammer tactics and, if you're not careful, you can filter out too many results with the wrong word filters.

AUCTION TYPO
www.auction-typo.com
★★★☆☆
Free
Online service

As with many similar services offered online, Auction Typo can help find eBay sales where the seller has misspelled the item description, usually meaning that you'd never see the result in your listings.

By typing in the correct spelling and then clicking the search button, the search engine will scour eBay for any similar, misspelled results, and will then take you to the corresponding eBay search results page. All correctly spelled results can be excluded, so you can browse through just the items you might not normally see.

You can filter results by choosing PayPal or Buy It Now items only, and you can elect to exclude words to further limit the results.

EBAY BUDDY UK
addons.mozilla.org/en-US/firefox/addon/11398
★★★☆☆
Free
Firefox

With eBay Buddy installed, you'll be able to use the Firefox right-click context menu to access all sorts of eBay functions and screens, regardless of the website you're currently on. There are quick links to selling and buying items, your 'My eBay' page, and the eBay community. In these sections are further menus, including links to the usual buying and selling tools, as well as web stores. You can even highlight text on a page and double-click eBay Buddy to search the auction site, all without touching the keyboard.

Any extra ways to access your tools or services above and beyond the norm are welcome, and integrating eBay with the Firefox browser so seamlessly here is a good thing indeed. Sadly, at the time of writing, eBay Buddy doesn't work with the latest version of Firefox, and we can but conclude that work on the software has ceased, sadly.

INVISIBLE AUCTIONS
www.invisible-auctions.com

★★★☆☆

Free
Online service

Being able to find auctions with misspelled titles can be a very good way to uncover some great deals among the thousands upon thousands of items on eBay, and using Invisible Auctions you'll be able to get the upper hand. The Invisible Auctions website allows you to search for particular items, such as a brand name or specific product, on the global eBay sites, and the results supplied include the misspelled versions for the item you're looking for.

Additional options in the search include the ability to view Buy It Now items only, eBay Shops only and completed auctions. You can also search in both the title and description. You can filter results

to wrong spelling, right spelling or both right and wrong, but the wrong spelling option is the best one to use to find better deals.

There are plenty of similar tools on the Internet, and Invisible Auctions is comparable to many of them. However, it's still a useful service to have when you're planning to purchase any items from the world's biggest auction, so take a look.

OS X DASHBOARD WIDGET
auctionmonitor.net/widget.php

★★★☆☆

Free
Mac OS X

Designed for the Apple Mac, this widget doubles up as both an eBay search bar and an auction monitor. When collapsed, the search bar functions like any other, and you can quickly browse eBay for any items of interest. By clicking the expand arrow, you can unveil a full list of any items that you're currently bidding on or watching, as well as those you're selling on the site. This information includes the prices and remaining time. The program also links to your 'My eBay' page, and is updated automatically.

Very similar to the Vista Sidebar Gadget (produced by the same team), this is a simple tool that provides simplified information. There's no advanced features as such, but for speedy updates of your eBay activities, this is a good tool to have.

SEARCH GNOME
www.searchgnome.com

★★★★★

Free
PC

With awards from many respectable software sites, Search Gnome is a powerful and

popular eBay search tool that contains many advanced search features not usually available to eBay users.

The program, once downloaded and installed, allows you to search through eBay as you'd expect, but also has a few nice extras. You can add searches to the application and save them, getting rid of the need to set up searches each time you need them, and you can quickly see any items that were added to eBay since the last time you searched. Even items that have been updated are clearly identified by the program, so you're always up to date. The program also makes it easy to search for items where the seller has spelled item names incorrectly. All this is handled via a single application window, and buttons will link instantly to the item pages that you wish to view.

SHORTSHIP
shortship.com/firefox.html

★★★☆☆

Free
Firefox

It's an age-old problem. You think you've found a bargain, only to get hit by tax or other unseen costs. Shopping on eBay isn't immune to this, and you'll often see a great deal, then reel back as the shipping cost offsets the 'bargain'.

ShortShip is a free Firefox add-on that will add an extra sortable column to the end of eBay search results. This will automatically total together the sale price and the shipping, so you can see exactly what the whole cost of an item is.

SportShip also performs currency conversion, so if you're browsing for items on the American version of eBay, then you'll be able to see what the items cost in British currency.

Listing Tools

ALIENFILES
www.alienfiles.net

★★★★☆

£39.99; free trial
PC/Mac

Ask any kind of seller, whether a shopkeeper, market trader or eBay merchant, and they'll all agree that one of the most important things to consider when selling items is appearance. This applies to both the item you're selling and yourself (or your shop). People are far more likely to buy a product that looks good, is presented well and is sold by someone who clearly knows what they're doing. Therefore, investing in a tool that can improve the look of your listings is a good idea.

Enter AlienFiles. No, this isn't a secret FBI department investigating extraterrestrial occurrences, but is instead a suite of tools that can give your item's listing a helping of sale bling. Using this program, you can change listings from simple text and images, to advertisements that feature image galleries, feedback displays, scrolling banners, Flash adverts and even embedded video clips. These listings are formatted in attractive templates, which can look far better than the usual white background, blocks of text and small images.

The program doesn't require any knowledge of HTML or other coding, and uses a simple interface that looks similar to a word processor, and even includes a spell-checker, so you can nail those ever present typos before committing anything to eBay. Most sections of the tool use a similarly straightforward interface, with plenty of guidance

and tabbed options. Even adding a map to your location is easy.

There are no image-hosting costs, and you can also add other files, such as Microsoft Office documents (.doc, .xls, etc.), and video clips use the now familiar YouTube Flash player embedded into your listings. All of your creations can be saved, so you can use them or edit them later for additional items.

AlienFiles is an accomplished and intuitive tool, and using it should be a cakewalk for even the most inexperienced computer or eBay user. More advanced users with HTML knowledge won't get much from the program, though, as they'll be able to achieve the same results for free.

GARAGESALE
www.iwascoding.com

★★★★☆

From $39.99 (£26 approx)
single user
Mac OSX

GarageSale 6 offers an alternative to eBay's own, often slow, listing tool and is tailored for eBay users who access the site on Macs. Versions are also available too for iPad and iPhone/iPod Touch.

The program itself makes full use of the usual, attractive Mac-style interface, and within this you can easily put together appealing ads for your items. Text can be added and formatted, font styles can be changed and images can be placed and manipulated.

The program features free image-hosting, 140 included templates, a built-in scheduler for automatically starting auctions, and compatibility

with iPhoto, so you can access your photos directly from the service for use in your listings. There's also a messaging system and full support for eBay stores. Newly added Twitter support, embedding of YouTube videos and Bonjour network sharing are also among the features.

GarageSale is a slick program with excellent support, including tutorial videos, FAQs and PDF manual resources, and the newest improvements make it an even more useful sales tool for Mac owners.

MISTER POSTER
classic.auctiva.com/products/
MisterPoster.aspx

★★★★★

Free
PC

Larger-scale eBay sellers will know that posting batches of items onto eBay through the default site tools can be a chore, taking up a ton of precious time. Mister Poster is a tool designed to alleviate this problem and can make the process far easier and, more importantly, faster.

Mister Poster lets you quickly create and preview item entries, and is able to create whole batches of items to be added to your eBay account. Items can be scheduled to be added at certain times and you can also import old batches from eBay's Mr Lister.

Mister Poster has been designed with bulk sellers in mind, so any users who have plenty of merchandise to list should find this a very useful tool indeed.

This is a great little program that really should save plenty of time. Adding hundreds of items in a day is made far, far easier and the addition of scheduled listings means you can even set items up ahead of time and the program will add them automatically at the

specified moment. This is great if you need to be somewhere and can't wait around.

LISTING FACTORY 2011
www.auctionlistingcreator.com

★★★★☆

$49.95 (£30.68 approx)
Standard, $89.95 (£55.25 approx) Pro
PC - Windows XP or later

Listing Factory 2011 is a step-by-step system to creating eBay listings. Like many other listing applications, the program is designed to make creating listings easier than using eBay's standard set of tools. It does this by letting users enter text and import images, to then tweak and arrange them into an attractive ad.

The program comes with a range of templates, and these can be tailored to your own needs, with images, galleries and other customisable content being available.

The interface is clean and efficient, and all the options are clearly displayed, rather than hidden away in awkward menus. Also, some of the supplied templates are well designed and implemented, offering some of the best examples seen in any listing app.

Along with the easy-to-use editor, the program offers free image-hosting (100MB with Standard and 400MB for Pro), no image dimension restrictions, no monthly fees, and one licence can be used on two PCs.

Listing Factory 2011 s a great little tool, and one that's been thought out well. All the tools included are useful, and the templates (and the ability to edit them so easily) are a welcome resource. It's a little expensive for this type of application, though, especially for the Pro version, which doesn't really offer all that much more than the Standard package.

Sniping Tools

AUCTION SENTRY
www.auction-sentry.com

★★★★★

$9.65 per year (£5.92 approx)
for three-year licence; ten-day trial
PC - Windows 95 or later

According to the program vendor, Auction Sentry is "the #1 eBay Auction Sniper", and to go along with this claim, the program has plenty of awards, which it isn't shy about.

In practice, the program stands up well too. Instead of the usual online service, Auction Sentry is an installed program that works in conjunction with the actual sniping tool provider, using its servers.

Once installed, the program uses a clear, colour-coded list to show you the status of any items that you're bidding on. Red entries mean that you've been outbid, green indicates that you're the highest bidder and yellow is used to notify you that Auction Sentry is waiting to snipe the corresponding auction.

The tabbed interface makes it easy to view your auctions, and you can filter listings to make things even easier. To snipe auctions, select the item you're vying for, and specify the maximum bid you're willing to make for it, as well as the time and date before the end of the auction. The program will then do the rest.

Notifications are displayed to keep you up to date, and there's a built-in browser that you can use to peruse eBay (or anywhere else).

There's no denying the power available in this bidding tool, and the actual program installation means you always have access to your current activity, without the need to visit a website. As it boasts on its website, "set it and forget it".

AUCTIONRAPTOR
ww.auctionraptor.com

★★★★★

$4.95 (£3.04 approx) per month,
$52.95 (£32.70 approx) per year;
one month free
Online service

AuctionRaptor is a nicely put together service that aims to be simple and user friendly. The service, which is free for the first month, offers unlimited bids on as many items as you like at once and e-mail notifications to let you know if your bid is too low to win the auctions, giving you the chance to raise your game.

You can utilise item grouping to bid on the same item from a number of sellers (with the other bids being cancelled if you win one of them), and you can add items to your AuctionRaptor account while browsing eBay. Best of all, AuctionRaptor can place bids as little as two seconds away from the closing time, giving you a great chance of winning (Internet traffic permitting).

While the subscription price is a little more than many competing services, AuctionRaptor's simple but effective features are usually worth it, and the last-second sniping is a real bonus that beats most other services hands down.

BIDNAPPER
www.bidnapper.com

★★★★☆

£7.99 per month standard
subscription; £19.99 (ten snipes)
£36.99 (25 snipes).
Online service

Bidnapper is a flexible and powerful online bidding service that supports not only eBay, but a wide variety of other auction websites (more than 40 in total). As you'd expect, the service allows you to place bids automatically during the last few seconds of an auction, and you can specify your maximum bid amount and also protect your username from searches, to stop your competition from locating you.

Bids can be changed or cancelled at any time, and using the tabbed interface of the service, as well as the included searches, makes it easy to stay on top of things, regardless of how many auctions you're taking part in. The service's interface relays plenty of information about each bid, along with the product image, and you can make notes as well, should you need to.

Bidnapper has won plenty of praise for it successes, and is a good service for users of multiple auction types. The payment methods are flexible too, and you don't need to be tied down to a subscription, which is a bonus.

EZ SNIPER
www.ezsniper.com

★★★☆☆

$11.99 (£7.90 approx) per month
subscription, ten snipes for
$21.99 (£14.50 approx).
Online service

Billing itself as one of the cheapest sniping tools around, EZ Sniper features a flexible pricing plan, with last-second sniping for as little as £0.05 per go. Although it charges 1% of your winning bid on top of that, it isn't too bad, and should you be unsuccessful, you don't pay a thing.

All bids can be changed or cancelled as you see fit, and all transactions are totally secure, with your privacy guaranteed.

After a simple registration process, you can use the online applet to add snipes and monitor the status of your auctions, and you can bid on as many items as you like.

EZ Sniper has a free trial that grants you three snipes, and if you register and then recommend the service to your friends, you'll be eligible for the free service, with a whole month of free bids on offer.

GIXEN
www.gixen.com
★★★★☆
Free
Online service

Sniping services, by their very design, usually have a lot in common, and similar features, as well as a price. Using them usually requires a subscription. Not so with Gixen. This is a totally free sniping tool that offers the same features as many paid-for options.

Using Gixen you can snipe auctions in the last few seconds and are able to use groups bids to make sure you grab that elusive item. The number of bids you can place at any one time using Gixen is ten, which is less than most other services. Considering it's free, though, you can't complain.

The developer claims that bids using Gixen are 99.5% reliable, which is a high level indeed and, should you wish to, you can pay for a Gixen 'mirror', which sends two snipes at the same time, effectively doubling your chances of getting that bid in at the last possible second. A downloadable desktop management Gixen tool is now available too, incidentally, also free of charge.

MYIBIDDER
www.myibidder.com
★★★☆☆
Free web-based
PC/Mac

Bid sniping is, of course, a very popular method of nailing that elusive deal on auction sites. Many eBay users now make the most of services that offer this

essential trick for snagging items, and if you want to ensure that you stand a chance of winning some of the more hotly pursued deals, then tools like Myibidder (formerly Myibidder) are very useful indeed.

Myibidder is a bid sniping and auction management tool. Using it, you can manage and organise your current auction activity, keeping track of time left, current prices and more. Integrated into the service is a sniping tool that can be set to increase your bid on an item automatically should you be outbid. Simply set your maximum bid, and the program will do the rest and attempt to sneak that all-important last-minute bid in for you.

Myibidder is available as a free (donations are welcome) service, using extensions, shortcuts and custom buttons for Firefox, Internet Explorer and Opera browsers. If you'd rather use the service locally as a client application, however, you can. You can download a Windows application that includes all the web service's features and free updates. The local version has the benefit of speedier performance, as it's installed on your PC, and may be a good choice for heavy eBay users. You do have to pay for it, though.

POWERSNIPE
www.powersnipe.com
★★★★☆
$3.95 (£2.42 approx) per month
Online service

PowerSnipe has won awards from various websites for its reliability, and is an accessible online service that comes with a 30-day money-back guarantee, so sure is its developer that it will help you win eBay auctions.

As is standard, the program only needs an auction number

and maximum amount (as well as your user details, of course) and it will then attempt to outbid other users by sniping at the last possible second.

Daily updates are sent to you by the service, and you can also use it to snipe multiple auctions, including group bids.

You can view your full order history via the Auction Manager, and bids can be altered or cancelled should you wish (up to two minutes before the end of the auction).

For under £30 per year, and unlimited snipes, PowerSnipe is a good service to try if you do a lot of eBay bidding. However, occasional users may do best with a token-based service.

Seller Tools

AEROLISTER
www.aerolister.com
★★★☆☆
$24.99 (£15.45 approx) for 30-day licence; $124.99 (£77.26 approx) 180 days, 14-day trial
PC - Windows XP or later

Some of the most time-consuming aspects of selling on eBay include sending buyer feedback, relisting items and other clerical tasks like sending out invoices and order confirmations. These can be tiresome chores, unless you simplify the process, and this is just what Aerolister does.

Once installed on your PC, Aerolister is able to automate a whole range of tedious tasks, including sending positive buyer feedback (after payment is received), invoicing and removing items from your lists. The program also makes relisting expired items that haven't sold effortless, as it can automate this as well.

Since the program runs on your PC, it's faster and more reliable than the eBay online interfaces,

and you can set up bulk jobs to handle masses of items at once.

This is a great program, especially for large-scale sellers, but the high monthly price is a bit steep for most. Casual sellers won't benefit from the software at all.

AUCTIONPIX
www.auctionpix.co.uk
★★★★☆
Free
Online service

AuctionPix is a long-running (since 1999) image-hosting service for eBay users. The service offers free image-hosting for all your item shots, and also offers a watermark function on uploaded images (to stop other people pinching your pictures), thumbnail slideshows, templates (both prebuilt and user-created) and image descriptions.

Because this is an online service, there's no software needed to make use of the abilities on offer, and users of any platform can take advantage of it, including Apple Mac and Linux.

There's more to the service than simple image-hosting, though. Indeed, you can actually edit and touch up your images online, and perform such functions as resizing, cropping and adjusting colours.

There are also some forms of protection. As already mentioned, you can watermark your images, therefore ensuring your photographs stay yours, and you can also use the HTML encryption function to protect your descriptions, so other users can't simply copy them and then use them on their own listings.

Other new features offered by AuctionPix include a hosted image that can be used as an eBay auction counter, and a user-customisable cross-promotion slideshow, which can be added to all of your listings to advertise your other items to potential customers.

AuctionPix offers a good level of service, and is one of the better image-hosting services around at the moment. As well as auction image help, the site also features a selection of other eBay tools and template creation facilities that should be checked out.

AUCTIONPIXIE GALLERY
www.auctionpixie.co.uk

Free
Online service

Scrolling galleries can help give your eBay sales potential a boost, as they look more impressive than a simple list of images, and can usually be inserted into any web page, including your own personal website or blog. This activates another route to your eBay items, meaning people can discover your wares without even being on eBay.

AuctionPixie is a free, Flash-based scrolling gallery that, although simple in appearance, looks attractive and impressive nonetheless. Once you set it up, the gallery will scroll through your current items, and potential buyers can click an image and be taken straight to your eBay pages. The gallery also contains item descriptions, current bid prices and time left, and you can change the colour to your liking.

AuctionPixie enables nice, clean-looking galleries, but when it comes to advanced features, it's a little lacking, so it loses some marks when compared against other similar options. Still, it's a nice addition to traditional eBay selling tactics.

AUTOMATIC EBAY FEEDBACK
www.auctionpixie.co.uk/
automatic-feedback.aspx

Free
Online service

Paying attention to feedback is crucial to any seller's success. Although it often seems the least fair area of doing business on eBay, it still needs to be dealt with daily.

AuctionPixie has another tool up its online sleeve in the form of feedback management for its members. Join up for free, and set the service to automatically respond to praise from your customers with like-minded good comments for them.

The way it works is you build up a bank of complimentary, generic comments (up to ten per eBay account) that can be applied to any successful sales scenario to be cycled randomly in reply to feedback received.

By using template tags, detailed on the site, you can customise feedback to include the eBay ID of the buyer, or item title, number, or price, for a more unique reply.

You'll also be advised by e-mail of any neutral or negative feedback that's been left for you, so you can quickly try to repair deals that have gone badly.

Automating feedback is fine, but it's advisable to keep an eye on things to know it's being handled professionally. With that caveat, this is a very good resource for sellers at no cost and a huge time savings.

BAYTOGO
www.baytogo.com

★★★★☆

Free (basic service)
PC

BayToGo is a small eBay tool that can keep you informed of auction status wherever you happen to be, even if you're in another country. It does this by sending text messages of any changes in your auctions to your phone.

As well as text notifications, the BayToGo widget can provide a range of information, such as

total sales in a period of time, customer information and more.

The service is fully compatible with wireless devices with e-mail/SMS capabilities and can be tailored to your needs, sending messages at any time, or only between times you specify (so you don't get bothered at night or when out with friends, for example). You can also choose which events you wish to be notified about, such as new bids, first placed bid and so on.

This is a great little tool, and with its free option, there's no reason not to give it a go. If you travel around a lot, and need to stay up to date with your eBay auctions, it's a must.

BOLDCHAT
www.boldchat.com

★★★☆☆

$29 (£17.92 approx) per month Basic; $49 (£30.29 approx) per month Pro; $99 (£61.19 approx) per month Premier; free trial
PC - Windows

The best eBay sellers know that customer service goes beyond packaging and a thank you e-mail. Anything you can do to build confidence in your products and services will go a long way towards a successful business.

E-mail contact is fine and marketing tools like newsletters can add a professional touch. Although those options can be fast, though, they're not nearly as instant and accessible as being able to chat live with potential buyers.

Adding a chat feature to your eBay store you can quickly answer questions, confirm details and firm up sales that may be lost in the slower to and fro of typed communications. Boldchat offers a wide range of seller solutions from less than $300 (approximately £185.43) per year for infrequent sellers to over

$1,000 (roughly £618) per year for serious sellers.

If you have the resources to have someone available to chat about your items and terms, you may also want to add Boldchat to your sales team.

DISPATCH LABELS
www.dispatch-labels.com

Free
PC

It's often the small things that can take time, and the more tedious the task, the more you'd like to see a computer do it for you. When selling goods via eBay, few things are as tedious as writing out reams of shipping labels for sold items.

Dispatch Labels can help alleviate this tedium, and using it you can enter full details of all your customers, and create a list of mailing labels, which the program can print out for you onto your own sticky labels.

As well as printing the usual shipping labels, the software can also print out warnings (such as "DO NOT BEND") and you can access a full history of previous labels, so you can reprint existing customer labels for repeat buyers.

This is a very useful app that should save you plenty of time. Label designs and customisation are minimal, though, so more professional sellers may need to look elsewhere.

EBAY MARKETPLACE
www.facebook.com/apps/application.
php?id=2554599077

Free
Online service

Facebook has become a huge, unstoppable juggernaut of social networking, and people can spend all day sharing their thoughts with friends. It stands to reason, then, that with so much coverage, advertising and linking to items you're selling on eBay through your Facebook profile is a good idea.

Using eBay Marketplace is one way of doing this. Available from Facebook itself, this service, once you've signed up for it, allows you to share your eBay listing with others on the social networking service.

You can share items you're selling with others, and you can also show people what you're bidding on. However, this may not be something you wish to advertise, so you can use the tool's settings to restrict what others can see, hiding your secret bids from everyone or a select few.

Once you link your Facebook account to eBay (by simply clicking a link), you'll be able to not only share your eBay info with others, but you'll also be able to view your friends' items using the built-in interface. All items can link back to the main eBay site, and listings found on the Facebook page include the usual assortment of information, such as images, descriptions and price.

A less useful feature, but one that some may find entertaining, is the ability to place a 'wacky' item into your friend's watch lists. This isn't all that valuable, granted, and is obviously intended solely for practical jokes. However, it could be used for subtly hinting at birthday gifts.

EBAY UK FEE CALCULATOR
auctionfeecalculator.com/uk_ebay_fee_calc.html

Free
Online service

The eBay UK Fee Calculator is an always-ready resource that you can access from anywhere. It will help you figure in the total cost of selling any item by working out both eBay and PayPal fees for the transaction, revealing what you can expect to retain and allowing you to adjust options or prices accordingly.

Simply tick the listing options, including upgrades, image details (hosting, Supersize, and volume discounts) and any promotional extras such as Gallery and Featured listings and the costs will be calculated for you.

There's even a handy eBay Breakeven Calculator to help you determine the absolute minimum sale price you need to charge to net your costs back - great for when you need to quickly clear merchandise without taking a beating on the sale.

ECAL AUCTION FEE CALCULATOR (FOR EBAY UK AND PAYPAL)
ecal.altervista.org/en/fee_calculator/ebay.co.uk

★★★★☆

Free
Online service

This online service provides free calculators to compute and compare listing fees and costs on many eBay sites. The UK page is dedicated to the fee structures for users in the United Kingdom, and has you choose from Auction, Buy It Now and eBay Store format tabs. It also includes a special facility to add or change VAT for European Union countries.

Simply enter the details of the intended sale item, (or Multi-item Dutch Auctions), and tick the listing upgrades and picture services you're interested in, such as Gallery, or scheduled, highlighted or bold listings, and the costs will be tallied up for you.

If they seem too high to get the profit you're hoping for, you can make changes that alter the features of your listing and affect your bottom line. Having this info in advance helps to plan for the cost of every item and to control each sale.

Frequent sellers should be using fee calculators on a regular basis. This is a good, up-to-date choice for the infrequent seller or if you're working away from your desk and need access to a service to plan sales strategies away from home or the office.

FAST PHOTOS
www.pixby.com

★★★★★

$24.95 (£15.42 approx); 21-day free trial
PC - Windows XP or later

This image editing program is as streamlined as they come and concentrates on the improvements that matter, helping users make good, clear, colourful, correctly cropped images at files sizes that won't slow shoppers down.

It includes an extremely handy watermarking feature for identifying your unique shots as yours, and a one-click thumbnail creator for building nearly instantaneous galleries.

An instant browser preview lets you test your images as they'll be seen. Once you've got your shots perfected, a built-in FTP feature delivers them to where they'll be stored.

The idea of an image editor made specifically for the needs of busy eBay sellers with many other chores to accomplish during their days is extremely appealing. The price is perfect, and it's easily recommended, even for those who own more fully featured image editors, where too many options may get in the way of good, quick, fuss-free item photo creation.

INSTANTFEEDBACK
www.merlinsoftware.com/
instantfeedback
★★★★☆
$19.95 (£12.33 approx); 15-day
trial
PC

Feedback management is
undeniably a major admin
headache for eBay sellers and
InstantFeedback may be the pill for
the job.

It's a small and simple program
that sits in the Windows System
Tray waiting and watching for
feedback activity on your eBay
account. When positive feedback is
found, it can automatically generate
positive feedback in return,
reciprocating the actions of your
buyers as well as sending along a
thank you e-mail message.

If you have a lot of feedback to
catch up on, the program can help
with that too by producing a list of
those needing your comments and
can also request feedback from
customers who have yet to give
their opinions.

InstantFeedback will also alert
you to any neutral or negative
feedback received, so you can make
amends should you need to.

Feedback tools are very
welcome, yet surprisingly few are
to be found considering the value
and cost of good and bad
comments. InstantFeedback is
recommended to those who prefer
an installed tool that's updated
often by its creator.

JUST SHIP IT
www.justshipit.co.uk
★★☆☆☆
Subscription - £29.99 monthly,
£149.99 one year; 3-day trial
PC - Windows XP or later

Taking care of shipping labels is
just a small part of the after-sales
tasks you need to perform when
using eBay (and Amazon) and
running your own business. There

are invoices, posting items and
keeping an audited list of all your
sold items. This can be a headache,
but a program like Just Ship IT
could help.

This app aims to take care of
everything, from producing
shipping labels (which you can
customise), to invoices and keeping
tabs on previous sales. It'll even
download your listing information
from eBay, storing it in one
easy-to-access place.

Shipping labels can include
images, such as your company
logo, as well as postage paid
impressions, should you use this
for easy posting. Likewise, invoices
are fully customisable, and you can
use existing templates or create
your own.

The history of sold items is a big
help to anyone wishing for an
easier time keeping track of orders,
and all details can be printed off for
archiving.

Just Ship IT is a very useful tool,
but at £149.99 per year to use the
service, the price isn't cheap,
especially as there are both
cheaper and free alternatives that
accomplish the same thing.

LABEL WIZARD
www.ledset.com/labwiz
★★★☆☆
£5.16; 45-day trial
PC

Printing your own shipping labels
via a dedicated label-making
program doesn't just save time, it
also adds an element of
professionalism to your sales. It
also gives you the chance to include
details of any other websites or
stores you that may run, further
extending the potential for sales.

Label Wizard, like many
label-making programs, enables
you to create your own custom
labels for use on your packages to
be shipped. All you need to do is
enter the customer's details and
you're away. Using the more

advanced features, though, you can
also add images to labels, as well
as business-card-like footers,
containing your company logo and
any other details.

Using the program is easy, and
adding extra info and images is a
breeze. Printing works with all the
most popular label formats, and
you can perform a search for any
previous labels, so you can quickly
print off labels for repeat
customers.

Label Wizard isn't free (and it is
quite old, with no update to the
software we could see over the past
few years), but it does provide some
great label customisation, and the
ability to advertise your services
with every sale.

KYOZOU WIDGET
www.kyozou.com/widget.html
★★☆☆☆
Price available on request
Online service

The coverage that can be gleaned
from a presence on social
networking sites is invaluable, so if
you're planning on reaching the
maximum amount of possible
buyers, then finding a way to
advertise your wares on these
well-trodden avenues is vital.
This is where Kyozou Widget
comes in. It's a specially designed
Flash-powered listing box that can
be slotted into any site that allows
custom content. By pasting the
required code into your page, you'll
publish an interactive panel that
contains all your current listings.
The information contained in the
widget includes a thumbnail image
of the item, description, price
and end time. The panel can also
include your own company logo and
description.
The widget can be customised by
the user, and different layouts can
be set up.

Sadly, the widget isn't free, and
you'll need to contact Kyozou for
pricing, which makes it a lot less

attractive for casual users. However, if you're interested in the widget, you can try it out by entering your eBay ID into the online demonstration. This will then show you a fully working widget, complete with your own current listings.

MERCHANTRUN GLOBALLINK 3.0

www.merchantrun.com/ MerchantRun/

★★★☆☆

From $29.99 to $374.99 (£18.54 to £231.78 approx) plus 1% of sales, which reduces with plan scales and volume
Online service

While most casual eBay users will be content with selling the odd item once in a while through their country's eBay incarnation, more advanced, larger-scale sellers may not be so easily pleased. For some, an adequate portion of the market isn't simply with their native eBay, and getting their listings placed internationally is key. This is where MerchantRun GlobalLink comes in.

With this service you can simultaneously upload listings to 21 eBay sites all over the world. This process includes category translations, currency conversion, cross promotions, prebuilt templates, and image-hosting. The translation services alone will make the it essential to many, making this a very interesting selling application to consider.

MerchantRun can also automatically relist items (including relist to store), and it can also keep a fixed number of listings active, and list according to a predefined schedule.

The ability to list items to 21 different international eBay sites is a huge bonus to anyone wishing to expand beyond their borders, and for sellers with truly international aspirations, this is a great tool to have close to hand.

Commissions are based on the item sale price only and don't include shipping, unlike other percentage-based offers - a detail often overlooked when choosing services.

PAYLOADZ

www.payloadz.com

★★★☆☆

Free Basic account (1GB storage), various Premium accounts
Online service

Not everything sold on eBay takes the form of physical objects such as collectable figurines, cars, clothes and compact discs. More and more people have opted to use the auction site to sell downloadable software. With eBay being so popular, you're almost guaranteed extra coverage compared to an independent website.

Payloadz is a service that aims to make the sale of electronically distributable items easier for both the seller and the buyer. It works in conjunction with eBay and PayPal, and once payment has been received, will send a thank you e-mail to the buyer, along with details of where and how to download the software.

Payloadz is a welcome service for small-scale software developers and distributors who need a simple, effective way of peddling their wares. Providing secure file storage using its servers, you can opt to supply downloads or even provide CD copies. The free account can help test the waters for the sale of e-books

and other digital files without long-term commitment.

PAYPAL FEE CALCULATOR

www.rolbe.com/paypal.htm

★★★☆☆

Free
Online service

With this PayPal calculator you can check the impact and effect of payment processing fees on your sales. It will quickly do the math for you and save your brainpower for other tasks.

This calculator has the added attraction of a 'reverse' feature to effortlessly arrive at the net amount you want to receive for items you sell. Enter the desired amount and it calculates the exact amount a person would need to send you. Of course, there's the more traditional, straightforward method of figuring fees as well.

With a handy percentage-to-decimal conversion feature for 18 different countries, including a Cross Border Payment function, and links to other equally useful calculation tools, this is definitely a site worth bookmarking for frequent use.

RELIABID BID ASSURE

www.reliabid.com

★☆☆☆☆

0.25% of total sale (including shipping), minimum $5 (£3.09 approx) per month; 30-day trial
Online service

Non-payment is a frustrating experience for sellers. Too many bad debtors and your plans for successful selling fall apart. The ReliaBid program's aim is to eliminate non-paying bidders. It does this with a warning sign (seal) that states that payment is expected. Then it claims to follow up on the threat with

action from a collections agency (for US buyers only).

This international seal service isn't recommended because, as any experienced seller can tell you, the chance of non-payers exists in any business, and you need to develop your own way of professionally handling it.

Plastering your pages with warnings is hardly welcoming to the trustworthy, and those bad bidders in the middle of collection proceedings are fobbed off with ReliaBid's website statement that it isn't responsible in any way. A poor choice for a solution to a common selling concern.

SOURCE CODE PROTECTOR

www.auctionpixie.co.uk/source-code-protector.aspx

★★★★★

Free
Online service

You work hard to stand out from the crowd of other sellers. Imagine the frustration of someone coming along and stealing your perfectly colour co-ordinated pages and poetic descriptions of your wares.

If you'd like to keep your hard work yours alone, stop by the Source Code Protector, enter your listing's HTML, press Encrypt and voila! Your code is transformed and written in a manner that's impossible to edit without decrypting, yet you can paste it, as is, into your listing and it will display as perfectly as the original.

If you're exceedingly proud of your work or have developed an above average look that you'd like to maintain as exclusive, this free service from AuctionPixie may appeal. It's only practical for infrequent use but, together with watermarked photos, helps keep your brand and style unique among the throngs of lazy sellers only too willing to copy and paste their way to success. Dedicated thieves can, of course, duplicate your look with some effort. Copying is done to save time and trouble, and this service could discourage those types.

TIME LEFT
www.nestersoft.com

★★★★☆

Free (Deluxe version also available, for $24.95, £15.32 approx.)
PC

eBay and time go hand in hand, and TimeLeft is a little application that's more than aware of this. Its purpose in life is to make sure that you don't miss out on anything because you weren't watching the clock!

It's not an application specifically designed with eBay in mind, as it has lots of other functions to it. It can serve as a stopwatch, for instance, or a countdown. It then appears on your screen in a small, floating box, and you get the necessary reminders when you want them. But there is an auction side to it, courtesy of an AuctionWatch function that's been built into the program. It's quite a nifty idea, too. You basically tell it what auctions you're wanting to watch, and TimeLeft will keep an eye on how long is left for them.

This is a useful tool for both buyers and sellers, and TimeLeft doesn't just display an indication of time, but it'll also tell you who the current high bidder in a certain auction is, as well as the current price. This information isn't presented in a massively attractive way, but it is functional, and it is useful.

There's nothing earth-shatteringly complex about TimeLeft, but then there doesn't need to be. It's a simple tool to do

a simple, but very useful job. And it's hard to grumble at just how well it does it.

AUCTIONBLOX
auctionblox.com

★★★☆☆

$99 ($61.19 approx) per month plus 1.0% transaction fee for Merchant account; prices available on request for Enterprise account (no transaction fees)
Online service (server-based)

AuctionBlox isn't a stand-alone solution for selling items on eBay. Instead, it integrates with osCommerce shopping carts, as a means of selling through eBay and a store or website.

All of the standard, must-have capabilities common among seller tools are present such as invoicing, e-mailing, and shipping help.

AuctionBlox automates listing chores like relisting of unsold items and immediate listing of new items on the close of successful sales. Also, the notification process for winning bids, feedback, and other communication is streamlined as well.

More advanced features are available in the form of Checkout Redirect, which can generate 'upselling' opportunities by enabling sellers to view additional items you have for sale, as they're stepped through the payment process. This has obvious benefits to sellers, but also offers buyers savings on shipping of their combined purchases. An Inventory Management feature monitors stock, cancelling eBay auctions when items are depleted in shops to avoid overselling.

There's a wealth of help available for installing and getting to grips with the software, including a wiki, a community forum, and even a

Feature Request Form via the website. But, at last visit, AuctionBlox has discontinued free trials (although they may be started again at any time) and the software looks complex enough to warrant a no-fee dry run before a long-term investment, especially as hosting services (for online storage of the software) aren't included in the Standard price package, but only with the Gold, Platinum and Enterprise editions.

T-HUB
www.atandra.com/Prod_THub.htm

★★★☆☆

$300 (£196 approx) Standard; $500 (£327 approx) Professional; $700 (£458 approx) Advanced; set-up and training ($200 to $300, £130 to £196 approx) and annual support ($200 to $300, £130 to £196 approx) additional; 15-day trial
PC (MS Access and QuickBooks software required)

If you're running a serious business, either solely through eBay or with eBay making up a part of your operation, then you'll no doubt need to keep track of your orders, including sales figures, card payments, shipping costs and so on. Doing this manually is no small task, and even if with accounting software, getting your eBay info into it can be tricky.

T-Hub is a special tool that's designed to effortlessly transport data from your online store into the popular QuickBooks software. It'll handle order management, credit card processing and shipping with just a few clicks, and should help to streamline the whole process.

T-Hub is a very useful tool for advanced, larger-scale sellers, but it's not for most eBay sellers. It's expensive and, of course, requires QuickBooks to function.

Management Software

AUCTION HAWK
www.auctionhawk.com

★★★★☆

$24 (£14.74 approx) per three months; 14-day free trial
Online service (server-based)

Auction management starts on day one of deciding to be an eBay seller. If you haven't had any tools in place from the first sale, it can be more difficult to make the move after the fact. Auction Hawk imports up to two months of listings "within ten minutes of sign-up". From then on you can continue with improved bulk relisting, scheduling and feedback tasks and get alerts on bad feedback.

You can produce, customise and track customers' e-mails (using an 'exclusive E-mail Ping feature'), and integrate bidder notifications with delivery tracking to streamline purchase through fulfilment stages. Sales, fees and full customer history reports are always at hand through popular financial and banking tools or Excel charts and graphs and can be searched easily on any criteria.

Listing duties are simplified through Auction Hawk's 1-Page Lister, which suits beginners as well as experienced sellers using professional templates, Item Specifics, and creation of customised shipping and payment profiles.

Its image hosting service, a substantial part of the pricing levels, includes scrolling showcases and galleries.

Flat-fee plans range from Basic with 220 listings, 50MB of A and 2,000 images to Unlimited listings, 500MB of storage and 20,000 images, with no percentage of sales due on any price or service category

Auction Hawk throws an hourly hit tracker into the package so you have an instant, visual indication of the number of page visits your auctions are achieving. A 14-day free trial is more than enough time to see if it's worth the monthly cost to carry on.

LISTING ANALYTICS
www.listinganalytics.com

★★★★★

Free
PC/Mac

This one's an official product from eBay itself, and it's been made available entirely free of charge.

The idea behind it is quite simple, too: using the software, you can get an added insight into just how many people are clicking onto your eBay listings, and what they're doing when they get there.

Even at a base level, it's an interesting piece of work. But if you're a dedicated eBay, Listing Analytics provides invaluable intelligence.

For instance, using the software, you can find out quite easily what your best and worst performing listings are. You can also find out where your buyers are coming from, and find how, effectively, what they do when they land on your listings page.

All of this is really useful information, but there's still more to what Listing Analytics can do for you. Perhaps the most valuable feature here is the one that lets you search for a listing keyword, so you can find out where it'll appear in eBay's search results. If you're the kind of trader who frequently gets frustrated that, no matter what you try, your listing seems to get hidden away behind everyone else's, then being able to do this kind of search before you've

committed to sell something is really quite important. You can quite easily use the information you gleam, to shape a much better, keyword-focused listing at the end of it all.

Some have noted that the work it does is simply common sense, and there is some substance to that criticism. But then, not everyone's an eBay expert, and if you follow what Listing Analytics demonstrates, then you can learn a lot from it, and hopefully enjoy more sales in the process. The fact that there's no charge attached at least means there's no obvious risk involved in giving it a try.

AUCTION WIZARD 2000
www.auctionwizard2000.com

★★★★☆

$100 (£61.81 approx) first year, $50 (£30.90 approx) per year thereafter; 60-day free trial
PC - Windows XP, Vista or 7

Some of the best software was developed to fill a need, rather than as a commercial effort, and if it's especially good it often reaches other customers by knowing just what the user wants to accomplish firsthand.

Such is the case with Auction Wizard 2000, a very fully featured seller management package that was originally designed by the owners to sell estate assets through eBay, and it includes the tools that proved to be the most helpful.

Choose from among dozens of included customisable listing templates, for professional pages without any previous experience of HTML, and select, resize, upload and remove images, all from within the same program.

A powerful database doesn't just sit there, holding onto your figures. You can generate equally powerful and useful reports for full control over financial decisions and directions. A built-in ledger tracks

income and expenses, and data can be imported or exported in CSV format for use in numerous software titles. You can import data from any supported auction site, and back-up and restore tools - essential to your peace of mind - are included as well as a purge and archive utility to keep all your vital records relevant and tidy.

Inventory management and invoicing are covered, and there's unlimited support for multiple User IDs. E-mail is produced automatically at each stage of the auction process and a spell checker will help maintain a professional presence.

With built-in image-editing capabilities and e-mail, FTP and HTML modules, it's an all-inclusive package that goes beyond typical management software and more than justifies the price, eliminating the need for separate software to handle those tasks, and consolidating work into one program rather than across many.

The maker claims owners recoup the cost of the software through the quick relisting feature alone, with reduced fees for second-shot listings of unsold items.

Multiple users working across a network are supported, although each workstation requires a separate licence, but it's good to know the software can grow with you as you grow your business. With 60 days to trial the package, there's plenty of time to have a good root around.

Miscellaneous Software

FEEDBACK ANALYSER PRO 2
www.feedbackanalyzer.com

★★★☆☆

$37 (£22.87 approx)
PC - Windows 98 or later

eBay feedback is one of the most useful ratings for anyone using the site. Knowing if the person you're buying from is reputable, or likely to take your money and run is important. It's also just as important for sellers to check out their potential buyers.

This research tool is able to provide you with full feedback information on eBay users, both buyers and sellers, and can split this feedback into neutral, good and bad, so you can quickly gauge the kind of feedback a particular person has received. These lists can then be saved out to several formats including text, CSV and HTML.

As well as this, the software can produce feedback ads for your own page. By using this HTML code, good feedback can be clearly seen on your page so people can see that you're a highly rated seller, and hopefully will be far more confident in buying from you. The program currently comes with ten free templates for these ads, all of which can easily be implemented in your page.

Seeing feedback ahead of time is useful, and this app makes this much easier by gathering details into one place.

FIREFOX EBAY-EDITION
pages.ebay.co.uk/firefox/

★★★★★

Free

PC - Windows XP, Vista or 7

Few would dispute that Firefox is the most popular alternative to Microsoft's Internet Explorer. One of the reasons for this popularity is its ability to accept plug-ins that augment its functionality. And yes, there are plug-ins for eBay too, such as this eBay helper add-on.

Billed more as a special version of Firefox (the download now includes the browser itself), this package adds an eBay sidebar that lets you stay in the know at all times while you're browsing the Internet.

The side panel includes a built-in eBay button, and pressing this opens up a menu with quick access to eBay's search, as well as links to buy and sell items, your My eBay page and feedback tools.

The actual eBay Companion Sidebar displays full details of current auctions and watched items, as well as feedback status. The eBay Alert Box does just that, and alerts you to any changes right away. Less intrusive 'Glow Alerts' can also be used, and if anything changes, the eBay logo in the browser will glow silently to signify an event.

There's a wide range of settings that let you take full control of the Companion, and automatic updates are included. Security is also given attention, and will show when you're on a real eBay or PayPal site, so you can avoid any dodgy fakes.

There are more accomplished tools available out there that feature a wider range of abilities, but few are as polished and as well integrated as this one, which is also free. A definite recommendation, and an essential tool for any Firefox and eBay fans.

GET4IT
www.get4it.co.uk

★★★☆☆

Free

Online service

A major question on both eBay buyers' and sellers' lips is, 'How much is it worth?' When you're looking to buy, you want to find the best price for the item you're looking for, and if you're planning to sell on the site, you don't want to price yourself out of the market by putting too high a reserve on your wares.

To help with this dilemma, you could visit Get4It. This website features a search function that lets you enter search criteria in order to see what specific items have sold for on eBay before, as well as

the most popular results. You'll see a graph that shows at a glance the price bracket similar items fall into, and you'll also get the minimum and maximum amounts people have paid.

You can narrow searches down by entering more detailed search criteria, and the engine even shows the maximum number of bids received for the item. A very useful research tool whether you're buying or selling.

RSS AUCTION
www.rssauction.com

★★★★★

Free

Online service

RSS (Really Simple Syndication) feeds are a fantastic way to be automatically notified of updates and additions to your favourite sites. And eBay pages can be treated to the same techie touches.

The RSS Auction page holds an online form that makes creating custom RSS searches simple by selecting categories and key words and choosing the length of time until the feed expires. Have your feeds fade after one month or up to a year, or never expire at all.

More advanced options include limiting item searches to your localation, setting minimum and maximum prices, selecting currencies and sorting by a number of factors such as price, distance and auction time remaining.

Buyers can be fed information about collectable items all year round, and sellers can keep up to date with competition selling the same or similar items. Receive and read feeds in the traditional way, through an RSS reader, or by having them sent directly to any e-mail address.

This is a brilliant, free resource that can be used in many creative ways by anyone with an eBay business or buying habit.

AUCTION WIZARD 2000

www.auctionwizard2000.com

$100 (£61.81 approx) first year, $50 (£30.90 approx) per year thereafter; 60-day free trial
PC - Windows XP, Vista or 7

Some of the best software was developed to fill a need, rather than as a commercial effort, and if it's especially good it often reaches other customers by knowing just what the user wants to accomplish firsthand.

Such is the case with Auction Wizard 2000, a very fully featured seller management package that was originally designed by the owner to sell estate assets through eBay, and it includes the tools that proved most helpful.

Choose from among dozens of included customisable listing templates, for professional pages without any previous experience of HTML, and select, resize, upload and remove images, all from within the same program.

A powerful database doesn't just sit there, holding onto your figures. You can generate equally powerful and useful reports for full control over financial decisions and directions. A built-in ledger tracks income and expenses, and data can be imported or exported in CSV format for use in numerous software titles. You can import data from any supported auction site, and back-up and restore tools are included as well as a purge and archive utility to keep all your vital records relevant and tidy.

Inventory management and invoicing are covered, and there's unlimited support for multiple User IDs. E-mail is produced automatically at each stage of the auction process and a spell checker will help maintain a professional presence.

With built-in image-editing capabilities and e-mail, FTP and HTML modules, it's an all-inclusive package that goes beyond typical management software and more than justifies the price, eliminating the need for separate software to handle those tasks, and consolidating work into one program rather than across many.

The maker claims owners recoup the cost of the software through the quick relisting feature alone, with reduced selling fees for second-shot listings of unsold items.

Multiple users working across a network are supported, although each workstation requires a separate licence, but it's good to know the software can grow with you as you grow your business. With 60 days to trial it, there's plenty of time to have a good root around.

BLACKTHORNE BASIC

pages.ebay.com/blackthorne

★★★★☆

$9.99 (£6.17 approx) per month; 30-day trial
PC

Here we have an official auction management tool that can be found in eBay's own selling tools section. Blackthorne Basic may sound like a simplified tool, but in practise it's actually far from simple. This application offers a range of powerful and flexible selling tools designed to help users get the most from eBay.

The package is an end-to-end selling system. You can use it to create and upload your new listings, using preset or custom-built templates. These listings can be uploaded in bulk, making it easy for sellers who shift items in higher quantities. Once listings are active, you can use the program to keep tabs on any activity, and once sold, the service continues, allowing you to go through the entire sales process, including payment, shipping and, of course, feedback.

You can save your previous sales and customer information, which can be useful in analysing your performance so you can improve in your sales techniques and follow-through. There's a reporting tool included too, which is always useful for tracking sales trends.

The program's interface is simple and easy to use, with a tabbed menu system and a straightforward step-by-step listing generator. The included templates are attractive, and the whole process of placing items up for auction is easy enough for even the most fresh-faced eBay seller.

This is the basic edition of the tool, so although it's still a powerful and excellent tool, more advanced and large-scale users may wish to upgrade to Blackthorne Pro ($24.99, approximately £15.45 per month). For most eBay users, though, Basic should suffice.

INKFROG

www.inkfrog.com

Free for 25 listings, unlimited subscription plan available for $14.95 per month (£10 approx.)

Any larger-scale eBay seller knows that it's important to keep accurate tabs on all of your items and auctions, and having a useful management tool to aid you is imperative. Therefore, a program like inkFrog is just the ticket.

InkFrog is a long-established management tool that allows eBay users to control and keep track of all their items from a single, easy-to-use system. The program stores and lists all your current listings, including updated 'time left' information and current bids, and it will also catalogue all previous sales too.

You can use the program to upload new listings using the interface, and it comes with a selection of prebuilt templates that can make your items look even better, and more attractive to potential buyers. Of course, you can also use your own custom templates should you prefer. The listing tool is billed as a 'one-step' system, and does make listing items far easier. You can also create stored profiles, which you can quickly select and apply to items. This makes listing multiple items a breeze.

As well as the management tool, it also comes with 1GB of image hosting, which is useful for eBay sellers who need to supply higher-resolution images of their wares.

With such large image-hosting space and powerful inventory and listing management tools, this is a great option for power sellers. And it's now available free of charge for up to 25 listings a year.

KYOZOU

www.kyozou.com

★★★☆☆

Price on request; demo available
Online service

Kyozou is an online auction management tool that contains a range of aids to allow eBay sellers to manage their business from a web browser, without the need for locally installed software. This effectively means you can run your business from any computer with an Internet, anywhere in the world.

The service includes support for inventory management, communications with buyers, payment collection, shipping tools, and support not only for eBay, but also for other outlets such as Amazon. You can create your own marketplace, provide ample support for customer feedback and even use the tool to manage any employees.

The web-based service delves into every area of online sales and is an impressive tool that advanced sellers will be able to use to capitalise on their business. You'll be able to stay on top of your auctions and grow your business beyond eBay, if you so choose.

BUYING &
SEARCHING
TOOLS

LISTING TOOLS

SNIPING TOOLS

SELLER TOOLS

MANAGEMENT
SOFTWARE

MISCELLANEOUS
SOFTWARE

MOBILE APPS

Mobile Apps

Over the following pages, we've tested a collection of products to help you with eBay, starting with buying and searching tools...

THE OFFICIAL EBAY ANDROID APP
iOS, Android, BlackBerry

The official eBay application takes the day-to-day PC experience of using eBay and places it within your smartphone. The application is completely free and is available on iOS, Android and BlackBerry.

eBay version 1.5 has been released for Android and brings the ability to list and sell items on your smartphone. Key features include built-in PayPal support, the ability to search, buy and sell items, notifications, barcode scanning and support for up to five languages, including English, French, Italian, German and Spanish.

eBay for Android, as well iOS and BlackBerry, is easy to use, intuitively designed and it enables you shop simply and securely while you're on the move. Updates to iOS and BlackBerry will bring the ability to list and sell items in time. So if you're looking for a way of using eBay on the move, look no further than eBay's official mobile app. You really can't go wrong.

POCKET AUCTIONS FOR EBAY
iOS, Android

Pocket Auctions For eBay lets users bid, compare prices, check on auctions, view pictures and read item descriptions from the comfort of their smartphone. One really cool feature is the 'What's Hot' section, which lists the best current auctions taking place on eBay.

The Pocket Auctions application may lack some of the features of the official eBay tool, but it's still a great little application that's well presented and easy to use.

Pocket Auctions For eBay is a perfect alternative to the official iOS eBay application, because it allows you to list and purchase goods - something that's not yet available in the official one.

Beauty does lie in the eye of the beholder, however. So having said that, if you're on Android and fancy something a little different, it's definitely worth checking on Pocket Auction For eBay - who knows, you might even prefer it?

DROID AUCTIONS EBAY
Android

Droid Auctions, as the name suggests, is an Android exclusive that does just about everything the official eBay application does - bar selling items, or course.

The app itself is free and is pretty comprehensive in terms of features. For instance, you can place bids, view feedback, send/receive messages, scan barcodes and even set up a widget for the app on one of your Android smartphone's home screens.

The layout is simple and easy-to-use, so novices and professionals alike will have no trouble getting to grips with the application. Our favourite feature of Droid Auctions is the barcode scanner, which puts thousands of items at your finger tips in an instant and ensures you always get the right price, wherever you are.

EBAY FASHION
iPhone

If you enjoy shopping and fashion, eBay Fashion is the for you. Not only does it put you in touch with up-to-the-minute fashion news and goods, it also enables you save and try items on via the app's Closet feature.

But that's not all. eBay Fashion takes you straight to the heart of

the action as well with an emphasis on vintage clothes, new modern styles, shoes, handbags and accessories. Users can also access the app's Style Gallery feature, which effectively brings the catwalk to your iPhone.

You can also check to see if sunglasses suit you via a preview in the app's 'See It On' Sunglasses feature. All in all, this is a very impressive application with a wealth of features that are perfectly tailored to the needs of today's modern fashion fanatic.

And because it's an official eBay application, it looks brilliant. Great care has clearly been taken in the development and design of the applications. The results really do speak for themselves - there's nothing else quite like this application available.

EBAY CLASSIFIEDS
Android
★★★★☆

eBay Classifieds for Android is all free listings. Once downloaded you can buy and sell items locally and it won't cost you a penny to list your products. The app's main draw is that it focuses on local sellers so you only deal with people near you, which means no shipping costs.

The application is completely free and because it's on your mobile you can simply take a picture of the item you want to

sell, upload it straight to eBay via the application and sell it quickly in your surrounding area.

Key features of the application include Auto-locate, which directs you to your closest eBay Classifieds area, view, reply to, or forward ads, a Watch List and Facebook and Twitter sharing, so you can maximise your chances of selling something by utilising social networking sites.

FAT FINGERS
iOS, Android
★★★★☆

Thousands of items listed on eBay never sell because no one ever sees them. The reason, as

we've discussed, is that people make spelling mistakes - and lots of them. Spelling the name of an item incorrectly when listing something on eBay can have a detrimental effect on that item's visibility.

What Fat Fingers does is to grant you access to all these hidden gems, which you can pick up for next to nothing. It's a unique angle and it'll certainly secure you some bargains, which otherwise would have completely gone under your radar.

The application, as you'd expect, is well presented and receives regular updates - so no bugs. Once downloaded, Fat Fingers lets you place bids from the get-go, so you can begin soaking up those bargains straight away.

All in all, this is a very useful and insightful application. It opens up an added dimension of eBay right before your eyes.

REDLASER
iOS, Android
★★★★☆

Comparison websites are very popular with consumers. So too are comparison apps like RedLaser, which allows users to compare items as they shop so as to ensure they always get the best deal by comparing it to items on eBay.

All the user has to do is scan an item in a shop - a pair of shoes, say - and RedLaser will scan eBay for comparable items. More often than not these items are cheaper on eBay, so users that implement applications like RedLaser into their shopping habits stand to save quite a bit of dosh in the long run.

And because RedLaser licenses out its barcode scanning technology, there's

plenty of affiliate partners tied into the service as well. So you get access to site listings from the likes of Coupons.com, The Knot and Shopkick, as well as eBay. Very nice.

EBAY CALCULATOR
Android
★★★☆☆

If you tend to use eBay as a quick way to generate a second income, but your current paper-based system is a little unorganised, then you need eBay Calculator in your life - it'll make keeping track of all your eBay-related financials a piece of cake.

The eBay Calculator application does all the hard work for you calculating your eBay and PayPal fees, as well as your profit, without you having to even lift so much as a

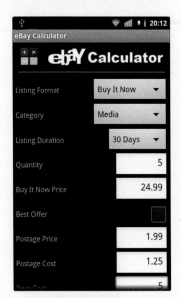

finger. The user interface is simple and easy to use too.

The app also takes into account all your costs and gives you a final breakdown of what your gross profit is. The only thing it won't do is your tax return, which is a shame.

EBAY PROFIT CALCULATOR US & UK
Android
★★★★★

eBay Profit Calculator US & UK does exactly what it says in its name: it works out your eBay costs and derives your overall profit margin, ensuring you're always in the green.

It's simple to use, free and makes light work of all the maths - always a good thing. When calculating your eBay profits, the app takes into account everything from insertion fees to final to value fees to Paypal fees and then even does your shipping expenses for you.

In short it's like having your own personal accountant. All calculations and cost breakdowns can be saved to the app's clipboard so you can keep all your records in one place and refer back to them at any point.

This application is indispensable - especially for aspiring eBay merchants.

EBAY ANNUNCI
Android
★★★★☆

Like eBay Classifieds, eBay Annunci lets you post ads for free and is focused on tapping into local deals, so it also saves you on shipping and hassle as well. eBay Annunci is ideal for locating and buying things like flats, cars, PCs, games, DVDs, bikes and furniture locally.

Simply log in, enter a search query and the appl will trawl over 270 categories to find exactly what you're looking for nearby.

Key features of eBay Annunci include the ability to browse and search any category by keyword, price or any attribute, view, reply to, or forward ads, Watch List and it's also extremely easy to post an item as well.

The eBay FAQ

To finish off, a recap of some of the most asked questions surrounding eBay

And so we round off with a look at some of the common questions that emerge regarding eBay. Many of these were covered in more detail earlier on, but the following four pages are a useful quick reference guide nonetheless to some of the more common questions that pop up...

BUYER TIPS

Is eBay safe, and will I get a good deal?

Yes, it's generally safe to buy on eBay, but it pays to employ a bit of common sense. Something that's too good to be true is generally too good to be true, and sellers with lots of negative feedback tend to have that for a reason. Sellers, too, who try to circumnavigate the eBay system and approach you directly should be treated with a degree of caution.

Yet the truth remains that millions of transactions are conducted on eBay every year, the vast majority of which go without a hitch. Are you going to get a good deal? Again, that depends on how good a shopper you are! It certainly pays not to get carried away with the euphoria of bidding, which often ends up with you feeling like you've won something, rather than bought something, at the end of a furious bidding war. Compare the eBay price to other outlets, set yourself a strict bidding limit, observe it, and you should be able to seek out some very fine deals.

Do watch out for the likes of postage charges, though, and remember to factor them in.

Should I bid on an item if someone has a poor feedback rating?

It's not a good idea, in general, and should absolutely be avoided on high-value items. If you can't afford to potentially lose the money on the item, then don't bid.

If it's a low-value item that you're keen on, then by all means read the specific feedback and make a judgement based on that. Also, if the seller is local, it might be worth seeing if you can pick an item up in person, which will get round potential problems.

Ultimately, though, the feedback system is there for a reason, and while all eBay purchases have an implicit level of risk, bidding with a low-rated seller enhances the chances that something will go wrong.

Can I trust a high seller rating?

You can certainly take confidence from it, but again, for high-value items, it's worth doing just a bit more

How can I be sure a seller will receive the item I send?

Short of putting it in their hands yourself, you can't. However, there are some precautions you can take.

Firstly, for higher-value items, use a trackable form of postage, one that has insurance built into it to cover any potential losses should your item go astray. Also, if it's trackable, your delivery company will be able to tell you if an item has been signed for or not. Royal Mail offers tracking services, as do other courier firms, whose fees may not be as prohibitive as you may at first assume.

Even for low-ticket items, it's worth getting a certificate of postage from your local Post Office, which at least gives you some small comeback should your item go missing.

The onus is firmly on you to ensure that the item concerned arrives with the buyer, and if it fails to do so, you will have to issue a refund.

Should I pay with PayPal?

It certainly gives you a level of protection, yes, although it's far from perfect. On bigger items, it certainly makes sense to use the PayPal service, as in the event of a problem, its own dispute channel is generally the most effective way to get your money back.

You should certainly avoid payment methods such as cash and bank transfer (both of which leave you no recourse if something goes wrong, and are regularly exploited by fraudsters), and Western Union transfers too should be setting off loud alarm bells in your head.

work. If, for instance, somebody is selling a £2,000 television, but all that seller's feedback is from people who have bought 1p e-books, then that should instantly raise alarm bells. The more homework you do (and you can click through and find out recent transactions that a seller has been involved in), the safer you will be.

That said, there's always a chance that things will go wrong. However, sellers with very high ratings, and large quantities of transactions, are invariably the safest to go with.

An item has arrived, and it's not as the seller described. What should I do?

Contact the seller immediately, but do so through eBay's communication channels, rather than private e-mail. That way, there's a communication trail which, should you need to escalate the dispute, can be easily referred to. Most problems are easily resolved this way.

You need to detail exactly how the item differs from the description, and take photographs to back up your claims. Do not start using the item. Tell the seller you want a refund, or a part refund if you still want to hang on to the item. If you don't hear back from them within 72 hours, then start a dispute with eBay and PayPal (if you paid with the latter). Again, keep the details clear, and include photographic evidence where appropriate. Tell eBay that the item was Significantly Not As Described.

I've won an auction, but the seller won't sell the item. What should I do?

This sometimes happens if an item, for instance, has

sold for less than the seller had hoped for, but it's still a clear breach of eBay's terms and conditions. Send the seller an e-mail asking them to supply the item, or else you'll have no option but to report them to eBay.

Should you not receive a satisfactory response, or any reply at all, then raise a dispute with eBay for non-supplying of goods. You should also leave them negative feedback. However, if someone doesn't want to sell you something, then no matter how hard you push them, you won't ultimately be able to get it. It's best, once feedback has been left and the matter reported, to chalk it up to experience and move on.

Someone has approached me about an item, and asked if I want to buy it outside of the eBay system. What should I do?

There's a clear advantage to conducting a transaction outside of eBay, given that it would save on both eBay and PayPal fees, which can ultimately be to the benefit of both parties. However, not only is this a practice that eBay frowns upon, it's a case of the risks far outweighing the advantages.

You lose the protection that eBay and PayPal offer on transactions, and should something go wrong with

a deal, then you're likely to be left high and dry. Clearly, eBay will not intervene in a problematic transaction that's taken place outside of its walls. It's thus recommended to refuse any such offer that a seller may approach you with.

SELLER TIPS

My auction has ended, but I haven't heard from the buyer. What should I do?

As soon as an auction ends, it's a good idea to send an invoice through the eBay system as soon as possible. If you don't hear from your buyer after a week or so, then something clearly has gone wrong. As usual, try the common-sense approach first: try to contact the buyer again and, if necessary, inform them that you'll have to go through eBay's reporting channels.

After seven days, you can file a report for a non-paying bidder with eBay (or you can do it instantly if the buyer has since left the eBay service and no longer has an account). If you still hear nothing back after a further seven days, you can at least claim your final value fees back (although you'll still be liable for any listing extras you bought, as well as the listing fee itself). To do this, you need to close your case with eBay within 60 days of the end of the auction. If you fail to do this, then eBay will not refund you.

Sadly, the eBay system doesn't allow you to leave negative feedback for the buyer concerned, thanks to controversial changes in the feedback system that were implemented in 2008. Those changes still rankle.

I've sold an item, but the buyer has left me negative feedback unfairly. What can I do?

Feedback can be mutually withdrawn if both parties agree, yet if your buyer steadfastly refuses to do so, then, unfortunately, you're stuck with it. At the very least, though, it's worth replying to the feedback to state your case. This will appear alongside the feedback on your transaction that future bidders will see, so you at least get to state your side of the story.

It seems to cost a lot of money to sell my item. What am I doing wrong?

Quite possibly nothing. However, it's important not to get carried away when putting together your listing. Only choose the extras that will genuinely help and enhance your listing, for instance, and be wary of overspending on low-ticket items. Be aware of the final value fee eBay will take at the end of your auction (10%, up to a maximum of £40), and adjust your pricing accordingly. There's little point allowing bids to start at 1p, when it's an item that you won't feel the financial benefit of until bidding reaches £20.

Don't discount using specialised alternatives to eBay, either, depending on the item you're looking to sell. For example, with a second-hand car, there are many outlets through which you might get a better ultimate price, once charges have been taken.

However, the best tip is this: be aware of what it's costing you to list your item, choose your listing enhancements with care, and set your pricing at a realistic level. You are, after all, getting your item in front of millions of potential buyers by listing it on eBay!

I've sold an item, and the buyer has now revealed that their address is outside of Europe. What should I do?

If you didn't list worldwide shipping in your listing, then you can refuse the sale. You should certainly do so if your buyer is located in one of the many hotspots for online scams - Nigerian, Thai and Indonesian addresses are notorious, for instance. If in doubt, it's best in these instances to not send your item out, as your chances of getting payment that won't bounce are much lower than usual, and also the chance of hearing from your buyer once a problem arises is virtually non-existent.

However, as noted earlier, you can't leave a reciprocal piece of negative feedback. Not surprisingly, this is not one of eBay's most popular policies, and you may end up having to simply dust yourself down and move on.

When should I post an item?

The ideal answer is when payment has cleared. With the likes of PayPal, that's straightforward, as you're informed when a payment has been made. If you must proceed with a bank transfer - and this is only recommended for traders you have some trust in - then again, allow three to four working days.

Cheques are trickier. When payment clears in this case varies from bank to bank, and even from cheque to cheque! Even when funds appear on a bank statement, that doesn't necessarily mean that a cheque has fully cleared, and said funds can still potentially be pulled. You can ring your bank if it's a

high-value cheque for guidance, but it's likely to recommend four working days at least, or perhaps even a couple of weeks.

Depending on your own financial situation, you might find it good practice to ship before this process is complete on lower-value items. At the very least, you need to advise your buyer throughout the process, and ideally list in your original auction that you will require a cheque to have cleared before you'll ship the goods.

SECURITY

I've had an e-mail from eBay asking me to confirm my account details. What should I do?

Ignore it. This is what's known as a phishing scam, where unscrupulous criminals will try to direct you to a plausible-looking eBay site. The problem? It's more than likely a fake designed to get your login details and password. Once a phisher has those, then they can log into your account, and potentially get access to your financial details too, as well as conduct fraudulent activity.

If in any doubt, don't click on the links in such an e-mail, and send it directly to eBay for analysis. It generally comes back to you quite quickly to let you know whether it's a fake or not.

AND FINALLY

eBay isn't the be all and end all, but used properly and intelligently, it can be a great source of bargains, and a good way to make some pocket money. Keep your expectations realistic, know when to walk away, and keep an eye on all the hidden costs. Happy bidding!

Reviews Index

THE INDEPENDENT UK GUIDE TO EBAY 2011

Editors:
Anthony Enticknap
Simon Brew

Writers:
Aaron Birch, Gaye Birch, Martyn Carroll,
David Crookes, Jason D'Allison, Sarah
Dobbs, Ashley Frieze, Ian Osborne, Mark
Pickavance, Mark, Pilkington, Kevin
Pocock, Jenny Sanders

Design & Layout:
Laura Passmore, Heather Reeves

Digital Production Manager:
Nicky Baker

Bookazine Manager: Dharmesh Mistry

Group Publisher: Paul Rayner

MD of Technology: John Garewal

Production Director: Robin Ryan

Managing Director of Advertising:
Julian Lloyd-Evans

Chief Operating Officer: Brett Reynolds

Group Finance Director: Ian Leggett

Chief Executive: James Tye

Chairman: Felix Dennis

MAG**BOOK**

MAGBOOK
The MagBook brand is a trademark of
Dennis Publishing Ltd,
30 Cleveland St, London W1T 4JD.
Company registered in England. All
material
© Dennis Publishing Ltd, licensed by
Felden 2011, and may not be reproduced
in whole or part without the consent of
the publishers.
The Independent UK Guide To eBay 2011
ISBN 1-907232-30-3

LICENSING
Please contact Hannah Heagney on +44
(0) 20 7907 6134 or e-mail
hannah_heagney@dennis.co.uk

LIABILITY
While every care was taken during the
production of this MagBook, the
publishers cannot be held responsible
for the accuracy of the information or
any consequence arising from it. Dennis
Publishing takes no responsibility
for the companies advertising in this
MagBook. The paper used within this
Magbook is produced from sustainable
fibre, manufactured by mills with a valid
chain of custody.

Printed at: BGP